50
SPECIALYEARS

50

SPECIAL YEARS

A STUDY IN SCOTTISH HOUSING

·

Tom Begg

Ḥ

Henry Melland
LONDON

Frontispiece: Scottish Special Housing Association Head Office
in Palmerston Place, Edinburgh.

First published in Great Britain in 1987
by Henry Melland Limited
23 Ridgmount Street, London WC1E 7AH

for Scottish Special Housing Association
15-21 Palmerston Place, Edinburgh EH12 5AJ

Distributed by

Canongate Publishing Limited
17 Jeffrey Street, Edinburgh EH1 1DR

Designed by Ann Ross Paterson

Hardback edition ISBN 0 907929 14 1
Softback edition ISBN 0 907929 15 X

Set in 11/13 point Palatino

Printed in Scotland by
Charles Letts (Scotland) Limited

Contents

Acknowledgements   vii

Foreword   ix

CHAPTER ONE   *Housing in Scotland in the Twentieth Century*   1

CHAPTER TWO   *The Origins of the SSHA*   43

CHAPTER THREE   *The Early Years*   61

CHAPTER FOUR   *1945-1955*   128

CHAPTER FIVE   *1955-1979*   167

CHAPTER SIX   *The Contemporary Period*   231

CHAPTER SEVEN   *Retrospect and Prospect*   261

References   273

Appendices

    A   *Completed houses – Scotland*   282

    B   *House completion under various programmes*   284

    C   *Multi-storey stock – West Region*   285

    D   *Erskine – Housing stock*   286

    E   *SSHA in Gear*   287

       Summary   290

    F   *SSHA Fixed Assets 1969/70 – 1985/86*   290

    G   *SSHA Interest Rates on Borrowings 1969-1985*   291

    H   *SSHA Capital Expenditure/Capital Receipts*   291

    J   *Housing Revenue Account – the last 10 years*   292

    K   *Characteristics of houses sold*   293

    L   *Awards for Design*   295

Index   297

To Professor J.T. Ward
and to the
Tenants
Members of Staff
Senior Officers
and Members of the Council of Management
who have been part of the SSHA

Acknowledgement and Author's Note

Thanks are due to many people who assisted with the preparation of this book. In particular, I am grateful to Len Ferguson for reading and commenting on the draft text and for helping to correct some of my errors. My gratitude goes also to Ian Small, Ian Ireland, Frank Colston and to the members of the Housing Management Directorate for advice and information, especially in formulating the appendices; to Sybil Laing of the Technical Library for digging out much useful material on the first and second Scottish National Housing Companies; to Gary Malone, Bill McCowan, Helen Legget and Una Kerr of the West Regional Office for their assistance with the Appendices on Glasgow, GEAR and Erskine; to June Moyes, Pauline Easton, Jill Ronald and Heather Ramsay for their patient help with typing; to Marjery Bruce, Val Howard and Ann Wells for innumerable cups of coffee and general secretarial assistance; and to the many other members of Association staff who passed on useful bits of information.

Donald Ross of the Association's Public Relations Department is responsible for many of the photographs in this volume and obviously I am more than grateful to him. Thanks also go to John Timms, Lorna Frost and Dan Miller for their continuous support and advice; to the *Glasgow Herald* Photographic Library and to the BBC Hulton Picture Library for permission to reproduce some of their photographs; and to the members of staff of Queen Margaret College Library for their unfailing assistance in obtaining works of reference.

I am much indebted to Ann Ross Paterson for the design and layout of the book and to Patrick Bowen of Henry Melland Limited for his expert guidance on many matters of detail. Thanks are also due to the Clydesdale Bank for their financial contribution.

In addition, I wish to acknowledge the enormous support and patient encouragement which I received from my wife, Mary.

Finally, I am extremely grateful to Malcolm Rifkind for contributing his kind Foreword; and to the chairman and members of the Council of Management for granting me unrestricted access to the Association's records. I wish, however, to make it absolutely clear that this is not an 'approved' history. Full responsibility is mine for the opinions and judgements made throughout the text.

Tom Begg
Queen Margaret College
Edinburgh

Foreword

Housing is a fundamental element of the environment of any society. As such it has always generated much political interest and attention in one form or another, not least over the last half century. The creation of the Scottish Special Housing Association was a valuable initiative and the Association has, over the years, proved to be a key instrument in the development of housing policy in Scotland throughout this long and often turbulent period.

It is fitting therefore that someone should chronicle the story of the Association as a contribution to the celebration of its Fiftieth Anniversary in 1987. This Tom Begg has done with clarity, insight and careful attention to detail, drawing also on his own knowledge of the Association through his membership of its Council. It is also very interesting how he has set the evolution of the Association against a backcloth of housing generally in Scotland in the twentieth century.

The Scottish Special Housing Association's responsiveness to government, its search for excellence, economy and practical solutions, and above all its persistence 'to make it work', throughout the ups and downs of politics, the constraints of men, materials and money, are all fairly covered.

Attention is also given to those figures who played a seminal role in developing the Association as an effective tool in the struggle against atrocious housing conditions in the early post-war years. A special place, however, is accorded, justifiably, to Walter Elliot, who, as the final chapter concludes, would have found much satisfaction in what the Association has achieved since its inception.

In all, this is a detailed and comprehensive history of the Scottish Special Housing Association painstakingly compiled and from which readers of different persuasions can learn much about the Association's past role, as well as speculate on what its future role may be. I congratulate Tom Begg on this work and commend it wholeheartedly to all those who have been associated with the Association in one capacity or another and to those who have an interest in the evolution of housing policy and practice over the last half century.

Malcolm Rifkind

CHAPTER ONE

Housing in Scotland in the Twentieth Century

The first point which a newcomer to the Scottish Special Housing Association has to grasp is that, despite its name, it is not a housing association at all – at least in the conventionally accepted sense of that term. Typically, in this country, housing associations are registered, controlled and funded by the Housing Corporation, which was set up in 1964 and which has grown rapidly in stature and effectiveness since the enhancement of its powers in the Housing Act of 1974. Most housing associations are relatively small, exist to serve a particular locality or specialised type of housing provision, and are of comparatively recent origin (although a few associations can in fact trace their roots back to nineteenth-century charitable and philanthropic organisations). By contrast the SSHA is directly funded and broadly controlled by the Scottish Office, dates from 1937 and is, in Scottish terms, a large organisation which makes its presence felt in almost every corner of the kingdom, literally from the Borders Region to the Shetland Isles. It has no connection with the Housing Corporation, beyond a tradition of friendly goodwill, which goes back perhaps to the 1960s when, briefly, the Association acted as Scottish agent for the nascent Corporation. Moreover, as will be shown throughout this narrative, the Association's range of provision covers almost the full spectrum of public sector housing in Scotland and its stock of accommodation includes examples of almost every type of dwelling which has been provided by the state in this part of the country throughout the twentieth-century.

To understand why the Association exists and to arrive at some kind of estimation of the extent of its achievement over the past fifty years, it is necessary to know something of the context against which it has operated. Although there are several useful accounts of the development of public sector housing in Scotland[1] it is worth here providing a brief description of the main elements of the background against which the Association's history must be set.

The Industrial Revolution in Scotland was more concentrated both in geographic terms and in time than was the case south of the border. By comparison with much of the English experience, the processes of industrialisation and urbanisation in Scotland perhaps more definitely merited the term revolutionary, since they affected an economy and a people which were, initially, infinitely less prepared. By any measure of wealth, personal income, standard of living, agricultural development, scale of capital formation, experience of international trade, or management of urban concentration, in general terms eighteenth-century Scotland lagged far behind England. It is not, therefore, surprising that the upheavals of the next century and a half affected a population which was both less demanding of tolerable standards of habitation and less able to secure and organise the resources with which improvements could be accomplished. The Highlanders and Irish migrants who crowded into Glasgow and its environs in the nineteenth-century, pushed by the realities of rural poverty and attracted by the hope of employment, brought with them an acceptance of low standards and, by their ever increasing numbers, collectively ensured that rapid improvement through better wage levels remained only a remote prospect for the majority.

The story of the destitution, poverty, overcrowding, criminality, drunkenness, dirt, filth and squalor of the slums of nineteenth-century Glasgow has been well recorded.[2] What is perhaps less widely appreciated is that conditions in the industrial cities were in fact paralleled by, and had their counterparts in, many of the older villages, towns and burghs throughout the country. It has to be remembered that those migrants arriving in Glasgow or Dundee or Edinburgh, or fleeing to England or North America, were in the main trying to escape from the poverty of old Scotland. Not surprisingly, therefore, vile housing conditions could have been found in

almost every corner of nineteenth-century Scotland, from the 'black' turf-roofed houses of the Western Isles, or 'pits' of decaying terraced village cottages, to the slums of the many closes or vennels of small ancient burghs.

If the permissive powers granted to municipalities by

nineteenth-century Parliaments were generally inadequate to deal with the problems of overcrowding, bad sanitation and urban deprivation in English cities, how much more feeble were they in Scottish terms. It was not that city and burgh Corporations did not try. Indeed, Glasgow (1866), Edinburgh (1867), Dundee (1871), Greenock (1877), Leith (1880) and Aberdeen (1884) all took powers to initiate improvement schemes and to get rid of the worst slums. But knocking down slums did not remove the problem; rather, it intensified it. 'The policy of not providing alternative housing for those displaced by improvement schemes was self-defeating. The poor were pressed into even smaller areas of greater densities, and any house suitable for subdivision was "made down"' (partitioned)[3].

It is true that Glasgow's City Improvement Trust, set up under the 1866 Act, did provide some houses as well as demolish the worst slums. However, as Professor Butt points out, it was 'untypical'[4] and its achievement up to the First War was very modest. 'Thus, the Corporation, through its Improvement Trust, probably housed about 10,000 people, one per cent of a total population of over one million and fewer in total than were housed in any one year by private builders in the periods 1867-78 or 1893-1902.'[5] Municipal schemes elsewhere were similarly limited in their scale of accomplishment.

Up to 1914, therefore, the provision of housing was, with a few minor exceptions, in the hands of private landlords who obtained their properties from speculative builders or acquired older properties which were modified for the purpose of renting. Unfortunately, however, income levels for a large proportion of working people were inadequate to permit them to pay rent levels which would have provided a reasonable return for good quality premises. Moreover, in Clydeside in particular, where so many workers were dependent on shipbuilding and related industries, industries which were often disrupted by cyclical depression, periodic unemployment frequently produced poverty.[6] The result was an almost inexhaustible demand for the cheapest possible accommodation: hence small, sub-standard dwellings were the normal habitations for thousands of Scottish working people, while many men avoided or postponed marriage and settled instead for a bed in a lodging house.[7]

But the basic difficulty for many labourers trying to house

their families was essentially a wage problem ... it was not the low percentage of income allocated to rent by this group which was the cause of their poor living conditions; it was that income level for labourers in a wide range of Glasgow's industries was too low to allow a man to keep his wife and children in decent accommodation.

The years immediately before the outbreak of the First World War were marked by an increase in social tension with several fierce and protracted industrial disputes. This period was also the occasion of the last great Liberal Government, while the general elections of 1906 and 1910 saw Labour members arriving in the House of Commons in significant numbers for the first time. The social and economic problems of the working classes were, therefore, assuming increasingly imperative proportions in political terms and, perhaps in consequence, a Royal Commission was established in 1912 to investigate the state of working class housing in Scotland.

In 1917 the Commission reported. It found –

[8] ... unsatisfactory sites of houses and villages, insufficient supplies of water, unsatisfactory provision of drainage, grossly inadequate provision for the removal of refuse, widespread absence of decent sanitary conveniences, the persistence of the unspeakably filthy privy-midden in many of the mining areas, badly constructed, incurably damp labourers' cottages on farms, whole townships unfit for human occupation in the crofting countries and islands, primitive and casual provision for many of the seasonal workers, gross overcrowding and huddling of the sexes together in congested industrial villages and towns, occupation of one-room houses by large families, groups of lightless and unventilated houses in the older burghs, clotted masses of slums in the great cities. To these add the special problems symbolised by the farmed-out houses, and model lodging houses, congested backlands and ancient closes. To these, again, add the cottages a hundred years old in some of the rural villages, ramshackle brick survivals of the mining outbursts of seventy years ago in the mining fields, monotonous miners' rows flung down without a vestige of town plan or any effort to secure modern conditions of sanitation, ill-planned houses that must become slums in a few years, old houses converted

without the necessary sanitary appliances and proper adaptation into tenements for many families, thus intensifyng existing evils, streets of new tenements in the towns developed with the minimum regard for amenity.

It was not, however, simply that the houses were insanitary or of bad condition. As we have seen the mass of Scottish working people could only afford to pay low rents, hence the typical dwelling which could be afforded was far too small by any reasonable standard. In 1911, the housing stock in Scotland was made up as follows –

12.8 per cent – 1 room
40.4 per cent – 2 rooms
20.3 per cent – 3 rooms
26.5 per cent – 4 rooms

In effect, this meant that almost three quarters of the population lived in houses with three rooms or less and almost half were in houses with only one or two rooms. 'The contrast with England and Wales is startling; even in 1911 only 3.2 per cent of the houses had only one room and only 8.3 per cent two rooms, while only 7.1 per cent of the population lived in these abnormally small houses; the great majority of the (English and Welsh) houses, 73.8 per cent, had four or more rooms'.[9]

On a standard of more than three persons per room, just over one million people – about a quarter of the Scottish population – were living in overcrowded conditions. On the contemporary English standard of two persons per room, 2,077,000 Scots (45.1 per cent) suffered from overcrowding. But even these figures do not fully reveal the extent of the problem since it has to be remembered that, in Scottish towns and cities, the habit of building tenements – restricting the amount of available light and fresh air – compounded the problems of interior congestion by adding extreme densities of population per acre.[10]

In order to replace houses which were totally unfit for human habitation and to ease the overcrowding problem the Commission estimated that 121,000 houses were needed immediately. In addition, half of the one-roomed houses and 15 per cent of the two-roomed houses needed to be replaced in an effort to bring some modest improvement in standards; hence, according to the Commission, a total of 236,000 new houses was required at once, and this took no account of the need to make good the deficiency caused by the lack of building throughout the war.[11] According to Marion Bowley the shortage of houses in Scotland in 1921 as a direct result of the First War was 95,000.[12] Not all of the latter would necessarily have been working-class housing, but if we assume a figure in excess of 60,000 for that section of the community, it is clear

Gorbals, 1948. Rooms could be shared by 4, 6 or 8 people, lavatories by up to 30 people, and water taps by as many as 40 people in such Glasgow slums.

Slum conditions in Glasgow.

that if one adds to the Commission's calculations the additional requirement caused by the lack of building between 1914 and 1918, not less than 300,000 houses were urgently required at the end of the war. This, of course, was in addition to the normal annual requirement of new houses as a consequence of new family formation.

In setting out the qualitative and quantitative nature of the problem the Commission also rejected the possibility of the remedy being provided by traditional private enterprise.

13   We are driven to the conclusion that the sources and forces that were available for the provision of working-class houses had . . . failed to provide anything like a sufficiency of houses, and that in particular they had failed to provide houses of a reasonable standard of accommodation and habitability . . . Private enterprise was practically the only agency that undertook the building of houses, and most of the troubles we have been investigating are due to the failure of private enterprise to provide and maintain the necessary houses sufficient in quantity and quality.

If the task of building the required number of reasonable standard houses could not be left to private enterprise, the alternative favoured by the Commission was for the state to hand the responsibility to local government. Central government should also provide subsidies which would make up the difference between economic rents for the houses and the actual rents which the local authorities would be able to obtain from their low income tenants.

In fact, however, even before the Commission had reported, the state had intervened in a manner which was to bedevil housing for many years to come. In 1915, in response to industrial unrest and what was perceived to be a potentially explosive situation in Glasgow, the government introduced the Increase of Rent and Mortage Interest Act which effectively limited rents to the levels obtaining at the outbreak of war.[14] Given wartime rates of inflation this was perhaps a reasonable, even inevitable, emergency measure. But subsequently it became almost politically impossible to remove these restrictions; hence for a generation the private sector for rented accommodation lost all responsiveness, and the rents of local authority houses – which were normally fixed in relation to house size and to neighbourhood rent levels – became, at times, wildly divorced from economic reality. It may be argued that these controls also helped to condition the British in general, and the Scots in particular, to expect housing subsidies of one kind or another and thereby to be unwilling to allocate a realistic proportion of their incomes to housing. Rent control was not partially removed until 1957.

In broad terms the government accepted the recommendations of the Royal Commission and responded by introducing the House and Town Planning (Scotland) Act in 1919. One of the curiosities of the inter-war period is that although the Royal Commission was concerned with Scottish housing conditions the subsequent Acts of Parliament were, in all but minor details, UK-wide measures and, as we shall see, this was to have somewhat unfortunate consequences from a Scottish point of view.

The Act of 1919 – sometimes known as the 'Addison' Act after Dr Addison, the then president of the Local Government Board – gave local authorities the specific task of determining the housing needs of their districts and of then submitting plans to the Scottish Board of Health to provide appropriate numbers of houses for the working classes. Advice and

1919 Houses in Dumfries.
(Photograph Alison Burgess)

administrative assistance was to be provided to the local authorities and, most crucially, the general taxpayer through central government, rather than local ratepayers, would accept responsibility for almost all of the cost of the losses incurred on these houses. Local rates could be increased by four-fifths of a penny (one penny in England) as a nominal contribution, but beyond that token level all of the difference between the expected income from rents and the cost of borrowing the funds to build the houses would be borne by the government.

At first building got under way somewhat slowly, as was perhaps inevitable since few of the local municipalities had much experience of providing houses, but, in the event, only 25,500 houses were completed under the terms of this measure. As early as 1923 the government felt compelled to change the rules.

Two things were fundamentally responsible for the – in some ways – regrettable early demise of the Addison Act. The first factor concerned the cost of building houses which, in the immediate post-war years, was roughly three times as great as had been the case in 1914 and, given the apparently almost unrestricted subsidy, the local authorities had no great reason to skimp on quality.[15] The results were expensive houses, but they were also examples of the finest public sector housing built in Scotland in the inter-war period and, arguably, a standard and character of house was achieved which was not matched until the 1970s. However, the rapid realisation of the probable magnitide of the financial burden which had been assumed was too much for the government.

The second problem was that Scottish housing policy had become hopelessly submerged by the general policy for the whole of the UK. It should be remembered that the Royal Commission had made its recommendations in the context of a study of Scottish housing conditions and the objective of making the local authorities into house providers for the working classes, and of organising special national funding support, was precisely 'to bring the Scottish standard up to a level approximating to that already achieved in England by private enterprise before the Great War'.[16] In 1918, however, a quite separate report was published by an English committee, headed by Sir John Tudor Walters, which had been set up a year earlier by the Local Government Board to consider the standards of English housing which would be required after the war. The 'Tudor Walters' report was particularly influenced by one committee member, Raymond Unwin, who was a main advocate of the Garden City movement and, in keeping with the ideals of the movement, the report attempted to promote a dramatic enhancement of English housing standards. Inevitably the war had also caused a significant fall-off in house-building in England and the popular mood of 1918 was one of determination to reward the returning soldiers by building the legendary 'homes fit for heroes'. The 1919 Addison Act – designed fundamentally to meet the special requirements of the Scottish situation – by its general application to the UK automatically provided the means by which English local authorities could attempt to give effect to the enhanced standards of the Tudor Walters' recommendations at very little cost to themselves. By 1921 the UK economy was experiencing the first surge of the inter-war depression; yet English local authorities were already building at a rate equivalent to 70,000 houses a year, and in the twelve months to September 1922 they completed no less than 85,976 houses.[17]

In these circumstances it is not perhaps surprising that the decision to terminate the Addison Act was taken as early as 1921, but when it was finally repealed in 1923 it left Scotland with an interesting little legacy of estates in various parts of the country. In Glasgow, for example, developments at Riddrie, Craigton and Moss Park date from this period, as does a part of Rosyth, which is of more direct interest to the SSHA (see Chapter 2 below).

In 1923 Neville Chamberlain, the Minister of Health in the new Conservative Government, secured a replacement Housing Act in which his main intention was to shift the responsibility for house provision back to the private sector. Again, in view of the findings of the Royal Commission, some variation in policy in respect of Scotland might have been expected, but in the government's haste to curb the levels of local government expenditure the Scottish problem was quietly returned to the shelf.

The Chamberlain Act provided a modest subsidy of £6 per house for a maximum of twenty years. Today the sum appears derisory, but it should be seen in the context of the low and rapidly falling house prices of the day, when a good three-bedroomed home could be purchased for around £400 (the same house might have cost more than £900 just three years earlier).[18] The subsidy could be paid in a lump sum of up to £100 and its effect was to provide a moderate boost to private construction. Falling prices and the wider availability of mortgages also stimulated private building, but, by contrast, local authority activity contracted.

The good quality houses built in England under the Addison Act were undoubtedly attractive to the middle classes and to the skilled artisans who could afford to pay the relatively high rents attached to them because of their substantial size and despite rent controls. Clearly this had made life very difficult for the private builder who found himself contending in this substantial portion of the market with a heavily subsidised and superior product. It was, perhaps, principally for this reason that house prices fell so sharply from 1920 to 1924. Some readjustment was obviously necessary, quite apart from the need to bring public expenditure under control.

In the years in which the Chamberlain subsidies were available (in England they were reduced to £4 per house from 1927) it is estimated that they yielded 438,000 houses in England and Wales, of which 363,000 were built by private enterprise, hence it is clear that Chamberlain's main objective was achieved.[19] It is equally clear, however, that the needs of low income working people generally, and of the Scottish problem specifically, were neglected. Not surprisingly, Scottish public sector house completions in 1924 and 1925 fell back to the lowest levels recorded in the inter-war years (see Appendix A).

In 1924 the Labour Party came to power for the first time as a short-lived minority government tacitly supported by the Liberals and under the premiership of Ramsay Macdonald. The only significant measure which they were able to enact was the Housing Act which takes its name from John Wheatley, the Minister of Health and a member of the Glasgow ILP.

By the nature of the government, Wheatley's room for manoeuvre was constrained, but realistically he attempted to encourage the local authorities to tackle the shortage of working-class houses without any undue inihibition or conflict with the private sector. The Chamberlain assistance to private builders was maintained. However, there was to be no return to the blank cheque centrally provided subsidy of the Addison measure. Instead the burden was to be limited and shared between central and local government. Wheatley's moderation was rewarded, for when the Conservatives returned to office within the year their codifying Housing Act of 1925 left the main elements of the Wheatley Act in place and thus accepted the necessary involvement of local authorities as main house providers.

Having struck a deal with the building trade unions to allow an increase in the numbers of apprentices to the skilled trades, Wheatley hoped to bring about a long-term plan to increase the production of houses to a UK output in excess of 150,000 per annum by the mid 1930s. The subsidy to local authorities was fixed at £9 per annum (£12 10s in rural areas) for forty years. Although rent controls were not removed, local authorities fixing new rents could now use average rent levels for similar houses as a guide and could charge a higher rent if it was necessary to cover costs in excess of a rate contribution equivalent to £4 10s per house for forty years. The effect of this was that local authority losses per house were restricted to a maximum of £4 10s per annum and that the maximum combined subsidy was limited to £13 10s (£17 in rural parishes). If losses exceed that level average rents could be increased accordingly.[20]

In the event, it was an ingenious scheme which appeared to give both local and national government the confidence that the problems of working-class housing could be tackled realistically without allowing public expenditure to get out of control.

The result of the Wheatley Act was a steady increase in building by the local authorities. The Exchequer subsidy was reduced to £7 10s in 1926, but the Act remained operative until 1933, by which time 508,000 council houses had been erected under its influence in England and Wales, while in Scotland in the same period just over 100,000 council houses were built.

The difference in the nature of the housing problems in Scotland and England is clearly illustrated by the operation of the Wheatley Act. What had formerly been minimum standards of housing design and layout became progressively, through the Acts of 1923 and 1924, to be regarded as maximum standards. The result was a marked qualitative decline from the Garden City specifications of the Tudor Walters Committee and

Bungalows at Janefield, Dumfries built under the 1919 Act.
(Photograph Alison Burgess)

this has been commented on unfavourably by almost all English commentators on the subject as well as by some Scots. Of the latter Douglas Niven, for example, says –

> [21] The Board of Health was compelled by the government of the day to reduce the costs of houses submitted to it for approval under the Act. Design standards were reduced to a minimum and builder-work specifications severely curtailed. The resultant product of these restrictions was a dreary rough-rendered brick box which was formless, practically shorn of all detail, colour or ornamentation and utterly lacking in imagination. This 'design' was reproduced by many local authorities...until the beginning of the Second War... Collectively they marred the approaches to all urban areas and completely destroyed the continuity of domestic architectural design in Scotland.

As Niven concedes, not all of the developments were of an unreasonably low standard and, for example, he exempts the Glasgow Corporation estates at Knightswood and Carntyne from the most severe of his strictures. However, it is also interesting to note that his views, which may be valid in retrospect, would have registered somewhat strangely with many Scots of the period. The fact was that these four-roomed local authority houses were considered to be significantly better than many of the existing older middle-class houses. Not surprisingly, therefore, many people who were by no means amongst the lowest paid scrambled to obtain a council house and, as the Department of Health for Scotland grumbled, the local authorities interpreted the term 'working-class' in no narrow sense in their allocation policies.[22]

Up to 1934 of all the mainstream houses built in Scotland '83.9 per cent were built with the aid of a subsidy, including 61.1 per cent provided by the local authorities. In England and Wales the corresponding figures were 48.8 per cent and 31.0 per cent.'[23] The significance of these figures is that the private sector in England was now well into its stride in the creation of middle-class suburbia; hence the overwhelming bulk of the houses being constructed by private builders in England were of a standard which precluded subsidy. By comparison the smaller subsidised private dwellings were suited to even the better-off Scotsman's purse. Similarly, while council housing represented less than one-third of the English output the equivalent figure for Scotland was approaching two-thirds. Nothing could more clearly indicate the variation between the problems and affordable standards north and south of the border.

Indeed, the difficulty in Scotland was even more intractable than the above comparison might suggest. The Department of Health for Scotland repeatedly sought to encourage local authorities to maintain a standard of three or more rooms to a dwelling.[24] The codifying Housing (Scotland) Act of 1925 had also laid down that plans for private houses with less than three rooms should only be approved in 'exceptional' circumstances. However, the pressure to meet the requirements of the low Scottish levels of income made it an uphill struggle to raise standards even with the help of the various subsidies. Eventually, in 1929, the Department of Health was forced to agree that 25 per cent of the local authority houses might have only two rooms.[25]

The problem was that the larger houses still involved rents which represented too sharp an increase to withstand for the tenants coming from small older rent-controlled properties. In fact, the truth was, as has been suggested, that the principal Scottish beneficiaries of this early phase of council house building were typically not the poorest working-class people on whose behalf the Royal Commission had protested.

As the country slid into the nadir of depression (1929-33), when three million were unemployed, high rents were also an increasingly important factor in England. 'The fundamental problem was the level of rents in relation to earnings. Although the heavy Wheatley subsidies had been specifically designed to reduce the level of rents, they could not bring council houses within the reach of the mass of poorer workers who everywhere continued to live in old, rent-restricted property, much of it turning into slums.'[26]

Nevertheless, even in retrospect, the Wheatley Act must be regarded, from a Scottish point of view, as a success, since it enabled the local government agencies to draw on national resources in the first major attempt to improve housing conditions for the mass of the people of Scotland.

As a result of the economic crisis the Wheatley Act was repealed in 1933 from when, once more, the general provision of working-class houses was to be left to the private sector.

Milldam Head. Note the stark appearance of houses built under the 1924 Act.
(Photograph Alison Burgess)

However, the Housing Act of that year, building on the scheme introduced by the Greenwood Act of 1930, concentrated public effort and attention on the business of clearing and replacing slums. In this case the subsidy was not granted to the house, but was instead related to the number of people displaced and rehoused. In some ways this was a reversion to late nineteenth-century practice, but with the crucial difference that local authorities had to provide replacement houses for the former occupants of the slums which had been cleared.

In England the system does not appear to have worked well since doubts remained about the definition of a slum, but in Scotland few councils had much difficulty in identifying slums; hence the withdrawal of the Wheatley Act produced no slackening in the pace of council house construction. In 1935, 18,814 council houses were completed in Scotland, which was the highest figure achieved thus far. By the end of 1938 55,000 out of the 63,000 slum houses identified in the 1934 programme had been cleared or demolished and 40,000 replacement houses built. A further 27,000 houses had also been erected and these would be allocated between slum replacement and ordinary needs.[27]

Considerably less progress had been made on the matter of dealing with the traditional endemic Scottish problem of over-crowding; however this matter will be looked at in greater detail in the next chapter when the origins of the SSHA are examined. For the moment it is enough to consider the broader perspective.

Over the period 1919 to 1939 337,173 houses were completed in Scotland and of these some 230,137 were provided by the public sector. Undoubtedly this marked a major revolution in the provision of houses and in the general improvement of the overall Scottish housing stock. Did it also mean that the objectives set by the Royal Commission report of 1917 had now been achieved?

The 60,000 houses condemned by the report as unfit for human habitation had certainly been replaced. But when due allowances are made for the need to make good the deficiency brought about by the lack of building during the First World War, for providing the additional houses required by normal new family formation throughout the inter-war years, and for dealing with the problem of overcrowding, the advance was not nearly as great as may be imagined.

A survey in 1936 indicated that 260,000 houses were over-crowded, a figure which represented abut a quarter of all Scottish working-class houses.[28] Later, in 1944, the Scottish Housing Advisory Committee calculated that to complete slum clearance and eliminate overcrowding required 321,000 houses.[29] By then, of course, the effects of the Second World War were complicating the situation dramatically, and even if the best inter-war building rates were subsequently achieved it was reckoned that it would take a further thirteen years to complete this programme alone.[30] But by 1944 the Advisory Committee also believed than an additional 148,000 houses were required for general purposes and to balance the increase in families in the period 1938 to 1943. Their total estimate of the Scottish housing requirement in 1944 was, therefore, 469,000 houses, and it was believed that it would take at least nineteen years following the end of the war to complete the task – *ie* to meet the objectives of the inter-war period and to retrieve the losses occasioned by the Second World War. And this was, of course, on top of the normal building which would be necessary to match the increase in new family formation.

Clearly the task which faced the post-war planners was a daunting one and those who had been involved nationally and locally in the inter-war programmes must have felt that, far from achieving the Royal Commission's targets in these years, they had merely held the line.

Could more have been accomplished in the 1920s and 30s? Given the low levels to which house prices sank and the fact that so many workers were idle throughout the period, one must conclude in the affirmative. However, the matter is not as straightforward as it might appear. House-building by traditional methods involved the employment of skilled craftsmen and, in the context of the contemporary unemployment, the building unions were not keen to render their members more vulnerable by accepting a rapid expansion in the inflow of apprentices. In addition, for obvious reasons the Scottish building industry was historically substantially smaller in proportion to its English counterpart, and growth was bound to be somewhat slow so long as the industry was confined to traditional techniques. By 1936 the Department of Health for Scotland were fully aware that something more was required if the kingdom's labour resources were to be more efficiently harnessed to the housing problem. Again, however, this takes us to the origins of the SSHA and the question will, therefore, be left for further discussion in the next chapter.

The twists and turns of government policy from the Second World War onwards form a main part of the history of the Association and there is little to be gained from a detailed description of the subject at this stage. However, it may help to highlight some of the general background features against which various policies, and the Association's specific operations, should be considered.

As will have been realised from the preceding paragraphs the Scottish housing problems which confronted the government at the end of the Second World War were particularly acute. It is true that of the UK total of 475,000 houses destroyed or permanently rendered uninhabitable by enemy action only about 7,000 were in Scotland, and these were mainly concentrated in Glasgow, Greenock and Clydebank.[31] However, many other houses in these areas were damaged, and once the residue of the pre-war housing programme was completed by 1940, the flow of new houses was reduced to a trickle, with

only 15,633 houses being erected from 1940 to 1945 – mainly for essential war workers. Furthermore, the condition of many of the older existing houses deteriorated significantly during the war, both from the scarcity of tradesmen for maintenance purposes and in consequence of the shortage of materials.

If the quality and condition of the housing stock was inadequate, it was also hopelessly short in quantity. The war years saw a recovery in both the rates of population growth and family formation. No census was conducted in 1941, but in 1945 the Scottish population was estimated at 5,150,000.[32] In 1931 it had been recorded at 4,800,000.[33] Similarly the number of marriages per year increased, while the average age at which people married fell.[34] Thus the demand for accommodation was growing rapidly at precisely the moment when the supply of new houses dried up.

Throughout the UK the housing shortage was severe.[35] And if this was particularly true in London and the heavily bombed cities of the Midlands, it was also true in Scotland, and the problem was by no means confined to the industrial heartlands. In the ancient Royal Burgh of Tain in the north east, so fierce was the scramble among potential tenants for the Burgh Council's meagre stock of houses in the immediate post-war years that the housing committee decided to co-opt the local minister as a sign of the honesty with which they dealt with the occasional allocation. It was a vain hope, for invariably he found himself baffled and beleaguered in having to explain why the rare lucky applicant was more deserving than any number of others who were crowded into a single room, sharing space in a disused railway carriage or 'putting up' in a former army hut.[36]

Similar stories could have been recounted throughout the length and breadth of the land and, in 1946, about 40,000 squatters were believed to have taken possession of disused service properties of one kind or another.[37] Moreover, throughout the war years it had become almost a patriotic duty to share any available spare accommodation space (compulsory powers could be used to enforce sharing if necessary). With the return of peace this practice naturally came to be regarded as increasingly burdensome and unsatisfactory.

The earliest attempts to increase the stock of dwellings as rapidly as possible involved the repair and adaption of war-damaged houses, the modification of various wartime buildings such as government hostels and service properties, the adaption and erection of huts which had originally been intended for war purposes, and the production of temporary houses – often the celebrated 'prefabs'. Nationally 'by the end of 1946, one-

Squatters at Duddingston Camp,
Edinburgh, as late as January, 1954.

third of a million such units had been provided: 80,000 in "prefabs", 45,000 in conversions and adaptions, 107,000 in repaired unoccupied war-damaged houses, 12,000 in temporary huts and service camps, 25,000 in requisitioned houses, and 52,000 in new permanent houses. About 1¼ million occupied dwellings which had suffered war damage and had been repaired'.[38] In Scotland about 30,000 prefabs were erected around this time.[39]

Looking to the longer term, however, it is interesting that in housing, as in so many other areas, the war seems to have stimulated rethinking on the grand scale, and throughout the years 1939-45 an astonishing number of committees and commissions were at work preparing to contribute to the reshaping of post-war society. Perhaps one explanation is that the emergency provoked by the 'total' war between nations seemed to demonstrate the organisational power and apparently limitless authority of modern governments. Could not the bureaucratic strength displayed in war be harnessed in peace to provide a better world for the ordinary citizen? A world from which unemployment would be banished, with health care freely available to all, with good pensions for the elderly and disabled, and with everyone decently housed in pleasant

Demonstration prefab in Kelvingrove Park, Glasgow, August 1944.

The first Scottish prefab erected in Glasgow under the government's temporary housing scheme, April, 1945.

surroundings. This was the prevailing mood and, despite the fact that the committees which planned to bring this dream into being had been established in the main by the wartime coalition under a Tory prime minister, perhaps it provides the best explanation for the unpredicted return of the first majority Labour Government in 1945.

The first committee to report, the Barlow Commission, had actually been set up before the war, and (in 1940), it produced its recommendations on the Distribution of the Industrial Population, urging the further redevelopment of congested areas, the dispersal of population and industry and the establishment of a national planning authority. It was followed in 1942 by the Uthwatt Report on Compensation and Betterment and the Scott Report on the Utilisation of Land in Rural Areas. The former encouraged the State to assume the right to take up undeveloped land for development purposes, while the latter looked at development and conservation in the countryside and made recommendations on the improvement of rural housing. In 1943, while the Ministry of Town and Country Planning was set up for England and Wales, its duties in respect of Scotland were devolved to the Scottish Office, and the Town and Country Planning (Interim Development) (Scotland) Act brought all land under planning control (planning procedures were consolidated in the post-war era by the Act of 1947). This enabled the Scottish Office to accelerate its own preparations for the return to peace. In 1944 the Scottish Housing Advisory Committee produced its report *Planning Our New Homes*, which investigated everything from numbers of houses required to the types of houses, standards of space and extent of equipment to be provided. (The Dudley Committee on the *Design of Dwellings* accomplished a similar task for England and Wales.) In the same year, the first of the Burt Committee reports on standards and methods of house construction was published, suggesting a variety of techniques and materials which might be employed while traditional resources remained in short supply. The Burt Committee's activities continued after the war and it produced further reports in 1946 and 1948.

Each of these committees – and many others on related subjects – contributed to the planning for the years after the cessation of hostilities, but they also confirmed in the minds of politicians, local and national, and of the general public at large, the notion that housing was a matter for the State. No longer was it mainly a question of leaving the provision of a reasonable house to the resources available to the individual family. Now, and increasingly, it was assumed that the attainment of decent housing was not mainly an economic problem for families, but was, rather, a social right to which every citizen could lay claim.

Nor was the idea that it was the government's duty to provide good quality housing for all one from which the Labour Governments 1945-1951 dissented. On the contrary Aneurin Bevan, the Minister of Health for England and Wales, and Joseph Westwood, Secretary of State for Scotland, were eager to fulfil the election pledge of 1945 that they would build 'five million houses in quick time'.[40] But the wish was easier than the fact. Not only was the country exhausted physically and economically from six years of war, its economy was also severely dislocated and distorted. It would take years to acquire and train the labour force; raw materials of various kinds were in chronically scarce supply; and the resources with which materials from abroad might have been obtained had long since been hawked to provide the munitions of war.

In these circumstances it is not surprising that the long term permanent housing programme seemed to gain momentum only slowly. 'During his first eighteen months or so at the

Ministry of Health, so little progress was made in relieving the housing shortage that it began to look as though Bevan's head would have to roll.'[41] Nor is it strange that the earliest dreams of building to the highest standards were gradually abandoned throughout the late 1940s and early 1950s. Speed of construction and quantity produced became the guides in the effort to meet the requirements of a population by now absolutely convinced that it was the government's business to provide the houses, and increasingly frustrated after years of rationing and restrictions.

To overcome the shortage of raw materials, to aid the speed of construction, and to offset the lack of traditional skilled labour, many novel house types and new construction materials and techniques were devised. Some of these were expensive solutions and the houses proved to be less than ideal. Others have, in fact, worked well and, suitably modernised, are still providing their occupants with accommodation of a good standard.

Gradually, therefore, the tempo of construction quickened. A glance at Appendix A will show that completions in Scotland increased from 4,310 houses in 1946 to 21,211 in 1948. In 1949, and again in 1950, just under 26,000 houses were erected and with the return of the Conservatives to power, when responsibility for housing in England and Wales was assumed by the new Minister of Housing, Harold Macmillan with a national

Weir Quality houses erected at Blackburn in the immediate post War period.

24

target of 300,000 houses per annum, the pace of construction in Scotland also accelerated still further. 1953 and 1954 were the peak years, when 39,548 and 38,853 were the respective figures for house completions.

Again, however, as is shown in the same appendix, the proportion of building being done by the private sector was inordinately low throughout these years. In 1950 only 782 private houses were built in Scotland, just three per cent of the total, and between the end of the war and the election of the Conservatives in 1951, the best annual record of private builders was just 1,541 houses, a little over seven per cent of the total for 1948.

These figures reveal the extent of the commitment to state provision of housing in the immediate post-war period. Indeed, it was then imagined by some local politicians that housing should be regarded entirely as a social service to be provided by the local authorities. Inevitably, carried to such extremes, this attitude, and the consequential domination of housing secured by local authorities, gave rise to many problems which have left their mark on the legacy of Scotland's current housing stock, and this is a subject which is discussed in greater detail later. However, for the moment it is enough to remark that the post-war government controls did as much as possible to discriminate in favour of local authority building and against the private sector.

In the 1950s the controls on private builders were progressively relaxed and their output increased, jumping from 2,608 houses in 1954 to 6,529 by 1960. In England and Wales the comparable returns are 88,000 and 162,000 houses respectively.[42] South of the border completions in the private sector exceeded the public sector in 1958 when 124,087 private houses were built as compared to 117,438 council houses.[43] Thereafter, while public construction remained overwhelmingly dominant in Scotland the lion's share of provision to the south was in the hands of private builders. In part the explanation of the divergence lay in the traditional problems of the inadequate Scottish housing stock, the comparatively low Scottish income levels, the marked reluctance of the Scottish population to devote a larger proportion of disposable income to housing – reflected perhaps in the greater continued strength of the Labour Party at local government level – and the comparatively under-developed nature of the private building industry in Scotland.

That these were genuine problems is revealed by an examination of the figures for the period 1954 to 1962. As early as 1954 the government was becoming convinced that the general post-war housing shortage was on the way to being solved and began to concentrate public activity once more on dealing with slum clearance. Mandatory rate-contributed subsidies were eliminated for general needs houses and were only to be available for slum clearance. In England the resulting slow down in public activity was substantially offset by the continued growth of private building. In Scotland, although slum clearance was more obviously necessary, and although private output almost tripled from 2,608 to 7,784 houses, this was not sufficient to counter the drop in public production from 36,245 to 18,977 houses, a net reduction in annual output of 12,092 houses.

In this post-war period one of the crucial problems concerned the need to disperse the population. As we have noted, the Barlow Commission report of 1940 had urged the redevelopment of the congested cities and the dispersal of the displaced population and industries to new satellite towns or to redeveloped older towns. In 1945 a New Towns Committee was established under Lord Reith to consider how new towns might be organised and administered and a year later the New Towns Act was passed setting out the legal framework within which these planned communities could be established. Subsequently six New Towns were designated in Scotland, East Kilbride (1947), Glenrothes (1948), Cumbernauld (1955), Livingston (1962), Irvine (1966) and Stonehouse (1972). The last named of these was cancelled in 1976 when only a handful of houses had been completed.

In the fullness of time the New Towns absorbed a significant proportion of the families moving from the old high density areas of Glasgow in particular. But for long Glasgow bitterly resisted the attempt to deprive it of large numbers of its citizens.

In 1946 the Clyde Valley Regional Planning Advisory Committee produced a plan which pointed out that over 500,000 people in Glasgow and 40,000 in Greenock needed to be rehoused.[44] It suggested that half of Glasgow's overspill be accommodated in planned communities on the periphery of the city and the remainder in four New Towns. The Glasgow Corporation did not agree and, in a minute of that year, declared 'that there was no overspill problem'.[45]

Glasgow, perhaps determined to remain the Empire's second city, drew up its own plans to tackle the housing problem of its citizens. It proposed nineteen neat community areas each accommodating 50,000 people in five neighbourhoods of 10,000 persons. This was the design of the city's Master of Works and City Engineer, Robert Bruce, who was hostile to the whole concept of overspill.[46] As a consequence of the city's adherence to this fantasy – with the exception of the designation of East Kilbride in 1947 – plans to confront overcrowding by means of planned overspill were delayed far into the 1950s, by which time the lack of available building space within the city was chronic and the pressure to build to a high density was intense.[47] Glasgow's congestion in 1956 was unparalleled in the United Kingdom: 700,000 people were living in the centre of the city, an area of 7.7 sq km at an average density of over 900 people per hectare, with 12,000 people huddled together in one area of 7 hectares. Housing standards in these areas were unbelievably low: 43 per cent of all houses in the city were of one or two rooms, compared with only 5 per cent in London and 2.5 per cent on Merseyside; 30 per cent of Glasgow's families shared toilets compared with 2.6 per cent in London and 1.1 per cent on Merseyside.

Ultimately central government intervened designating Cumbernauld in 1955 and, while Glasgow was encouraged to build outwith the city boundaries, the Housing and Town Development Act 1957 set out procedures by means of which the city's overspill population might be exported to other towns. Grants for industrial location, for the erection of shopping centres, for enhancement of sewage services and – as we shall see – the assistance of the SSHA, were all offered as inducements to receiving authorities to persuade them to accept large numbers of people.

The overspill programme never assumed the proportions for which its originators hoped, principally because the intended migration of the country's older industries proved almost impossible to effect. With the economy of the region under-

'The forgotten Gorbals,' 1948. The original caption says 'in thousands of rooms like this some Gorbals folk sleep four to a bed. In many others there are no beds.'

27

going fundamental long term structural change the fate of many of the traditional firms was decline and decay rather than migration: hence the new towns quickly tended to become dormitory towns or to rely on their ability to attract firms active in new industries. Perhaps the most spectacular failure of an old industry which was intended to support a new town occurred at Glenrothes where the development programme throughout the 1950s was directly linked to the opening up of the Rothes Colliery. As early as 1962, however, the presence of heavy underground flooding aborted that project although, paradoxically, in the absence of the planned influx of coalminers, Glenrothes became more dependent on Glasgow overspill for the growth of its population. Equally unsuccessful – in the longer term – were the attempts to coerce the motor vehicle industry to locate in factories at Bathgate and Linwood to provide employment for people dispersed to these areas, and the history of the futile attempts to nurture these transplanted ventures over a period in which the pressure from foreign competition became ever more intense is, in retrospect, extremely sad. However, the establishment of the Scottish Development Department in 1962 and the identification of growth areas in and around the new towns and at Grangemouth produced a much more hopeful phase in which the emphasis was to stimulate the development of new industries rather than the relocation of the old.

Nevertheless, from the mid 1950s to the 1970s, much of the story of Scottish housing is connected with the migration of the population out from the old industrial urban centres to new planned communities within the new towns, to peripheral greenfield sites on the edge of the cities or to smaller developments in older towns in or near the central belt.

As we have seen, the pressure for building space in Glasgow and, to a lesser extent, in Dundee was severe, and the Glasgow Corporation only reluctantly acquiesced in overspill after much delay and procrastination. The inevitable consequence was high density building. In 1947 a team from the Corporation visited Marseilles to inspect multi-storey housing in the Le Corbusier mould and thereafter both Glasgow and Dundee enthusiastically encouraged multi-storey construction.[48]

Architects and planners of the day in fact needed little encouragement since steel and reinforced concrete provided the

Opposite *Tenements in the Gorbals, 1956. The Scottish Office expected to demolish 37,000 slum buildings by the end of 1958 and this was the background to the Glasgow overspill programme.*

technological means by which they could express some of the most ambitious of their urban planning concepts. Traditionally the origins of this development are credited to the European Modern Movement which drew much of its inspiration from the work of Le Corbusier and Gropius in the 1930s.[49] Insofar as such ventures were almost invariably in the hands of public authorities in this country, the connection with the Europeans is apt since their concern was as much with social engineering as with problems of constructional design or building techniques. Equally important, however, was the North American influence. To a generation addicted to the film images of the United States, the towering buildings of the cities of that part of the world seemed to represent visions of the future. The cinema pictures of the stunning North American townscapes made a vivid impression on a generation accustomed to the grimy horizons of Britain's Victorian cities and, since the inhabitants of this film-world seemed to live opulent lives in superbly appointed and equipped apartments, few doubted the sophistication and quality of life which would be offered by high-rise or flatted dwellings. Moreover, to the cost-conscious public authorities industrialised building appeared to promise distinct economic advantages once the initial production techniques had been mastered.

Thus it was that throughout the latter part of the 1950s and 1960s large-scale high density flatted developments appeared in the inner cities, in peripheral estates and in the new towns of Cumbernauld and, to a lesser extent, East Kilbride. Some of the buildings, particularly in Glasgow and Dundee, were high-rise (rising to 31 storeys in Glasgow's Red Road), but more common were large blocks of flats of from three to five storeys.

Subsequently, high-rise flats attracted an extremely bad press and after the 1970s there was little or no construction of this type in Scotland. It is, however, difficult to generalise about such developments. Some, for example, the Falkirk District Council blocks at Callendar Park or the SSHA's Broomhill high flats, provide excellent accommodation and are extremely popular with tenants. Good management arrangements, correct identification of appropriate tenants and a pleasing external setting seem to be the main factors in determining the success or otherwise of this type of dwelling, but this is a subject which will be discussed further later. For the moment it is sufficient to

note the phase in which they were produced and perhaps to add the comment that, if Glasgow and Dundee had some excuse for building high in an effort to confront the problem of population density, no such defence can be offered to the many other Scottish cities, towns and burghs which constructed high flats in odd corners for no apparent reason other than the pursuit of municipal prestige.

If the high-rise dwellings built in the 1950s and 1960s are the structures of that era which have excited some of the most hostile comment, of considerably more serious dimensions, in terms of the legacy to the present generation, are the large numbers of three-, four- and five-storey tenemental properties which were constructed typically in the peripheral estates in the same period. Indeed, if the current English problem is inner city decay, its Scottish counterpart is certainly rooted in the huge estates of tenement flats which are to be found around Glasgow in estates such as Drumchapel, Easterhouse or Arden, at Edinburgh's Wester Hailes or, at inner city sites of the same period, such as Glasgow's notorious Hutchesontown.

As the years passed and the immediate post-war period faded into memory so too did society and its expectations begin to change in many far-reaching ways. By 1961 Scotland's population had almost stabilised at about 5.2 millions and, after the brief upturn between 1940 and 1959, average family size began once more to decline.[50] With more people living longer, the average age of the population began to rise, while the

Blocks of flats at Faifley, Clydebank.

divorce rate increased sharply from the 1960s. Moreover, as the dispersal of people from the old urban industrial centres proceeded the process not only broke up whole communities, it also contributed to the weakening of traditional extended family ties. The result was a significant increase in the overall number of Scottish households.

The implications of these changes for housing were vast. In Scotland, in 1921 average household size was 4.4 persons, in 1931 it was 4.1, in 1951 it was 3.5 and today it is 2.7.[51] The main reason for this is the remarkable increase in the number of small households of one or two persons. In the past typical family houses had to accommodate not only parents and young children, but also, often for many years, adult sons and daughters and/or at least one elderly grandparent. Today family formation is concentrated into a shorter period so that married women now look forward to far more years of life after their children have grown up. The result of this has been to increase household formation at both ends of the spectrum. Young single adults often wish to set up on their own at an early stage and young married couples – marrying at a younger age – immediately expect to find a home of their own. This leaves an increasing number of small households of middle-aged people while the rising incidence of divorce has had a similar effect. Again, greater longevity has naturally produced growth in the number of small households of elderly citizens, many of whom may have special housing requirements.

Such factors make their impact over a prolonged period of time and are likely only to be obvious in retrospect. From the end of the Second World War to the 1970s the thrust of housing policy in Scotland was to increase the stock of family-size dwellings in order to meet the needs of society in these years as well as to resolve once and for all the traditional Scottish problem of overcrowding in consequence of excessively small houses. Inevitably, therefore, building throughout this period gave the country a large number of three- or four-bedroomed dwellings. Gradually, however, it became apparent that such a housing stock was not going to be the main requirement of the succeeding generation. Instead the relentless growth in demand was for more and more smaller houses and the effect of the resulting mismatch remains a major problem for housing authorities today.

In addition to these demographic factors, other profound changes were making an increasing impact and this is particularly true in terms of income and living standards. Despite the periodic economic crises experienced by governments, and despite the discontent provoked by the awareness that other countries were faring even better, the fact remains that the quarter of a century following the Second World War was a period of unprecedented prosperity in which the real wealth of the UK virtually doubled. Overall, these years were characterised by sustained growth, by full employment bordering at times and in certain industries on chronic labour scarcity, and by low rates of inflation for most of the period. The principal beneficiaries were the working classes – particularly clerical, semi-skilled and unskilled workers – who gained most from the high levels of employment and the well developed system of social security. Real earnings of this group increased more than for others hence there was a general narrowing of differentials between professional and manual workers, between skilled and unskilled. In addition, the buoyant labour market combined with wider access to education to produce a marked growth in employment opportunities for women and an increase in the tendency of married women either to remain in paid employment or to return to employment after having their children.[52]

The characteristic features of this era, perhaps summed up by Harold Macmillan's 'never had it so good' slogan for the 1959 general election, were a massive growth in consumer spending and steadily rising living standards. In the years 1961 to 1973 alone consumer expenditure in real terms increased by 39 per cent, and growth in spending on household durables was particularly spectacular – up 119 per cent on electrical goods and 50 per cent for other household items.[53] Increasingly the demand was for equipment – such as automatic washing machines, spin driers, vacuum-cleaners, refrigerators, food mixers, television sets and so on – which tended to enhance the convenience and quality of household living. Nothing, however, was more remarkable than the growth in demand for motor vehicles, the number of licensed vehicles in the UK increasing from 4.3 million in 1951 to 16.5 million in 1973.[54]

Again, the impact of these developments on housing was considerable. The motor car accelerated the tendency for people to live further and further from their place of employment and this, for a time, strengthened the movement of the population away from the old urban centres. In terms of the layout of housing estates the need to accommodate the family car made for a requirement which would have been almost (but, as we shall see, not quite) unimaginable in respect of working-class housing just a few years earlier. Similarly inside the house the pressure for available space became much more intense.

In total the cumulative effect of the prosperity of these years was massively to enhance the expectations of people right across the community. The standards of the past would simply no longer suffice. Moreover, concepts such as 'poverty' or 'need' typically ceased to be absolute questions and became rather more matters of relation. 'Deprivation' came almost to be used as a synonym for poverty while increasingly economically meaningless terms such as 'relativity', 'comparability' and 'fairness' were notions which figured in wage bargaining or in the determination of elements of the 'social wage'. In a sense the political mood of the period is summed up by the Rent Act of 1965 which introduced the new principle of 'fair' rents into the rent-fixing process.[55]

Decades of controlled rents had by now drastically reduced the stock of private accommodation available for renting and the partial decontrol of 1957 – for better properties with a rateable value greater than £40 – appears to have done little to halt the decline.[56] By the 1960s governments were tentatively attempting to find measures to increase the quantity of dwellings available for rent to people with higher incomes who would not normally qualify for local authority housing. In 1961 a fund of £3 million was created for Scotland to provide housing associations with the means of constructing houses for economic renting. This was a pilot project which led directly to the setting up of the Housing Corporation in 1964 to promote cost rent and co-ownership housing on a larger scale.[57] Changes to the rent fixing system for housing associations (1972) and to the subsidy arrangements (1974) subsequently enabled the Housing Corporation and its associations to assume greater and greater significance, and, to the present time, one of their major preoccupations has been with restoring older properties for renting.

From the 1960s rising expectations in respect of housing standards, a reaction against the continued large scale demolition of interesting older buildings in the cities, the desire to encourage home ownership and the obvious enthusiasm of governments to reduce the public cost of housing, led to the introduction of a wide range of grants for the improvement of older dwellings. Grants typically were linked to the installation of certain specified amenities such as a fixed bath or system of hot water supply, and were variously made available to institutions and private individuals.

With the return of Labour to power in 1964 there was once more a sharp recovery in the rate of completion of new houses by local authorities. From the low point of 16,245 completions in 1962, local authority output in Scotland jumped to 24,814 in 1964 and, after a brief pause, to 27,092 in 1967. Total public sector output reached 33,960 in that year and the figure was over 34,000 in both 1969 and 1970. Much of this construction was connected with the new town, dispersal and growth point movements discussed earlier. Again it is interesting to note that private construction in Scotland grew only slowly throughout the 1960s, from 7,147 in 1961 to 8,220 houses in 1970 (see Appendix A).

Gradually, however, the attempt by governments to sustain greater and greater real levels of public expenditure foundered. The Labour Governments 1964-70, Conservative 1970-74, Labour, together latterly with their Liberal allies, 1974-79, each, to greater or lesser degree, attempted to support huge levels of public expenditure on various social programmes in an effort to secure what was perceived to be greater social justice and to maintain full employment at all costs. The hope was that public expenditure could be sustained by accelerated economic growth through 'the white hot technological revolution', through more efficient industrial and economic planning, and by entry to the European Common Market.

In the event, although growth rates were more or less maintained up to the oil crisis of 1973-74, the experiment was foredoomed to failure since it unleashed unprecedented and insupportable levels of inflation – in excess of 20 per cent in 1975-76 and again in 1979-80 – and progressively undermined the competitive base of UK industry. The various prices and incomes policies to which well-meaning governments had resort merely had the effect of institutionalising inflation, while the social cohesion of the country was severely threatened, both by frequent and vicious industrial disputes (especially 1973-74 and in the 'winter of discontent' in 1979) and by a tendency towards political fragmentation.[58]

In the effort to keep public expenditure under control, inevitably the public authority housing programme was curbed. Local authority house completions in Scotland fell to just over 13,000 in 1974, recovered briefly to 16,086 in 1975 and then declined sharply to 4,755 in 1979. By comparison, private construction increased to 11,614 in 1971 and in 1978, for the first time since 1925, private builders erected more houses than the combined public sector – the respective figures being 14,443 and 11,316 (see Appendix A).

In general terms, the dramatic slow-down in public construction was justified. Crudely, the kingdom's stock of dwellings was now more than sufficient to match the numbers of households. Indeed, this had been the case from the late 1950s on and thereafter the gap between numbers of dwellings and households had steadily widened (by 1985 there were 2,012,000 dwellings as against 1,786,000 recorded households).[59] However, as the government's Green Paper, *Scottish Housing*, noted in 1977, it did not 'follow automatically from this that Scotland has

Houses at Kirkintilloch.

38

too many houses'. When allowance was made for second homes, empty houses waiting for modernisation, houses officially classified as sub-tolerable, and the impossibility of offsetting shortages and surpluses in differing localities, it was argued that 'a simple comparison between households and houses is only the first step towards an assessment of housing need'.[60] While this line of argument was, and is, correct, the fact remained that it was becoming impossible to argue that there was any general housing shortage in Scotland.

Another factor which tended to validate the sharp contraction of new public building was the marked trend towards private home ownership. From 1973 to 1978 the proportion of owner occupation increased from 32 to 35 per cent (the equivalent figures for England are 54 and 56 per cent) and, given the financial protection which private home owning provided in an age of high inflation, it was reasonable to expect more private individuals to want to own their own houses in future. (By 1983 the respective figures for Scotland and England had become 38 per cent and 62 per cent; and the trend has continued so that the relevant Scottish figure is now 42 per cent.)[61]

Nevertheless there were bound to be problems occasioned by the dramatic restriction of public sector construction. In some areas housing shortages remained, notably in the north-east where oil-related development was proceeding rapidly, while in Glasgow the long years of dispersal had left large areas of the city with dereliction and decay reminiscent of the bomb sites of the war years.

Indeed, reviews conducted in the 1970s indicated that there were still several major areas of difficulty requiring urgent attention, and this was particularly revealed by the government report, *Urban Deprivation Working Note 6, Great Britain*, which was based on an analysis of the 1971 national census figures, and concerned information on overcrowding, lack of exclusive use of basic amenities and male unemployment. Here it was shown that Scotland, with just over 11 per cent of the British population, nevertheless contrived to possess 77.4 per cent of the 'worst 5 per cent' of the nation's most deprived areas. In particular, Clydeside had 95 per cent of the worst '1 per cent' areas in Britain. By comparison the boroughs of Inner London, the second most deprived area, had a mere 3.5 per cent in this category.[62]

Much of this dereliction was concentrated within the old communities of the east end of Glasgow and, in 1976, the remarkable GEAR (Glasgow Eastern Area Renewal) project was initiated by the Secretary of State. (The outcome to date of this venture is considered in Chapter 6.)

Generally the state of the older houses of the Glasgow area was abject. In 1975 the West Central Scotland Planning Committee estimated that 127,500 pre-1919 houses were in need of immediate rehabilitation or replacement and that two-thirds of the 256,000 pre-1919 houses lacked at least one basic amenity.[63] However, with the cut-back in public sector construction the traditional policy of demolition and dispersal, which had reduced Glasgow's population from 1,057,000 in 1961 to 816,000 by 1974, was no longer an option.[64] Now, and greatly to Glasgow's benefit, attention turned increasingly towards the restoration of the remaining properties.

By this period the state of the local authority houses built in the inter-war years and immediately after the Second World War was also giving rise to concern. Inevitably there had been deterioration in the condition of the dwellings which, in many

cases, had been of indifferent quality in the first place. By contemporary standards they were depressingly inadequate and often in need of radical reconstruction.

Overall, these various concerns were confirmed when, in preparing the 1977 Green Paper on Scottish Housing, the Scottish Development Department concluded that about a quarter of a million Scottish households were still unsatisfactorily housed either for reasons of overcrowding or because of the lack of exclusive use of basic amenities.[65]

Another matter of growing attention was the special housing needs of particular groups within the community. For example, in an age when more thought could be given to the quality of life of seriously disabled or handicapped citizens, the improvement which could be brought about by suitably designed or modified houses was appreciated. Similarly, by the mid 1970s more than 700,000 Scots were aged over 65 years and their numbers were increasing year by year. Here again, it was realised that specialised housing provision was required for a significant proportion of these older citizens, particularly in a society in which many of the elderly were, for a variety of reasons, becoming more isolated.

Thus by the end of the 1970s, when public sector construction had been sharply reduced, several serious housing problems remained to demand the attention of public authorities.

The contemporary period from 1979 on is discussed in detail later in this book (particularly Chapters 6 and 7) and there is, therefore, nothing to be added by describing it at this stage. Rather it is appropriate, now that the general background terrain has been mapped out, to concentrate on the SSHA and to begin by examining its origins.

CHAPTER TWO

The Origins of the SSHA

Although the SSHA itself dates from 1937 its roots, and some of its stock of houses, are actually considerably older and extend right back to the heart of the Garden City movement at the beginning of the century.

In 1898 Ebenezer Howard published his little volume *Tomorrow* (renamed *Garden Cities of Tomorrow* in 1902) in which he set out his vision of planned, balanced communities of 50,000 people who would live in cottages with gardens, surrounded by extensive open spaces and protected green belts.[1] Although such communities could obviously have only limited applicability, Howard's ideas were enormously influential in shaping notions of town planning and, in due time, gave rise to the later enthusiasm for New Towns.

The Fabian Society eagerly embraced the concept, publishing various tracts including Raymond Unwin's *Cottage Plans and Common Sense* and, between 1904 and 1906, the first residential sections of Letchworth were completed to designs prepared by Unwin and Barry Parker.

In practical terms there was little chance of developments of this kind achieving much in the way of resolving the urban problems of the mass of the industrial population: however the ideas did excite great interest in Scotland and, when in the years leading up to the First World War, there was need for the construction of a major naval dockyard at Rosyth, the chance occurred to create a small-scale Garden City – a Garden Village – in this part of the country.

Since the eighteenth-century Rosyth had been recognised as an excellent site for a dockyard and it was an obvious choice when, in the period after 1900, naval tension between Britain and Germany increased the need for a large east-coast facility to accommodate the rapidly expanding Royal Navy. The decision was announced in March 1903 and thereafter land and fore-shore were purchased and, from 1908, access roads laid down. The task of constructing the dockyard was no light one, and by 1913, 3,500 men were employed in this activity. Already the numbers were more than could be housed in the locally available accommodation and it was evident that the pressure for houses would be greatly increased once the dockyard became operative.[2]

Indeed, the living conditions of the construction workers became something of a scandal. As was customary at the time, the responsibility for housing these people rested with the contracting company, Messrs Easton Gibb and Sons, and this firm, using materials provided by the Admiralty, erected two hutted encampments, known officially as Bungalow City East and Bungalow City West, but referred to locally as Tintown. Conditions in the huts of Tintown were primitive with up to twenty-six people to a hut – single men at one end, families at the other. In these circumstances the need for permanent housing was pressing.

The problem was, however, that there was no consensus as

Portion of Rosyth Village

to whose job it was to create the required New Town. In 1910 the Admiralty had proposed the building of Rosyth on Garden City lines, but would not accept the responsibility – and financial burden – involved. The government in general was eager that the task should be done properly since it would be the first major test of the Town Planning Act of 1909 and, as such, would be closely scrutinised by local authorities all over the country.[3] But there was no agreement as to which branch of government should fund and deal with the matter. Dunfermline Burgh council were also keenly interested. They knew that they did not themselves have the resources to house the incoming workers, but were equally determined that 'no part of the area should become the "happy hunting ground of the jerrybuilder"'.[4] Accordingly the Burgh Council submitted its own impressive plan for the New Town which was approved by the Local Government Board for Scotland, but again, without any clear guidance as to how it should be brought to life.

Eventually the Edinburgh and East of Scotland Branch of the Garden Cities and Town Planning Association offered their help and, in December 1913, Raymond Unwin was appointed by the Admiralty to prepare a detailed plan using the Garden City concept. This involved low density housing – approximately ten houses per acre – each house having its own garden and boundary fence. A green belt was designated around the whole town, provision was made for the protection of local woodland areas, and planned shopping facilities were designed to make the town tolerably self-sufficient in that respect.

With the approach of war the need for progress was becoming increasingly imperative. The dockyard managers expected to be employing 2,000 of their own people by 1915-16 on work on the fleet and these would be in addition to the construction workers engaged in completing the various dock facilities.

Tenders were invited from private contractors interested in building the town, but no satisfactory offer was received. As a result it was decided to form a quite novel organisation to take on the task and on 15th October 1914 the Scottish National Housing Company was incorporated for this purpose.[5]

Even then, however, delays occurred with disputes involving local landowners and the local authority. With King George V due to open the base on 8 June 1915, no further argument could be tolerated; hence in May the government pushed through the Housing (Rosyth Dockyard) Act of 1915 which brushed aside the normal Scottish building acts and by-laws and enabled the Garden City plan to be progressed.

The Scottish National Housing Company was intended to be, and remained, a single purpose organisation. The Dunfermline Burgh Council held the majority of the shares in the Company, but a small proportion were owned by private individuals. Ninety per cent of the funds for the building operations were loaned by the Local Government Board, with the balance being provided by the Company.

The original plans were to erect 3,000 houses over six years, but in the event the Company only completed 1,872 between 1916 and 1919. From then on, under the Housing Acts of 1919 and 1924 the Burgh Council were able to take over the task of completing the town and this was virtually finished by 1930.

The SNHC initially built 150 dwellings in blocks of two, four and eight houses within the triangle of Admiralty Road, Backmarch Road and Queensferry Road, and thereafter, over the next three years, completed approximately 500 houses per year. This was a fair achievement, particularly when viewed against the background of competing wartime priorities for materials and labour, and the prevailing high rates of inflation in the prices of building materials.

The first 150 houses were actually completed to designs prepared by the Edinburgh based firm, Greig and Fairbairn, but the work was overseen by one of Unwin's pupils, A.H. Mottram, and many of the subsequent houses were designed by him.[6] Later, Mottram was to become the first architect on the staff of the SSHA.

Looked at today, the interesting thing is the astonishing range and variety of house types and the evocative sense of the Garden City which they convey. In fact, of course, the buildings are seminal in the history of housing in this period since this was one of the projects which were conceived by Unwin immediately prior to the setting up of the Tudor Walters Committee. Presumably, therefore, Rosyth acted as something of a test-bed for his ideas and perhaps also for the planning of Welwyn Garden City in 1919-20. Curiously, however, despite the pleasant architectural character of the houses, the trees,

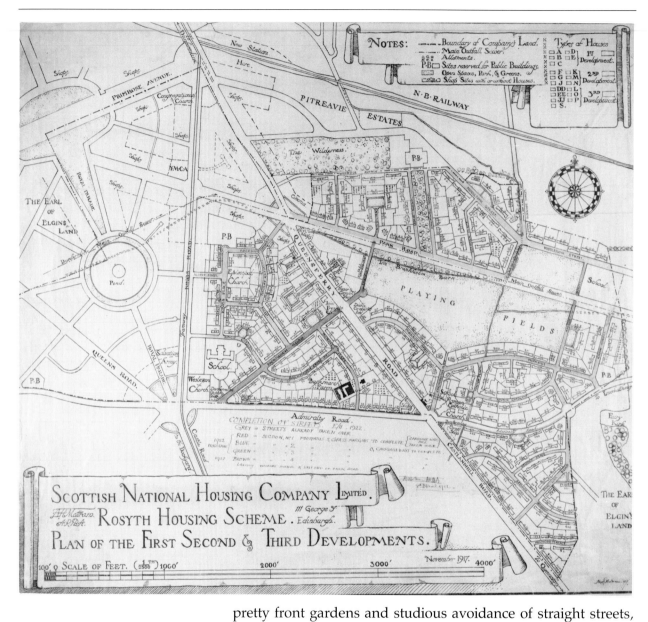

SCOTTISH NATIONAL HOUSING COMPANY LIMITED.
ROSYTH HOUSING SCHEME. *111 George St. Edinburgh.*
PLAN OF THE FIRST SECOND & THIRD DEVELOPMENTS.

100' 0 SCALE OF FEET. ($\frac{1}{2500}$) 1000'   2000'   3000'   *November* 1917. 4000'

Above The plans of Rosyth.

pretty front gardens and studious avoidance of straight streets, the houses at Rosyth were not at first popular with the tenants who complained that the rooms were awkwardly shaped and that the terraced houses had no rear access. They also objected to what they regarded as the excessively high rents (in spite of which, the Company consistently failed to achieve its targeted maximum annual dividend of 5 per cent). Today the area is

quite properly a designated conservation area and the houses are prized by their tenants or owner occupiers. (Just over 24 per cent – 455 houses – of 'old' Rosyth has been sold to sitting tenants since 1980.)

With the introduction of the Addison Act, giving local authorities the financial support to build their own houses, there were moves to dissolve the Scottish National Housing

Company, but these were rejected by the Local Government Board on the striking grounds that 'we may need such bodies as the Company in the event of the local authorities failing to undertake housing schemes'.[7] These were prophetic words and thus it was that this odd organisation survived, maintaining its houses at Rosyth until the properties were taken under SSHA management in 1963. The SNHC was formally wound up in 1969, but interestingly, the Scottish Special Housing Association may be known by its full name, by its initials or as the 'Scottish Special', in every other part of Scotland, but in Rosyth it has inherited its predecessor's title – 'the Company'.

As it happens, as early as 1925 the government – or at least one member of the government – did believe that local authority failings required the use of the Company, and this brings us to the next key link in the chain leading to the creation of the SSHA. In this case, however, the houses, though interesting, were to be very different from Unwin's classical cottages.

As we saw earlier, the withdrawal of the subsidies of the Addison Act produced a sharp drop in local authority house completions in 1924 and 1925, when the replacement Chamberlain measure attempted to shift the emphasis back to private construction. In Scottish terms this was not a viable option because the independent Scottish building industry was simply not capable of delivering the volume of houses required and, even if it had been, the generality of Scottish working people could not have afforded to buy the houses. Chamberlain, however, did not believe that there was any reason for making Scotland a special case, a view which was not shared by Walter Elliot*, the Parliamentary Secretary for Health at the Scottish Office. On the Bill's passage through the Commons Elliot was given the job of winding up for the government. He made clear his opinion that Scotland had been badly treated.[8]

The short-lived minority Labour Government improved the prospects with the introduction of the Wheatley Act, but this

Sir Walter Elliot, 1888-1958.
Educated Glasgow Academy and Glasgow University (1st class Hons Science, 1910 and Medicine, 1918). MO with Royal Scots 1914-18 (MC and bar). Conservative MP for Lanark 1919-23; for Kelvingrove 1924-45 and 1950-58; for the Scottish Universities 1948-50. Secretary of State for Scotland 1936-38, Minister of Health 1938-40, Director of Public Relations War Office 1941-42. Rector of Aberdeen University 1933-36 and Glasgow University 1947-50.

had not had time to have much effect when the return of the Conservatives brought Elliot back to the Scottish Office, this time as Parliamentary Under-Secretary of State. He was, in time, to prove himself one of the most outstanding and vigorous Scottish politicians of his day and it has been said of him that he belonged to those 'independent-minded Tories for whom Conservatism was a matter of ideas and principles rather than class interest and party tactics'.[9]

If Elliot was aware that a separate initiative was required in respect of Scottish housing, he was also deeply concerned by the depressed state of the traditional heavy industries in this part of the country. In particular, the shipbuilding yards of Clydeside were in a sad plight and, by turns, this had affected the local engineering, steel and coal industries. Part of the problem was a reaction to the cessation of the massive naval construction programme of the years before and throughout the war, during which time the industry had been grossly over-expanded. With the coming of peace many ships were cancelled or broken up on the stocks and there was naturally little new building to be expected for a time. But a predictable recession was turned into something larger by the Washington Conference of 1922 which restricted the Royal Navy to two new battleships in the next ten years (neither of these ships were built on the Clyde). Moreover, first the Labour Government of 1924 and subsequently Winston Churchill, as Chancellor of the Exchequer in the new government, bitterly resisted the Admiralty's plans for new cruisers and succeeded in limiting them to four ships under the 1925-26 estimates. Only one of these came to the Clyde – to Fairfields – and although, in the following year, an order placed with John Brown's for two similar ships for the Australian Government brought some temporary relief, these were bitter years for the naval shipbuilding companies and their employees.[10] Moreover, the slack could not be taken up by the construction of merchant ships since the international trading position was very poor (in 1925, UK exports amounted to a mere three-quarters of the 1913 level[11]).

In all of these circumstances, the idea of using steel and unemployed shipbuilding and steel workers to attack Scotland's housing problem appealed strongly to Elliot and to the industrialists of the region. However, given the opposition of Chamberlain – now back at the Ministry of Health – to any special housing policy for Scotland, it was going to be necessary to elicit some powerful support if such a project were to stand any chance of success. It was in an effort to obtain such backing that the new Scottish Secretary, Sir John Gilmour, persuaded the Prime Minister, Stanley Baldwin, to have a private look for himself at the slums of Cowcaddens and the Gorbals.[12]

Elliot accompanied the Prime Minister on his visit to Glasgow on 1st October 1925 and, although it was supposed to be informal, did not hesitate to keep the press informed as to his purpose. The *Glasgow Herald* commented –

[13] Major Elliot said that housing was a subject engaging the closest attention of the Prime Minister and the Secretary for Scotland, and he hoped it might be possible, especially after Mr Baldwin's visit to Glasgow, to get the justice of the Scottish claim admitted, namely that we in Scotland had a special problem and should, if necessary, be allowed special consideration in dealing with it.

The plan worked to perfection and that evening Baldwin announced an offer of a subsidy of £40 per house to Scottish local authorities which would erect steel houses prefabricated by local firms normally active in the shipbuilding and engineering industries and using labour of which only 10 per cent would be conventional building trade workers.[14]

When the news broke Chamberlain was furious. 'The Scottish Office', he wrote to his sister, 'will always make a bungle of it, if it is possible to do so...', and he went on to berate Elliot outrageously.[15] A fortnight later he came himself to inspect the slums of Dundee, to 'extol the virtues of owner occupation, and at the City Chambers that evening (to) speak not at all playfully of the need of his Department to be "exceedingly watchful" that the Scottish Office got no more out of government than its due share'.[16]

Having discomfited his formidable Minister of Health, Elliot now found fresh opposition to his project arising from two opposite directions. The ILP Clydesiders in the Commons noisily objected that he was proposing to replace bricklayers with less skilled and lower paid workers. On the other hand, some of the right-wing Tories in his own constituency sarcastically complained about the excessively high standards of council housing.[17]

Perhaps those opinions from the opposite flanks of the

political spectrum were shared by many local councillors; or perhaps it was that the Wheatley subsidies were once more enabling local authorities to plan to build significant numbers of traditional houses; but whatever the reason, the initial response to Baldwin's offer of a special subsidy for building steel houses was meagre, with few councils declaring an immediate interest.

Elliot, however, was not prepared to let the project languish. In the view of his department there was a current shortage of some 80,000 working-class houses in Scotland.[18] Accordingly, if the local authorities were not interested in building steel houses, the government would find another way. Thus the offer of an additional subsidy was withdrawn and Baldwin announced on 18th December 1925 that the government themselves would build 2,000 prefabricated steel houses.[19]

A few days later the Secretary of the Scottish Board of Health wrote to the Scottish National Housing Company proposing that it should erect the houses on behalf of the government. The Board of Health offered to meet any loss sustained by the Company and to provide additional protection to ensure that the hoped for 5 per cent dividend would be honoured in respect of the Company's operations at Rosyth. If, however, it was felt by the Company that the construction of steel houses in various parts of the country was incompatible with its present functions then the Board of Health suggested that an independently funded subsidiary company be formed for which the SNHC would provide office accommodation and administrative and technical staff.[20]

In the event, the latter option was preferred, perhaps because the Dunfermline Burgh Council and private shareholders of the SNHC were not much interested in building novel houses in different localities, but perhaps also because its own Articles of Association linked the Company to the creation of a Garden City type of development and steel houses may not have seemed to fit the appropriate image. As a result, in January 1926, the Second Scottish National Housing Company was formed as a separate subsidiary company. Its activities were funded by a loan from the Public Works Loan Board equivalent to 50 per cent of the cost of the houses and repayable over forty years at fixed interest. The remainder would be contributed by the Scottish Board of Health by a loan to which 5 per cent annual interest was attached.[21]

The original purpose of the Second SNHC was to erect, complete, maintain and let 2,000 houses in several parts of the country.[22] Later, an additional 500 houses were added to the programme and, between 1926 and 1928, a total of 2,552 steel houses were constructed in a variety of industrial locations. Specifically, as a letter to the Treasury explained, the purposes of the venture were to assist in relieving the housing shortage, to alleviate unemployment in the steel and kindred (shipbuilding) trades and to induce local authorities to follow suit, thus enhancing the impact of the effort.[23] The latter hope was regrettably not fulfilled since few councils responded and the effect on unemployment was, therefore, not sustained.

The three firms involved in the provision of the houses were Cowieson, Atholl Steel Houses Limited, and G. & J. Weir (Cardonald). In the case of the Atholl houses the management of the operation appears to have been in the hands of the famous naval shipbuilding company, Wm Beardmore and Company Limited*.[24] The managers of the SNHC do not seem to have been thrilled by some of the Weir house designs in particular and in a letter of 28th December 1925 to the Secretary for Scotland, complained that 'whenever Weir houses are built trouble is likely to ensue'. However, a visit by the Company's architects to the Weir factory dispelled some of the fears, and approximately 1,500 of the houses were built to Weir designs – mainly Weir 'Douglas' cottages, 'Eastwood' bungalows and 'Blanefield' flats.

Entry to the first site was secured as early as February 1926 and by October of that year the first 404 houses had been completed and 382 were occupied, which is a good indication of the strength of demand from potential tenants. The contracting firms provided the foundations and superstructures while the Company arranged for all services such as gas, water, drainage, fencing, footpaths, and clothes poles. In the event, costs were competitive with traditional costs and it was argued that the introduction of these houses would help to keep general house prices down.[25]

The building unions, however, were not happy with the labour arrangements. A condition of the scheme was that not

*Beardmore's had employed no less than 42,000 men in its heyday in 1918 – a figure which shows something of the scale of the problem caused by the recession in shipbuilding.

more than 10 per cent of the workers should be drawn from the traditional building trades both to avoid taking people from the conventional building industry's labour pool and, of course, specifically to take up men from the distressed industries. The result was that, to the annoyance of the unions, plumbers, electricians, joiners, etc from the shipyards were employed on the houses. In reaction the building unions objected to their members working with new materials but in the prevailing climate of employment and in the immediate aftermath of the General Strike in 1926, it is doubtful if they were in any position to make their views prevail. However, when shipbuilding temporarily picked up in 1927 the 10 per cent stipulation was abandoned.[26]

The houses themselves were built mainly in the west of Scotland and in Glasgow at Springboig, Shettleston and Rob-royston. The remainder were erected in Edinburgh (350) and Dundee (300). In terms of external appearance the houses did not look especially unusual. The majority were two-storey, either semi-detached or terraced, and usually topped with a pitched roof. In general, the external walls consisted of large steel plates with turned flanges which were bolted together on the bottom, over which a U-sectioned steel stiffener was welded to provide additional strength.

The original predicted life of the houses was assumed to be forty years and almost all easily reached that target. Sixteen, located in Greenock, were flattened by enemy bombs during the war and a handful of the remainder succumbed to the normal risks of destruction by fire. Otherwise, they are all still in use. Indeed, some of the 250 houses constructed at Lochend in Edinburgh were fashioned from steel of such strength and quality that when their modernisation was planned the Scottish Development Department – probably unwisely – declined to sanction the introduction of external cladding on the lines normally applied to the enhancement of post-war steel houses. A more restricted modernisation of these houses – comprising renewal of kitchen fitments and sanitary ware, rewiring, renewal of internal doors and installation of partial central heating – was carried out between 1980 and 1983 at a cost of £1.8 million. That they are excellent dwellings is borne out by the fact that approximately 20 per cent of the Lochend houses have been purchased by tenants.

Meanwhile, in 1926, Walter Elliot was reasonably pleased with his achievement. Addressing a by-election meeting in Kirkintilloch 'he hammered home the point that Baldwin's had been "the first government to admit the justice of the claim that Scotland had a special case in the matter of housing, and to make special provision for it"'.[27] As has been suggested, however, the local authorities declined to follow the example which had been set, hence the eventual outcome of the project was considerably less than Elliot had intended. Nevertheless, it is interesting to note that Elliot himself had won favourable opinions. In September 1928, no less a judge than Winston Churchill told the Prime Minister in a private letter that Elliot was 'by far the best' of the government's junior ministers.[28]

In 1929 the Labour Party returned to power, again as a minority government, but with the general support of a greatly reduced Liberal membership which was disinclined to rock the boat. This was a tragic period as it was the year in which a catastrophic economic crisis first struck the United States and then cast its malign shadow across the Atlantic. The slump which followed – and which virtually destroyed democracy in Germany – was of unprecedented ferocity and produced heart-breaking levels of unemployment in many parts of the country. In Scotland in 1931-33 unemployment varied between 26.1 and 27.7 per cent – the latter meaning that no less than 400,000 Scots were out of work.[29] And what made the situation so horrific was that much of the distress was concentrated into certain areas, namely the heartlands of the traditional heavy industries of shipbuilding, engineering, steel and coal.

The government did not survive the crisis and when, in 1931,

The steel houses at Lochend, Edinburgh.

Ramsay Macdonald accepted the premiership of a National Government, the move ruptured the Labour Party which was shattered in the subsequent General Election. Sir Godfrey Collins, a businessman and former Liberal Chief Whip, became Secretary of State for Scotland and, in 1934 he secured a victory in Cabinet which was soon to be significant. In that year a Ministry of Labour *Investigation into the Industrial Condition in Certain Distressed Areas* was followed by the Special Areas (Development and Improvement) Act. This resulted in the appointment of Commissioners whose job it would be to promote schemes to aid the recovery of those parts of the country which were most severely depressed. Although the Commissioner for England was appointed by the Minister of Labour, Collins successfully persuaded the Cabinet that the Scottish Commissioner should be under his jurisdiction and this, in some ways, was the beginning of the economic development function of the Scottish Office.[30]

In 1936 Sir Godfrey Collins died in office and was succeeded as Secretary of State by Walter Elliot, 'his prestige high from the work he had done as Minister of Agriculture in building an enduring edifice of controlled agricultural marketing and support'.[31]

The problems confronting Scotland were enormous for, proportionately, the depression had struck her more severely than England, as was perhaps to be expected given her greater dependence on a small number of particularly vulnerable industries. However, with Elliot as Secretary of State, vigorous action was not likely to be long delayed. Sure enough, almost immediately he persuaded the government to extend the boundaries of the 'special areas' – which already had included nearly one quarter of the Scottish population – and to empower the Commissioner to build industrial estates, to let factories, subsidise new industry, and widen the range of public utilities to be helped. Thereafter, Elliot turned his attention to housing.

Reviewing the situation, he was not satisfied with the progress which had been made either by the Scottish building industry or by the local authorities and concluded that the shortage of houses in the kingdom still amounted to something of the order of 250,000.[32] The survey on which he made that estimate was into overcrowding as assessed on the new standard introduced by the Housing Act of 1935.[33] If the problem was now attacked more effectively he believed this could also make a major contribution to reducing the level of unemployment. Given the background of his experience 1925-28, described in the preceding pages, Elliot had little doubt as to how the job should be tackled. Accordingly, he set out his views to the Cabinet in a memorandum dated 18th January 1937.

[34]   I have been deeply impressed by the deplorable condition of Scottish housing, but also by the recent falling-off in the rate of housing progress... The possibilities of using steel are at present being explored, but the present strain on the steel market makes it doubtful whether any substantial use of this material can be made for the time being*.

Neither concrete nor timber is likely to be a practicable alternative of any magnitude for house building in the core of large towns. The suburbs and the less thickly populated areas generally offer the best opportunity for the use of these materials. Experiments in construction with new materials would increase the already serious difficulties facing local authorities in carrying through their housing programmes, and I propose that a separate agency should be used to carry out this work. This separate agency at present exists, namely, the Scottish National Housing Company...

...The Company's organisation could rapidly be expanded to deal with a minimum programme of say 1,500 to 2,000 houses a year, and once it gets into full swing, it would be possible for the Company to provide if desired as many as 4,000 houses annually over a period of seven years. The Company's work would be complementary to and not in competition with the work of local authorities and it would release labour for ordinary building in areas where alternative methods of construction are less appropiate and where stringency in the labour supply might be experienced. On the programmes suggested, a substantial direct contribution would be made to the solution of the housing problem and, indirectly, the Company's work would, I hope, be so arranged as to have a salutary effect in

*Many blast furnaces had been lost during the depth of the depression and, with the cautious rearmament programme now under way, demand for steel was increasing faster than output.

stimulating local authorities to press forward vigorously their organisation for ordinary construction.

He then went on to plead for a dispensation to provide the Company with special financial arrangements to offset the fact that it would not be able to obtain a rate-borne subsidy, and called for a campaign to upgrade some of the existing sub-standard older houses.

It is clear, therefore, that Elliot was no longer prepared to leave the resolution of Scottish housing problems to the stunted private building industry or to local authorities which, in some of the most stricken parts of the country, already had their hands more than full. Now, in his view, the major drive must come via central government and, if traditional houses could not be produced in sufficient number for lack of skilled labour, or if the vast legions of the unemployed were to be enabled to join in the effort, fresh thinking should be applied to devise new house types of timber or concrete.

In view of his earlier activities it was natural for Elliot to look to the Scottish National Housing Companies as the means, but in the interim the management experience of the Second SNHC had not been happy. Financially it had fallen into severe difficulties. Although its rents were considered to be high and tenants seem to have had difficulty in paying them, the Company had enormous problems in repaying its debt. In 1934 the Treasury had had to waive arrears of interest and to suspend payment of future interest to the Public Works Loans Board, but with an increasing tax liability, with rent control and with many tenants in difficulty, there was little prospect of rapid improvement.[35] In these circumstances, and perhaps also because of the nature of the Companies' Articles of Association, Elliot's first thoughts on the matter had quickly to be dropped. Instead, consideration now turned to the creation of a new custom-built organisation.

By 1937 the English economy was pulling steadily out of the Depression but, by comparison, Scotland was still in the toils and Elliot, therefore, was desperately keen to do everything possible to stimulate the inflow of new growth industries. It was for this reason that he had persuaded the Cabinet to allow the Special Areas Commissioner to establish industrial estates and it was no great leap to connect his housing plan to the Commissioner's activities. This idea was backed by Sir William

Douglas, the Secretary of the Department of Health for Scotland, and so it was that the Scottish Special Areas Housing Association Limited was born in the autumn of 1937, with the specific task of building working-class houses within the Special Areas of Scotland.

Within a few months, however, Elliot realised that it was unwise to restrict the Association exclusively to operations within the defined Special Areas; hence in the Housing (Financial Provisions) (Scotland) Act, 1938, the Association was empowered to undertake the erection of working-class houses elsewhere 'for experimental or demonstration purposes'.[36] This was an obvious attempt to encourage and stimulate the activities of local authorities wherever such help might be required. As we shall see, the new Association was intended to embark on no negligible programme, 'and so there was now the heady prospect of a Scotland without slums by 1942. A Scotland without rural slums as well, for there was now legislation to require much better standards of housing for the farm-worker and country dweller; with his agricultural background Elliot was insistent on this.'[37]

In fact, Elliot had probably moved just in time. In May 1937 his old adversary, Neville Chamberlain, became Prime Minister and when, some months later, the Secretary of State drew the Cabinet's attention to the continuing depression and social distress in Scotland and pleaded for a greatly increased programme of action, he was rebuffed. Shortly thereafter he was transferred, but the record of achievement in his two years at the Scottish Office is remarkable.

[38] Overall, the recollection of those who were closest to him – and it is one which has not faded with the years – is that so much was owed to Elliot's questing, argumentative mind in the imparting of a sense of purpose and cohesion in the sectors of Scottish administration over which he presided... And he was greviously disappointed when the Prime Minister moved him to the Ministry of Health... To Elliot this was no promotion; rather it seemed to him an exasperating interruption in what he hoped would be his continuing work for Scotland.

Nevertheless, if any one man can be said to have created the SSHA it is certainly Walter Elliot and, in no small way, its achievements must rank as a part of his legacy to the kingdom.

CHAPTER THREE

The Early Years

The records of the earliest months of the Association's history are understandably somewhat sketchy, but certain things seem evident. First, Sir David Allan Hay* resigned his position as Commissioner for the Special Areas and accepted the appointment as the Association's chairman. Thereafter a Council of Management was selected, presumably by Walter Elliot in consultation with Sir David, and perhaps also with Lord Nigel Douglas-Hamilton, who had succeeded to the Commissioner's office. Technically membership of the Association had to be obtained by the purchase of a £1 share so that the Council of Management was (and is) formed by the Association's members. The seven other men on the original Council each brought to the task a wide range of appropriate experience and standing. John A. Inglis* was a King's Counsel and the pay-master in Scotland; J.C. Welsh MP* was Labour member

Sir David Alan Hay KBE CA (1878-1957)
Commissioner for the Special Areas in Scotland 1936-37; chairman of the SSHA 1937-39; president of the Institute of Accountants and Actuaries in Glasgow 1944-46; president of the Institute of Chartered Accountants of Scotland 1952-53; Lord Dean of Guild in Glasgow 1950-52.

John A. Inglis KC (1873-1941)
Called to the Scottish Bar in 1898, and appointed King's Counsel 1926. Assistant Commissioner for Food Control 1918-20; trustee of the National Library of Scotland; vice-president of the Royal Society of Edinburgh; chairman of the Scottish History Society; and King's and Lord Treasurer's Remembrancer in Scotland.

James C. Welsh MP (1880-1954)
Official of the Lanarkshire Miners' Association; Labour MP for Coatbridge

for Bothwell; Colonel Shaw-Stewart* was a retired soldier; David Ronald a civil engineer; Alexander McKinna*, a former senior official at the Scottish Office; William C. Davidson* a chartered surveyor; and A.W. Brady. Their services were given on an entirely voluntary basis.

The first offices were obtained at 14 Calton Terrace, Edinburgh and the Commissioner advanced the sum of £42 19s 2d to have these redecorated.[1] At the first meeting at the office on 3rd December 1937 Mr George Ross – who had been seconded from the Scottish Office – was appointed secretary at an annual salary of £750 and other appointments were an accountant, J.F. Torrance (£350 per annum), a junior clerk, Charles King (25 shillings per week) and a shortland typist, Miss Janet G. Steel (£2 15s per week). Mr A.H. Mottram was appointed as consultant architect, although it was agreed that other architects would be contracted as required, and it was decided to recruit an engineer and a quantity surveyor as soon as possible. These individuals were to be paid fees in accordance with the scale laid down by the Department of Health for Scotland. At the same meeting the Clydesdale Bank was formally appointed as the Association's bankers and the story goes that this decision was reached after the office junior, Charles King, had carefully measured the distance from the office to the banks in the district and discovered that the branch of the Clydesdale Bank in Easter Road had it by a few yards.[2] Thus commenced a relationship which has survived amicably to this day.

Exactly what the Association's initial target was is not clear, but in the minutes of the first meeting, under the heading 'Financial Estimate for the Commissioner' the following state-

1922-31 and for Bothwell 1935-45. Author of a number of books on the mining industry.

Colonel B.H. Shaw-Stewart CMG EOS (1877-1939)
Educated at Marlborough and the Royal Military Academy, Woolwich. Served with the Royal Artillery, retiring from the Army in 1925.

Alexander McKinna
Sometime Housing Secretary to the Scottish Board of Health. As such he had been involved in the setting up of the Second SNHC.

William C. Davidson OBE JP FRICS (1886-1957)
Native of Cullen, Banffshire. Member of Stirling County Council and Convener of Property and Buildings Committee. Factor of Bannockburn, Barnton and Sauchie Estates. President of the Estate Factors Society and member of Scottish Housing Advisory Committee. Chairman of Scottish Farm Buildings Committee. Deputy Chairman of SSHA 1944-46.

ment is made.

3   'The Secretary was instructed to base the estimate, for which the Commissioner had called, on 3,000 houses having been commenced in that period, including 750 completed.'

It is probable that the Commissioner was preparing his estimates for the financial year 1938-39, and that is presumably the period in question. In any event, it is obvious that the Association was being encouraged to push ahead as rapidly as possible with a substantial programme.

Advancing from scratch to the kind of rate of construction which was being envisaged was no straightforward task. Two major problems seemed to have preoccupied the Council in these early days and neither of them were easily resolved. First, there was the problem of the acquisition of suitable building sites. Second, there was the need to identify and select an appropriate range of non-traditional houses whose forms of construction would lend themselves to the employment of workers not normally recruited by the building industry.

Theoretically sites from which the Association could choose were nominated by the local authorities and the Commissioner, but some local authorities were initially dubious about, or hostile to, the Association's activities and the situation could be further complicated if a reluctant landowner was involved. As a result, the selection of land for development often seemed to be something of a Hobson's choice and was invariably a slow business. The annual report for the year 1938-39, commented that 'many difficulties have been encountered during the year in the acquisition of sites, which has proved to be a long and laborious process in many cases, not made less so by the known desire of the Association to acquire land as soon as possible'.[4] It was for this reason that the Association asked the government for powers of compulsory purchase, a request which was to be frequently repeated, but the answer then was, as it remained until 1966, that the Association should not have such powers, but should rely continually on its ability to work harmoniously with the local authorities.

At that first meeting in December 1937, it was reported that members of the Council had already inspected possible sites owned by the County Council of Lanarkshire and it was agreed to ask for land at Tannochside, Carluke and O'Wood, Holytown. Thereafter various Councillors were deputed to examine land at Forth, Douglas and Coalburn in Lanarkshire, at Johnstone in Renfrewshire, at Slamannan in Stirlingshire and at Bathgate and Armadale in West Lothian, which had been offered by the respective local authorities.[5]

The selection of suitable non-traditional house types was also no simple matter. By definition, apart from steel houses, which were not then an option, there was very little experience or knowledge available in Scotland of houses which might meet the required criteria, but the best bet seemed to be houses constructed either of concrete or timber. In the case of the former, the Second Scottish National Housing Company had built two concrete houses at Springboig to replace two steel houses destroyed by fire and it was decided to ask the Company for the services of their Mr Bennett and perhaps one or two of his colleagues, to assist with the proposed first developments at Tannochside and Carluke.[6] At the same time it was agreed that timber houses would be erected at Holytown.

Today, houses constructed of wood in the post-war years are a common enough sight in various parts of Scotland and most people are familiar, at least from photographs, with some of the attractive wooden dwellings of Scandinavia. In 1937, however, even among members of the Council, there was a great deal of uncertainty about the risks involved in housing of this kind. The Forest Products Research Laboratory at Princes Risborough was consulted,[7] as were the Bug Infestation Committee of the Medical Research Council and the London County Council, which was known to have experimented with timber houses.[8] The principal concerns were with the level of sound insulation, the risks of vermin infestation and, above all, the danger of fire.

Over the following months information was gathered from many quarters and Mr McKinna and Mr Mottram embarked on a tour of inspection in various parts of England to examine houses which might be regarded as suitable. They were impressed by poured concrete cavity wall houses which had been erected twelve years or so earlier in Ipswich by Messrs Whatlings and it was decided to adopt this method for 200 houses which were to be constructed in Johnstone. Similarly, they were satisfied with some solid wall red cedar houses which Messrs Tarran, in conjunction with the British Columbian Timber Commissioner, had built in Hull.

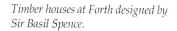
These were expected to be better at resisting damp and rot than European timber houses and to have a lower cost of upkeep. The decision was made to experiment by constructing solid walled European houses at Coalburn and the Canadian cedar houses at Forth, and for the latter site the appointed architect was a certain Mr Spence* of Edinburgh. Timber framed houses were to be erected elsewhere.[9]

And so it went on, with a few designs being selected for trial, while many others were exhaustively examined before being eliminated from further consideration for one or another reason. A close relationship developed with the Department of Building Research and by March 1939 three basic constructional forms had been adopted and were in use. These were:-

1   Poured cellular concrete, solid wall;
2   Poured dense concrete, cavity wall;
3   Timber, solid and framed, with outer wall of timber.

Sir Basil Spence (1907-76)
Professor of Architecture, Royal Academy, 1961-68. Designer of Coventry Cathedral, 1951, and of many estates, theatres, schools, university buildings, churches and factories throughout Britain. Perhaps the most famous British architect of his day.

In addition, Council had also agreed that provided the prices were acceptable at the time of going to tender, two other types of concrete house and steel houses could reasonably be adopted. In respect of the use of steel the British Steel Association had submitted proposals, but Council were not yet fully satisfied that the necessary standard of design could be achieved economically.[10]

Part of the problem in the choice of house types was that the Association was not simply trying to find good quality non-traditional buildings which could be constructed at reasonable cost. A key matter was also connected with the contribution which its operations were expected to make to the economic relief of the distressed areas. Sometimes a compromise had to be made. For example, in January 1938 when the Council discussed the sources of supply of timber houses the chairman reminded them that, while they could not ignore sources which could promise early delivery, their duty was to do what they could to encourage industry in the Special Areas.[11] Thereupon Council agreed that the following clause should be included in all contracts placed with companies operating on behalf of the Association.

[12] Preference must be given to articles, goods or materials obtained from or manufactured in the Special Areas provided that the price and quality compare favourably with those outside the Special Areas. Purchases from outside the Special Areas will require the specific approval of the Association.

As was indicated in the last chapter, when steel houses were erected by the Second SNHC the traditional building unions reacted with some hostility, and in an effort to prevent any repetition the Association immediately sought to establish a high standard of labour relations both in respect of direct labour and contracting firms. It was decided, for example, that all contracts should include a 'Fair Wages' clause in line with that normally applied to government contracts.[13] On 12th April 1938 a meeting was held with the Joint Council of the Building Industry, at which the chairman explained the purposes of the Association and expressed the hope that the Joint Council would give its support and advice should any matters of difficulty arise. He was assured of such assistance provided 'that the Association did nothing to disturb the traditions and agreed conditions within the industry'.[14]

However, as had been the case with the operations of the Second SNHC, the Clydeside ILP Group within the Commons were anything but sympathetic to the Association and remarkably, as it seems today, on 28th March, just four months after the organisation was set up, the chairman drew Council's attention to the questions which had been asked in the House alleging that the Association was dragging its feet and failing to produce any houses.[15] He impressed on his colleagues the need for speed.

As it happened, blinding speed was what followed; although whether this was because Walter Elliot was determined to quench political opposition in Parliament, or, as is more likely, he simply saw the opportunity for a first-class piece of public relations, is unclear. What is certain is that a day or two later the Association was requested to erect a block of two timber houses at Carfin by the end of April. The immediate reason for haste was that the King and Queen were coming to open the Empire Exhibition at Bellahouston Park in Glasgow in the first week of May and had agreed to visit Lanarkshire on the following day to look at the work being done in the Special Areas. An industrial estate was being developed at Carfin and the chance, therefore, existed to erect two houses on the site which Their Majesties could be invited to inspect.

Council were informed on 12th April that Sir David Allan Hay had responded immediately by ordering the erection of two Canadian timber houses and by the 9th April the framing for the walls was already in position. Naturally Council approved the chairman's action and, since it was felt that the houses should, if possible, be occupied, the secretary was instructed to ask the County Clerk to nominate two suitable tenants. That day the Department of Health for Scotland telephoned to suggest that one of the houses might be furnished for exhibition purposes by the Council for Art and Industry and this was agreed.[16]

The visit of the royal couple to Glasgow and to Lanarkshire in May 1938 was important not only to the SSHA or to the Scottish Office; it was also of major significance to the people of these battered parts of the country and to the King and Queen themselves. 1936 had been the year of the abdication crisis and the visit to Scotland almost coincided with the first anniversary of the coronation. Today, there is no more revered person in the kingdom than Queen Elizabeth the Queen Mother, and her husband's memory is honoured, particularly for the dignity with which he led the country through the war, but at the time there remained some uncertainty in respect of the divided loyalties which the public were assumed naturally to have following the abdication of King Edward. In the event, the visit seems to have been a triumph from start to finish with huge crowds turning out in glorious sunshine to cheer them on their way. 'Lanarkshire has never made a greater demonstration of loyalty', commented the *Glasgow Herald* in an extensive report covering three full pages.[17] The King made it his business to enquire into everything which was being done for the relief of unemployment and, of course, they visited the two houses.

Wherever she went it was the habitual custom of the young Queen Elizabeth to take a particular interest in housing and, for example, it was not unknown for her to make quite unofficial tours of inspection to see what action was being taken to relieve slum housing conditions in various parts of the country.[18] She must therefore have enjoyed the opportunity of seeing these two unusual prototypes. The *Motherwell Times* carried the following report:-

[19] The next stage of the visit took King George and Queen Elizabeth to the timber houses built for the Special Areas Housing Association Ltd by the Red Cedar Supply Company Ltd, Glasgow. First they entered the house which was furnished for display purposes but is not as yet occupied.

Next door live Mr and Mrs George Taylor, who until Monday lived in a single apartment at 83 Carfin Street, New Stevenston, in property which is to be demolished. Mr Taylor, who is an engineer, is well known in the district and is a native.

Lord Nigel Douglas-Hamilton informed Mr and Mrs Taylor of Their Majesties' desire to see round their new home – a request which was speedily granted.

Presented by the Commissioner, Mr and Mrs Taylor and their three daughters, Grace, Myra and Joyce, shook hands with the royal visitors.

Mr Taylor informed them that he had taken up occupancy only on Monday and the Queen remarked that Mrs

Taylor had certainly got things in spick and span order. They then visited each apartment in turn and Queen Elizabeth was greatly interested in the kitchenette range. Entering one of the bedrooms, the Queen remarked, 'Isn't it lovely?' and the King agreed. Before leaving Their Majesties and the Secretary of State for Scotland expressed the wish that Mr and Mrs Taylor and family would be happy in their new home.

At the site Sir David Allan Hay, chairman, and Mr James Welsh, MP, director *(sic)* of the Housing Association were presented. Their Majesties shook hands with Mr Mac-Dougall and Mr Alex Douglas, who superintended the building of the houses...

Thirty-three years later, Mrs Taylor remembered in an interview for the Association's Staff Journal that, since she had only been in residence for two days she had been unable to answer many of the Queen's questions. She also recalled the circumstances of the letting of the houses. 'We were chosen out of forty other tenants from our old houses – then we had to receive King George VI and Queen Elizabeth.' Interestingly, she was also consulted as to whom she wanted as neighbouring tenant and chose Mr and Mrs Gwynne, who had been their previous neighbours. In the same report Mrs Gwynne described the 'bus loads' of visitors who came for months afterwards to look at the houses.[20]

Mr and Mrs Taylor lived out their lives at Carfin and, at the time of writing, it is a matter of great pleasure throughout the SSHA that Mrs Gwynne, now sadly a widow, remains the Association's senior – though not necessarily most elderly – tenant. The houses, too have worn splendidly and are still much admired by contemporary visitors. A few months after the Royal visit the Association commenced the construction of somewhat similar houses at Watling Street in Motherwell.

If the Taylors, the Gwynnes, the Secretary of State, the Commissioner and the Association were all delighted with the timber houses, their views, predictably, were not endorsed by the ILP members in the Commons. In addition to the SSHA houses, the Swedish Government had erected two demonstration timber houses in Carntyne in Glasgow, and James Maxton, MP, – perhaps the most generally admired of the Clydesiders – challenged the government.

A modern view of the houses at Carfin.

Timber houses built at Watling Street, Motherwell.

21 Mr Maxton: As the people of Scotland could be housed in good solid granite and sandstone a hundred years ago, will the right honourable Gentleman see to it that he does not descend to this inferior substitute now?

Mr Colville: I understood that the hon Member's colleague a few moments ago wanted me to investigate every method which would help the housing conditions in Glasgow.

Mr Maxton: I hope that the right hon Gentleman will not understand that he is expected to start jerry building.

Coincidentally, just four days before Maxton got to his feet, the Association had noted that so many local authorities were now interested in timber house construction that 'it could no longer be regarded as an alternative available to any great extent to the Association...'. The trouble was that the demand for joiners was likely to quickly reach the point where there would be insufficient numbers for normal house construction. In these circumstances it was decided that concrete was likely to provide the main solution, since the latter method enabled the maximum use to be made of unskilled workers.[22]

Thus it was that the Association turned its attention increasingly to a method of house-building for which it was to become world famous. As early as January 1938 the appointment had been made as master of works of Mr Leonard Pond, at a salary of £550 per annum.[23] Having studied Dutch methods of building, Pond was acknowledged to be something of an expert in the use of concrete and he was recruited primarily because it was realised that private contractors in Scotland did not typically have the knowledge or experience to build by this method and that the Association would, therefore, have to do much of the construction by direct labour.

Leonard Pond's first action was to design steel shutters and five sets of these were ordered from two Glasgow firms – even although their tenders for the work were slightly higher than the figure quoted by an English company which was not located in a Special Area. Previous shutter systems were normally constructed of timber and, at the time, there was some discussion as to whether or not Pond's design should be patented, but the idea was later abandoned on the grounds that the design was not sufficiently novel.[24] Thereafter various experiments were conducted to decide on the best form of aggregate and Pond eventually selected crushed local whin-stone which was cemented together in a mixture without sand, thus producing the SSHA's particular form of 'no-fines concrete'.[25]

There was a frustrating delay while the shutters were being made, but when they were delivered to the Carluke site in October 1938 better progress followed. In the next seven months the whole of the walling for 222 houses was completed.[26] There was great interest in this operation and by the following March, Council had arranged for specifications to be made to enable contractors to tender for such work in future. 'Although...the Council of Management adopted direct labour for the first cellular concrete schemes they have always borne in mind that any form of construction, if it is to be of permanent value, should be capable of being carried out satisfactorily by contractors under the usual supervision.'[27] However, since the cost of a set of shutters (£642) was considered to be high Council believed that the system was likely only to be viable in a large contract. Accordingly a contract for erecting no less than 2,600 houses in six sites in the West of Scotland was put out to tender and eventually awarded to Messrs William Arnott McLeod and Company.[28] It was realised, of course, that this scale of activity increased the danger of creating estates of crushing uniformity; hence variety was insisted on by the selection of eight different house designs for use on each of the various sites. In the event, costs of no-fines houses were reasonably competitive and comparative costs per house were eventually estimated as: cellular concrete solid wall £127, cavity wall £164 and traditional brick £123.[29]

The first year or so of the Association's existence had been both exhilarating and frustrating. Exhilarating, because there had been so much to do and so many plans to be laid, and because (as is obvious to the modern reader of minutes which, despite the dry formal language, convey an unmistakable atmosphere of excitement) everyone concerned had a deep sense of the value, of the rightness, of what they were attempting to achieve. Frustrating, because everything had seemed to take so much time and because the slowness with which ideas could be translated into the reality of visible houses occupied by tenants had exposed the organisation to irritating and unfair criticism from those who purported to speak for the very people whom it was the Association's object to help.

However, by the end of March 1939, as the summary below shows, the Annual Report was able to declare that significant momentum was being gained.

Summary

Method	Completed	Under Construction	In Contracts but not yet commenced	In Preparation
Poured cellular concrete	–	586	– .	192
Cavity wall concrete	–	338	2,026	–
Timber	2	440		854
Not yet decided	–			1,095
	2	1,364	2,026	2,141

Total 5,533 houses[30]

In this programme work had been commenced at sites at Carluke, Tannochside, Holytown, Douglas, Coalburn, Forth, Polbeth, Crofthead, Johnstone and Greenock (Bow Farm); contracts had been placed for developments in Airdrie, Kilmarnock, Greenock (Maukinhill) and Coatbridge; and schemes were in preparation for Bathgate, Kirknewton, Motherwell (Watling Street, and Muirhouse), Dalry, Bonhill, Armadale, Hurlford, Stevenston, Carluke and Douglas.

In March 1939 the Council learned with regret that one of their number, Colonel Shaw-Stewart, had died and in the same month, Sir David Allan Hay reluctantly resigned, 'for business reasons'.[31] Bearing in mind that these men had been giving their services voluntarily and that the job had been time-consuming and extremely demanding, the Council persuaded the government to change the regulations so that the office of chairman could become a full-time salaried appointment.[32] But it was on a basis of the Association having first call on his time

in return for an honorarium that Viscount Traprain – later the Earl of Balfour* – succeeded to the chairmanship.

At the same time two other significant changes occured. First the word 'Areas' was deleted from the Association's name and its Memorandum of Association was altered to enable it to build anywhere throughout Scotland.[33] This was in response to the appeals for help from local authorities outwith the Special Areas which had persuaded the government to agree that the organisation's remit should be broadened. Second, with the clouds of war gathering and with fears of the unknown effects of aerial bombing on cities in mind, the government decided that some attempt must be made urgently to provide emergency accommodation. Again therefore, the Association's Memorandum of Association was altered to enable it to provide, maintain and manage 'camps of a permanent character in Scotland' either by new building or by acquiring and renovating existing premises.[34] The word 'permanent' is worth noting and although the annual report refers to camps being used by schools in time of peace, it describes them 'in times of

Third Earl of Balfour (1902-68)
Educated Eton and Cambridge. Chairman of SSHA 1938-44; Chairman of Scottish Division of National Coal Board 1946-51 and a director of the NCB 1952-62. Chairman of Royal Commission on Scottish Affairs 1952-54. Governor of BBC in Scotland 1956-60 and director of Scottish Gas Board 1958-65.

emergency as evacuation camps'.[35] It was subsequently agreed that the annual report could not be shown to the press because 'certain items were of a very confidential nature',[36] and one can only conclude that the government did not wish the public to learn just yet that it was taking the precautionary step of erecting evacuation camps.

In 1938, Walter Elliot had been succeeded by Sir John Colville*. The Secretary of State met with Council on 10th March 1939 and thanked them for agreeing to take on their new duties. He explained that the provision of housing remained the major objective and asked the Association to press ahead with the recruitment of new staff as quickly as possible. He said that a special branch of the Department of Health for Scotland's Housing Division was being established to deal with the Association's work and that henceforth it would no longer require to operate directly under the Special Areas Commissioner.[37] It is obvious that the government were now satisfied that the Association had prepared the base from which a fundamental assault could now be launched to overcome Scotland's housing problem once and for all. A few days later Council learned that they had been given an immediate programme of 8,500 houses in locations outwith the Special Areas [38] and at the end of July news came of a further allocation of 20,000, this time for houses to be erected within the Special Areas.[39]

Rt Hon Sir John Colville – later first Lord Clydesmuir

Thus on the eve of war the government and the Association were clearly poised to embark on the major initiative which, had it proceeded, would have produced a very different housing pattern in Scotland from the one with which we are familiar today. Recently, reviewing the post-war housing period in the context of his history of the Scottish Office, John Gibson concluded that after the war 'too much had to be done too quickly...the enlightened legislation of Walter Elliot's years might have saved the day. But the coming of Hitler's war was the final misfortune; for Scotland the enforced stop to house-building in the autumn of 1939 had been a national disaster'.[40]

Meanwhile, in that last summer of peace, the Council had come up against a portentous problem. As part of the allocation of houses to be built outside the Special Areas the Association had offered to build a first tranche of 1,750 houses in Glasgow. This offer Glasgow had been unwilling to accept and some of the City's councillors were actively campaigning against any co-operation with the SSHA, with one councillor having written a hostile and misleading article in the ILP Journal *Forward*. In an effort to reconcile the dispute the chairman and Mr Wedderburn, the Parliamentary Under-Secretary of State, had a meeting in London with their sternest critics, the ILP Glasgow Members, Mr Campbell Stephen, Mr J. McGovern and Mr J. Maxton. At this meeting the chairman explained the Association's difficulty in obtaining sites without the Corporation's assistance, and the problem of trying to make maximum use of unskilled labour without falling foul of trades union regulations on some of the sites. It seems unlikely that they got a sympathetic hearing for, on learning of the outcome of the meeting, the Council agreed that if Glasgow were not prepared to co-operate within a reasonable time they should reallocate the houses amongst the many other local authorities which were eager to have their help.[41]

With the outbreak of war there were several changes in personnel. Florence Horsburgh MP*, who had served on the Council for a few months, resigned on her appointment as

Baroness Horsburgh PC GBE (d 1969)
Conservative MP for Dundee 1931-45 and for Moss Side division of Manchester 1950-59. Life peeress 1959. Parliamentary Secretary Ministry of Health 1939-45; Parliamentary Secretary Ministry of Food, 1945, and Minister of Education 1951-54.

Parliamentary Secretary to the Minister of Health. The Secretary, George Ross, and the Administrative Officer, Peter Cairns, returned to the Department of Health for Scotland from which they had been seconded. The Annual Report for 1940 noted the Association's 'desire to place on record their appreciation of the services of these gentlemen. From the date of the Association's incorporation, and even prior thereto ... Mr Ross laboured assiduously to achieve the object of the provision of new houses for which the Association had been established. His extensive knowledge of housing in Scotland was invaluable to the Association and he was largely responsible for laying the foundations of the Association's work.'[42] Mr Norman J. Campbell, formerly Town Clerk of Kilmarnock, succeeded to the post of Secretary. Lord Traprain, a Royal Naval Volunteer Reserve, departed within a few weeks and although he remained nominal chairman until 1944, and attended an occasional meeting, he never subsequently took a direct part in the affairs of the Association. (Later in the war he was to become Controller of Coal for Scotland.) From 1939 to 1944 Alexander McKinna, therefore, assumed responsibility as acting chairman. Gradually several of the younger members of staff also trickled off into the services and it is interesting to note that when a shorthand typist, Miss Christie, joined the Women's Auxiliary Air Force she sparked off a row between the Association and the Treasury which rumbled on for many months. It had been decided that members of staff in the services for the duration of the war should have their service salaries topped up to maintain their civilian rate of income – as was believed to be the case for civil servants who joined the forces – and, quite properly, no exception was made in the case of female employees. This was unacceptable to the Scottish Office unless the women concerned 'joined the Hospital or Nursing Services'. In the event the Association lost the argument since Miss Christie had not been in its employment for six months[43] An interesting newcomer to the Council, who was to prove himself extremely useful, was Mr J. Coutts Morrison, MA, director of Education for Stirling, and his appointment was in the light of the future management of the evacuation camps.

On 8th September 1939 the Department of Health for Scotland issued a circular to local authorities indicating that, for the meantime, housing activities should be reduced to a minimum. The Association was required to follow suit and work ceased on all houses where no more than foundations had been provided. The intended programme for the construction of 20,000 houses within the Special Areas came almost to a standstill and typically negotiations for the acquisition of land were abandoned. In some cases land had already been obtained, or dealings were so far advanced that purchases had to be completed, and in these cases it was decided that, as opportunity arose during the war, technical staff would complete layout plans so that an early resumption could be effected whenever possible.[44] However, nothing further was done in respect of the programme for houses outside the Special Areas.

Inevitably, building operations throughout the war years were difficult and it may here be worth mentioning a few impressions of the kind of problems which occurred.

Immediately on the outbreak of hostilities the government took control of supplies of building materials, some of which became extremely scarce. This was particularly true of timber, the shortage of which, in fact, remained a problem for many years after the war. At first, no timber at all was allocated for houses which had not reached damp course level at the outbreak of war and for many months the scarcity of timber slowed down the work on even these few houses which had been earmarked for completion.[45]

Early on cement was also difficult to obtain and permits, licences or letters of authority were required for all types of materials. The Department of Health for Scotland introduced a quota system which helped, but the Report for 1940-41 notes that even War Building Priority A schemes did not always receive sufficient cement, although things improved later in the year.[46]

In the opening months of the war independent contractors were particularly severely hit by the shortage of materials and by a rapid increase in costs. 'Prices of materials and wages continued to rise during the year. Substantial rises have taken place in the price of bricks, cement, steel, fire clay goods etc'.[47] There were many appeals to the Association or to the government for relief from the losses incurred on contracts and usually some compromise was reached, but sometimes only after months of heated negotiations.

The biggest problem concerned labour. In 1941 it was noted

that 'contractors cannot, in the present state of the labour market, select their men but are obliged to accept whatever labour is available and the quality is often unsatisfactory'.[48] Since many of the younger men were in the armed forces and others were often deployed to make good air-raid damage it is not altogether surprising that the best workers were not always available. Labour also became more expensive and in 1941 and again, in 1942, it was noted that in each year the wages of workers had increased by a penny an hour.[49] By 1942 there were still many shortages of materials and, for example, 'copper piping became quite unobtainable'. Some materials, such as hardwall plaster, were scarce because of direction of labour – in this case from gypsum quarries to coal mines – while with manufactured articles, such as electrical fittings, scarcity was attributed to factories being damaged in air raids. [50]

The 1942 annual report noted the introduction of various Ministry of Labour Controls over the deployment of labour, and the application of a guaranteed 44-hour week and a system of payment by results. 'Labour cannot now be engaged or even transferred from one site to another except through the Ministry of Labour and National Service.' The payment by results scheme was applied at first to bricklayers and their labourers and then extended to joiners, plasterers and so on, and these conditions were accepted by contractors and employees alike with reluctance, and were 'strongly resented for some considerable time'.[51]

By 1944 the national management of resources of men and materials was better organised and the report for that year comments on the 'smoothness with which the central machinery is now operating'. It was noted, however, that labour was much harder to find in Renfrewshire than in Lanarkshire. It was also remarked that 'the poor physique of much of the labour available tends to hold up work', and that, with the payment by result system in operation, contractors, preferring 'to employ a small number of good men rather than a larger number including men of poor quality', were inclined to reject some of those sent to fill vacancies.[52]

With the main weight of the country's resources being flung into the war there was no hope of obtaining significant quantities of materials for ordinary house construction, hence the 1,226 houses which had been earmarked for completion in

September 1939 were not in fact finished until 1943-44.[53] In February 1943 the Secretary of State authorised the Association to complete the construction of a further 300 houses on five sites where work had been discontinued at the outbreak of war.[54] By the end of the year 1944-45 all but nine of these houses had been finished and the opportunity had been taken to conduct some constructional experiments, such as incorporating concrete floors and roofs, which the Department of Health thought might be essential immediately after the war in consequence of the scarcity of timber.[55] In total, however, that was the extent of the Association's additions to its stock of permanent houses during the war. At the same time some reduction was caused by the requisitioning by various government departments of 260 houses at Greenock, Kilmarnock, Airdrie, Motherwell and Johnstone.[56]

Understandably the war meant a considerable amount of new building in the vicinity of military bases or where factories were opened for war purposes, but beyond the erection of 372 houses (and some walling for huts) for the Admiralty at Rosyth[57], and the construction of 18 houses in Edinburgh – at Learmonth Gardens and St Johns Road – in which the Ministry of Aircraft Production housed staff from Ferranti's[58], little work of this type of a permanent nature was awarded to the Association. In fact, this was something of a sore point. In January 1940 the Association was invited to build 1,500 houses for workers who were employed at the new Rolls Royce Engine factory at Hillington in Glasgow. Initially the City Corporation were believed to be 'unwilling to erect the houses', but after technical staff had expended 'a considerable amount of work in connection with the type and layout plans', the Corporation abruptly changed its mind and insisted on taking over the project. Not even a war, it seemed, was going to persuade Glasgow to accept Association activity within its boundaries.[59] Thereafter the Association offered its help to various government departments, but without avail and for some months after the work at Rosyth was completed some of the plant was laid up in store.

In August 1941 the Air Ministry asked the Association for the hire of its plant, machinery and shuttering for use in the erection of new RAF stations. At the time some of the equipment was in use at Rosyth and could not be spared, but

A famous photograph of units of the fleet at Scapa Flow in August 1940. (The battle cruisers in view, L to R Repulse, Renown and Hood – were just three of the many major warships completed on the Clyde in the decade to 1920. Not until 1937 did Clyde shipbuilders resume work on two ships of similar size and complexity and this was a major factor in the severity of the region's unemployment between the wars.) Imperial War Museum.

with little normal building work going on the Association eagerly offered to take on the job of constructing the required buildings for the RAF. The Air Ministry declined – all they wanted was the equipment and the secondment of the key personnel such as Mr Pond and his staff – and they explained that their system of contracting precluded the Association's direct involvement. Reluctantly all but one set of shuttering (retained for use at Rosyth) was handed over at a fee of £100 per set per month and on condition that the equipment was returned in good order. The appropriate staff were also released.[60]

In 1942 the equipment which had been kept back was put to an interesting use when the Association was asked by the Ministry of Works to erect the structure of a hostel for 100 Post Office workers at Kirkwall in Orkney, where the latter were occupied in handling the huge volume of mail for the Fleet at Scapa Flow. The Association was asked to take on this job since construction by no-fines using local aggregate obviated the need for a large shipment of normal building materials from the mainland. The equipment loaded onto a ship at Leith Docks consisted of:

1 Reliance lorry; 2 Reliance dumpers; 3 giraffe cranes;

1 junior concrete mixer; 18 wheelbarrows; 1 saw; 1,453 posts; 7,648 steel panels; shutters; and shovels and other loose tools.

The two men in charge of this job were Bob Minto, general foreman, and Jimmy Attwell, clerk/timekeeper, and although an acute shortage of labour made for a slow start the hostel, which consisted of an administration block, garage, store, dormitory blocks, canteen and sick bay, was substantially completed by March 1943. Thereupon the squad was asked also to build a sorting office and this was finished in July. The report of Alex Foote, the appointed architect, after his second visit of inspection, is noteworthy.

[61] I was particularly satisfied with the able and efficient way in which Mr Minto had tackled a very difficult problem, namely, the construction of a large-span reinforced concrete roof over the garage building. It was most desirable that the comparatively large amount of timber shuttering necessary should be avoided in view of the shortage of timber generally. Mr Minto undertook to dispense with such normal shuttering in carrying out these large and heavy roof constructions using only the Association's steel pans and wooden posts. The finished concrete roof work has much exceeded my expectations under such circumstances, the resultant job being a first class one. In this work at the Post Office depot, Mr Minto has carried out the Association's first attempt at special work in either reinforced cellular (no-fines) concrete or reinforced dense concrete and with notable success, in my opinion.

(In regard to the Sorting Office)…the cellular concrete work at this building in my opinion is the best work of that nature which I have inspected.

If the Association's building activities were interesting, but very limited, particularly in the early years of the war, its operations in other directions kept the staff and council members fully occupied. In 1939 the SSHA were asked to build and manage seven holiday camps of a permanent character which could be used as evacuation camps should the need arise. Initially, there had been considerable debate as to where the camps should be located, but it was agreed that four should be near Glasgow, two near Edinburgh and one in the vicinity of Dundee. The camps themselves were to be in the form of

timber hutments.[62] Later the number was reduced to five and discussions were held with representatives of the Education Authorities of Edinburgh and Glasgow and with the Society for the Preservation of Rural Scotland to ensure that the locations and the appearance of the camps would meet with the widest levels of general approval.[63] Eventually, through the autumn and winter of 1939-40, the camps were built at Broomlee, West Linton; Middleton, Gorebridge; Glengonnar, Abington; Dounans, Aberfoyle; and Belmont at Meigle in Perthshire. The choice of Dounans Farm at Aberfoyle apparently produced 'a great number of letters' to Miss Horsburgh complaining that the site was not suitable 'because of the large number of midges...', but since Glasgow Education Committee approved the choice and since 'most places in the West of Scotland were similarly troubled', it was decided that the objections should be disregarded.[64]

Shortage of joiners slowed down the construction work for a few months and it was agreed that, if need be, unskilled workers would be employed.[65] In the meantime, however, some uncertainty arose as to the use of camps, with the suggestion being made that perhaps they should be reserved for physically or mentally handicapped children. Council were very much opposed to this suggestion, because the camps had not been designed for that purpose, and urged that proper arrangements should be made for such children.[66] Late in December 1939 a meeting was held with the Department of Health for Scotland to discuss the matter and it was reported that the 'Department had been giving special consideration to the cases of children who had proved troublesome to house-holders under the Evacuation Scheme as well as to the possibility of accommodating in the camps, as a purely temporary measure, physically or mentally defective children who might, in an emergency, require to be removed from their present quarters'.[67] The government had not yet reached a decision as to the long term future of the camps, but it would seem that the uncertainty was to some extent the product of the 'phoney war' in 1939 when, for months, little war-like activity seemed to be happening and the initial fears concerning the devastation likely to result from mass bombing of cities appeared to be diminishing.

By May 1940, with the fall of France imminent, the attitude

Opposite *Part of the evacuation camp at Glengonnar.*

was very different and everything possible was being done to expedite the completion of the camps. It was reported that 'owing to the serious war situation, and to the possibility of the Association being called upon at any moment to take in the full number of children at each camp, although the camps were not yet really complete, arrangements had now been made for all the furniture and equipment to be delivered immediately and for the camp managers, matrons and assistant matrons to take up residence at the camps, or in the respective villages in cases where their quarters at the camps were not completed'.[68]

Already, on 22nd April, the first 100 children had arrived at Broomlee Camp and four days later this camp was officially opened by the Secretary of State.[69] In June one of the dormitory blocks at Aberfoyle burned down, but fortunately no children were in residence at the time.[70] (It proved impossible to obtain sufficient timber to replace this block: hence Aberfoyle remained the smallest camp, although later its occupancy rate was to become the highest of the five.) By July 1940 the numbers of children in residence were – Broomlee – 281, Middleton – 138, Belmont – 155, Glengonnar – 106 and Aberfoyle – 55.[71]

Attitudes to evacuation seem to have varied very much in accordance with parents' perceptions of the state of the war and the likely levels of risk from air raids. For example, late in September 1940, people seem to have been taking a slightly more relaxed attitude and it was noted that 'many children were being withdrawn from the camps'. Accordingly it was agreed to accommodate the children for a month or so at a time

Broomlee as it appears today.

where this was preferred to a prolonged stay.[72] By comparison, in May 1941 after 'recent heavy bombing of industrial cities' (the main raids on Clydebank and Greenock took place in March and May 1941) the Secretary of State made an urgent request to the Association that the accommodation of the camps be increased and at least one new camp be constructed immediately – Balfron, Killearn or Fintry in West Stirlingshire were suggested as possible sites. In the event, when things calmed down again, the proposals were abandoned, primarily because of the impossibility of obtaining timber.[73] At this time it was put on record that the normal capacity of each of the camps was 240 children, although subsequent alterations reduced this to 222. (174 in the case of Aberfoyle.) To begin with the children were eight to twelve years of age although older children were also included at a later date.[74]

Typical occupancy rates later in the war are indicated below.[75]

	15.1.43	28.5.43	27.8.43	31.3.44
Broomlee	183	178	109	138
Middleton	82	81	83	136
Aberfoyle	107	123	139	153
Glengonnar	125	173	122	–
Belmont	85	97	95	60

Meanwhile, in the summer of 1940 the Association got down to the business of looking after the children and minute attention was paid to every aspect of their health and well-being. In July, for example, it was noted with satisfaction that the average increase in weight between 22nd April and 10th June was 1½lb per child 'and that there has been a marked improvement in the behaviour of the children while at meals'. Great care was taken over diet with the calorific value and amounts of protein, fats, etc being properly measured. Council were satisfied to learn that the cost of food for children and adults at Broomlee Camp worked out at 6s 8d per head.[76] Interestingly, when the Edinburgh School Medical Officer visited Broomlee Camp in December 1940 he found 'that there was very little to criticise in the diet...and that he had stated that it was extremely gratifying to find that the protein and animal fat contents were so high, since those items were of such extreme importance to the growing child'.[77]

Right throughout the war, the children were given detailed medical examinations and the most frequent problems which were revealed were the high incidences of 'dirty heads' and scabies. In severe cases the children were hospitalised for treatment and then permitted to go home for a week or ten days' holiday before returning to camp. Much to the frustration of the camps' management this often meant that the children were reinfected by the time they were brought back. Some of the locally appointed camp doctors took a fairly relaxed view of this matter and regarded the children as being privileged, in that they were given far more careful attention than would normally have been the case. However, the condition of the children, and the reinfection problem does make for a very interesting commentary on the prevailing standards of the homes from which they came.[78]

There were many visitors to the camps. For example, in October 1940 a deputation from the Glasgow Central House-wives' Committee 'expressed themselves as being very satisfied with the conditions obtaining at (Aberfoyle) and that the children were in good health and were being well looked after'.[79] The District Commissioner for Civil Defence, Glasgow, Sir Steven Bilsland, and Lady Bilsland also visited Aberfoyle and 'were very much impressed with the arrangements made for the children, and with the practical results shown by their healthy and happy appearance'. Between 26th and 28th November a major tour of inspection was carried out by Mr Joseph Westwood, MP*, Parliamentary Under-Secretary of State, with various officers of his Department, the Association and the local Education Committees in train.[80] At the end of that quarter there was great pleasure among members of the Council when the various reports showed that the physical condition of the children generally was very good and that 'the medical officers were of the opinion that the health of the children had considerably improved as a result of residence at the camps'.[81]

One problem concerned the poor state of the clothing possessed by many of the youngsters and it was noted that the

Joseph Westwood
Miner. MP for Stirling, Falkirk and Grangemouth Burghs. Under-Secretary of State for Scotland 1940-45. Secretary of State 1945-47.

task of carrying out repairs to garments was much greater than had been expected. In order to assist 'in keeping the work up to date' a portable electric sewing machine was purchased for each camp at a cost of £14 12s 10d per machine.[82] An incident worth mentioning – since it reveals an example of the generous support which was now flooding across the Atlantic – occurred in November 1940, when 'Council unanimously agreed to record their appreciation of gifts of pots of jam from women and children in Port Dover, Ontario, Canada, which had recently been received at the various camps through the Women's Voluntary Services'.[83] Later, in 1943, Broomlee and Middleton camps were also in receipt of a similar gift of 15 churns of dried milk from the Kinsmen's Club of Canada.[84] (Another interesting gift consisted of 450 Lawson's cypress plants from the Forestry Commission to the Aberfoyle camp and these partially account for its most attractive appearance today.[85])

As early as December 1940, however, the first signs were visible of strain in the uneasy relationship which existed for much of the war between the Association and the relevant Education Authorities. At that stage, and on several occasions thereafter, the Education Committees of Glasgow, Edinburgh and Dundee asked the Department of Health for Scotland to allow them to take over management of the camps.[86] Following his recent tour of inspection, the Parliamentary Under-Secretary of State was well pleased with the efficiency with which the camps were being run and concluded that the Education Committees 'had not made out any case against the Association's management'. For their part, the Council stuffily responded by alleging that any trouble was 'largely due to the appointment of head teachers who were not sufficiently experienced or otherwise qualified for the work of school camps'.[87] No doubt there were faults on either side, but it does seem that the root of the problem lay in the tension which sometimes existed between the local camp managers and the head teachers. In cases of dispute the managers occasionally asserted their responsibility and authority and presumably this was resented by the teachers. In the summer of 1942 the quarrel flared up again with a delegation from the Education Committees of the three cities appealing once more to Mr Westwood[88], but after thinking the matter over, the Under-Secretary of State

remained of the opinion that the camps were being well run and that the management arrangements should remain under the Association's control. He urged both sides to work together harmoniously.[89]

A few weeks after this latest tiff there came a general confirmation of the success of the camps in the form of a report on the height, weight and health of the children from Doctor J.R. Grant Keddie, of the Department of Health for Scotland. Council noted with satisfaction Dr Keddie's conclusion that 'residence in the camps had had a very beneficial effect upon the children'.[90]

As the war years passed and the risks of heavy bombing decreased so the numbers of children at the camps declined. For a time they were made up by using the camps as convalescent centres for children or as holiday camps for entire school classes and their teachers.[91] Towards the end of 1943, when yet another dispute with the local Education Committee resulted in withdrawal of some children from Glengonnar, the remaining children there were transferred to Aberfoyle and the former camp was temporarily closed.[92]

Later, in March 1945, Glengonnar was re-opened to accommodate 250 Dutch refugee children and a staff of 30 adults.[93] The people of many parts of the Netherlands had suffered extreme privations through the last winter of the war and Broomlee camp was also made available to enable children from that country to recover their health and strength in the peace of the Scottish countryside. For a time both camps were placed at the disposal of the Dutch Government and, when it was noted that staff at these camps were being paid at an increased rate, the Association asked the Department of Health if salaries at the other camps could also be increased.[94]

In 1944 the Evacuation Scheme was formally terminated and the camps assumed their originally intended permanent identity as holiday camps for children. In 1947 they were handed over to the Scottish National Camps Association Limited and it is interesting to record that, at the time of writing, they are all still in existence, which is remarkable since, when they were first being evaluated for insurance purposes, their expected life was estimated at 15 years.[95]

The evacuation camps were not the only facility of this kind which the Association provided during the war. Towards the end of March 1941 (after the first heavy raid on Clydebank) the Association was instructed by the Secretary of State to acquire, adapt, furnish and manage hostels 'for the accommodation of workmen engaged on essential war production who have lost or may lose their homes as a result of enemy action'. A few weeks later it was similarly asked to construct, furnish and manage 'hutted camps in the Clydeside area, which will be available, when necessary, for the accommodation of homeless single workmen in essential industries or married workmen whose families have been accommodated elsewhere and whose homes may be destroyed or rendered uninhabitable as a result of air raids'.[96]

Whitecrook School in Clydebank was converted into the first hostel and it was opened on 25th April 1941 by the Right Honourable Thomas Johnston, MP,* the Secretary of State for Scotland. Just a few days later, on 6th May, the hostel was damaged by a parachute mine[97], but the damage cannot have been too severe since it was soon back in operation. The cost of the adaptions and of making good the bomb damage was £9,417 1s 8d.[98]

Thomas Johnston (1881-1965)
Born in Kirkintilloch and educated at Lenzie Academy and Glasgow University. Journalist, started *Forward* in 1906. MP for West Stirlingshire 1922-24, and Dundee 1925-45. Under-Secretary of State at Scottish Office 1929-31; Secretary of State 1942-45. Later Chairman of North of Scotland Hydro-Electric Board and Scottish Tourist Board. Refused Peerage 1945.

The original terms of reference were soon modified to enable men to make use of the hostel who were engaged in essential war work and were simply unable to find accommodation elsewhere. Throughout 1941-42 the average number of residents per night was 163 and the largest number accommodated on a single occasion was 220, when, at the request of the Ministry of Labour, room was found for a party of dockers. It must have been a tight fit since the theoretical capacity of the building was 210 men, with 168 being provided for in twelve open dormitories with double tier beds and 42 in five cubicled dormitories. The charges were 20s per week for the open dormitories, 22s per week for cubicles containing two beds and 24s per week for the single bed cubicles. These charges covered two meals per day. In the Annual Report of 1942, the Association expressed its gratitude to the Lord Provost of Glasgow's Relief Fund for the gift of a billiard table and a supply of games, and to the WVS (Glasgow Branch) for gifts of suitable furniture for the recreation rooms.[99]

The majority of the residents at Whitecrook were employed in the local shipyards and engineering shops, at the Singer works, on repair work to houses in the district damaged by enemy action, and on other essential war work. By 1942 it was concluded that 'there can be no doubt that the accommodation provided by the hostel has in some small measure relieved the housing problem in Clydebank, especially when the town is probably busier than it has ever been, and the proximity of the hostel to important yards and works has also eased the transport problem.'[100]

Immediately after the heavy air raid on Greenock on the night of 5th-6th May 1941, the Association were asked to consider creating a similar hostel in that town, but rather than to provide for the victims of bomb-damage, the hostel which was eventually produced by converting the Highlanders' Academy in Mount Pleasant Street and which was managed by the Association on behalf of the Ministry of War Transport, was specifically to cater for dockers brought to the town to deal with the loading and unloading of convoys.[101]

Throughout 1941, work went on to produce the hutted camps, mentioned previously, at Kirkintilloch, Balloch, Hamilton and Johnstone. Originally the proposal was for buildings of plasterboard to be obtained from the Ministry of Supply, but eventually the Association convinced the government that something more substantial was required to face the Scottish climate and brick buildings were approved. However, even although the construction of these camps was scheduled as Essential Work under the (Building and Civil Engineering) Order, 1941, there were serious delays in progress as a result of a shortage of bricks and strikes at Kirkintilloch[102] and Johnstone[103]. In the latter case the joiners argued that the fixing of asbestos roof tiles to the wooden purlins was their work and that the task should not be done by fitters employed by the manufacturers of the tiles. The Secretary of State met with the Association to discuss the unsatisfactory labour position, since he was anxious to have the first camp available by 21st June 1941. However the meeting cannot have had much effect for it took a further seven months to complete the job. Interestingly, it was decided that camouflage paint should be used to obscure the camps from aerial observation.[104]

Each of the camps was designed to accommodate about 500 men in 25 dormitories and their intended function was to provide for men engaged in essential war work who had been bombed out of their homes. But again, by the time they were ready for occupation – the spring of 1942 – bombing raids on Scotland were mercifully rare and, therefore, other uses were found for them. As soon as it became known that the accommodation was available the Association was approached by several government departments to grant the use of the facilities for essential war workers for whom accommodation could not be found elsewhere. This was readily agreed, hence 'the greatest use of the hostels has been made by squads of dockers who are moved at intervals into the Clyde area for work. The other classes of men ... are aircraft fitters, employees in various government works, and groups of tradesmen and labourers employed by contractors carrying out essential work for government departments. The hostels were also made available, on very short notice, for the accommodation of a large number of distressed seamen from Russian convoys, and later on for a large number of distressed Indian merchant seamen (Goanese) whose ships had been put out of commission in the North African operations.[105]

The report on the occasion of the stay of the American seamen makes interesting reading. Warned on 23rd September

1942 of the imminent arrival of a 'very considerable number of survivors from sea convoys' the Association made ready the accommodation at Johnstone and Hamilton. (It was decided not to use Kirkintilloch since the latter hostel was located in a 'dry' area.)

[106] The Association kept closely in touch with Commander McLuckie (Chief Superintendent of the Mercantile Marine Office) and other officials in Glasgow ... It ultimately become known that the men would arrive in the Clyde on Monday 28th September 1942. Small unexpected groups, however, arrived in advance of the main body and were housed in the Johnstone Hostel. The first group of 69 arrived at 9.50 pm on Friday 25th and were given a hot meal right away. Other groups of 14 and 55 reached the camp during Saturday 26th. On Sunday 27th, 95 arrived in the morning, 24 in the afternoon and 40 late at night. On Monday there were 30 more, and with stragglers the total number in the camp was 335. At Hamilton the men arrived in two groups, 230 on Monday, and 20 on Tuesday. The men were in very poor condition, the bulk of them having had no proper sleep or regular meals for 14 days. They were also deficient in many necessary articles of clothing. The Warden at Johnstone communicated with the local Women's Voluntary Services who immediately sent to the hostel a parcel of clothing for distribution. As the men were without money or kit, he made a further effort to ease the situation by providing a number of razors, razorblades, a free issue of cigarettes, stationery and other small comforts.

At a civic reception in Glasgow the men were provided with a meal and were addressed by Nr Noel Baker, MP, Parliamentary Secretary to the Ministry of War Transport, who, on behalf of the government, thanked them for the services they had rendered...

The men were the survivors of American ships, flying the American flag, and also of American ships transferred to the Panamanian Registry, and they represented a cross section of the United Nations. There were Americans, (white and coloured), Danes, Norwegians, Czechs, Filipinos, Cubans, Brazilians, Chinese and others – several of the party could not speak English.

In view of the condition of the men and their lack of essential clothing, the Warden of the Johnstone hostel called upon the County Women's Voluntary Services and the Merchant Seaman's Comforts Fund who willingly sent large quantities of clothing, both new and secondhand, which was issued under the supervision of Mrs Roberts of Women's Voluntary Services, Bishopton. A similar distribution of clothing was carried out at the Hamilton hostel by the Voluntary Services. An official from the Ministry of War Transport attended and provided the men with the necessary clothing coupons to enable them to refit. At a later stage, the agents for the various ships concerned also attended at the hostel and paid the men quite large sums on account of wages.

What the men required on arrival at the hostel was sleep and food, and the catering resources of the hostel were called upon to provide four meals a day, and every effort was made to provide meals as near to the American type as possible. Sample menus of the meals are annexed to this report ... and it should be recorded that meals on this scale could not have been provided but for the action taken by the Ministry of Food ... in issuing the necessary permits. Nearly 10,000 principal meals were provided for the men during their stay at Johnstone, in addition to about 4,000 snacks served daily at 11.00 am and 3.00 pm. A corresponding number of meals were provided at Hamilton for the 250 men there. Sandwiches were issued to the men as they left camp on their homeward journey...

Some of the men were in need of medical attention and at Johnstone, Dr Keys was called in. He examined and prescribed for a number of men; one serious case ... had to be removed to Paisley Infirmary for immediate operation. Nurse Esplin of Johnstone Nursing Association attended at the sick bay.

(ENSA concerts and outings to Edinburgh, Loch Katrine and Loch Lomond were laid on and 'much appreciated by the seamen'.)

Immigration Officers attended at the hostels on Monday 5th October, and made the necessary arrangements for the men's papers being in order. The men left the hostels for repatriation the following morning. Before leaving the majority of the men expressed to the wardens, and also to the chairman and the general manager of the Association, who visited the hostels, their warm thanks and the high appreciation of the way they had been treated, and it is apparent that they will take with them pleasant recollections of their stay in Scotland...

When it is borne in mind that there was very little time during which to make the necessary preparations it will be appreciated that the wardens and the staff of the hostels concerned worked with keen interest and great energy and put forward their best effort to make this opportunity of real war service a success. This could not have been accomplished without the co-operation of Commander McLuckie and his staff and the officials of the Ministry of Food.

The Association wish to place on record the valuable services of Mr J.W. Fraser, one of their Administrative Officers, who took an enthusiastic interest in the arrangements for the welfare of the seamen. He spared no effort to ensure that all the arrangements worked efficiently and harmoniously

N.J. Campbell, General Manager and Secretary
17th October 1942

A few days earlier a letter had been received from the American Embassy at Grosvenor Square, London, from Charles A. Hogan of the US War Shipping Administration. He wrote 'I want to express the thanks of the United States War Shipping Administration and of the survivors who were so admirably housed in and looked after in your camps at Johnstone and Hamilton. A most extraordinary job was done in meeting a real emergency and the men were most appreciative and full of praise for the work of Mr Thomson, and especially of Mr and Mrs McGregor, and their staff. I visited both of the camps and found them admirably suited for the purpose.' [107] There were other letters of appreciation from the Ministry of War Transport and the Anchor Line Limited.

The two specimen menus attached to the report would have aroused a fair amount of attention among members of the UK public at the time, since the latter were, of course, then subject to the rigours of wartime rationing.

Tuesday 29th September

Breakfast   Cornflakes and prunes, sausage and bacon, cur-
             ried rice, fried potatoes, bread and rolls, margar-
             ine, marmalade, tea, coffee, cocoa.

11.00 am   Coffee, rolls and margarine.

Dinner   Celery soup, curried mince and cauliflower, pota-
             to pie, custard, semolina, stewed apples, tea,
             coffee, cocoa, bread and rolls.

3.00 pm   Coffee, rolls and margarine or jam.

Tea   Cold meat, tomatoes and lettuce, bread, margar-
             ine, tea bread, jam, tea, coffee, cocoa.

Supper   Meat rissoles and chips, bread, margarine, coffee
             and cocoa.

Sunday 3rd October

Breakfast   Cornflakes and prunes, cheese turnovers, bacon
             and chips, bread rolls, margarine, marmalade, tea,
             coffee, cocoa.

11.00 am   Coffee, rolls and margarine.

Dinner   Potato soup, cutlets, mixed veg, roasted potatoes,
             rice and raisins, tea, coffee, cocoa, bread and rolls.

3.00 pm   Coffee, rolls and margarine.

Tea   Steamed kippers and chips, bread, margarine,
             marmalade, tea bread, tea, coffee, cocoa.

Supper   Hotdogs and chips, tomatoes, bread, margarine,
             jam, tea, coffee and cocoa.

Bearing in mind the relative privations being endured by the
people of this country in 1942, these menus merit some
reflection, for little could more clearly indicate the generous
appreciation deservedly accorded to Allied seamen at that time.

From March to May 1943 the distressed Indian seamen
(Goanese) were billeted at Kirkintilloch. They were followed by

240 mobile dockers, but when the latter left, this camp remained empty for several months. Thereafter it was used for a time to house labourers brought from Southern Ireland to work on various housing schemes. Later still, at the request of the Ministry of Fuel and Power, a bath-house was installed and part of the accommodation was earmarked for trainee miners – 'Bevin Boys' – but their numbers were never more than about 25. Greek and Chinese seamen were also housed at this camp.[108]

At Balloch, the main regular residents were men employed at the Blackburn Aircraft Factory and at the Royal Naval Torpedo Works, but other essential war workers stayed from time to time. This camp was also used to provide holiday accommodation for Rolls Royce factory workers from Hillington. The canteen here provided daily meals to the employees of the Royal Naval Victualling Depot.[109]

In 1943 the Hamilton camp virtually became the Civil Defence Rotational Training School, with the 'Column' typically numbering between 150 and 200 men. Periodically squads from the school were rushed off to carry out special repair duties in London or other bomb-damaged cities in England. Indeed their particular skills were called into use in the spring of 1943 when a severe storm damaged the roofs of some of the camp buildings. Relations between the Civil Defence Column and the camp management were excellent and several dances and concerts were held to raise funds for various war charities. Early in 1945, the school gradually became 'non-operational' and a few months later it was formally wound up.[110]

Johnstone remained the most active of these camps up to 1945 housing, variously, seamen from the Cayman Islands, St Helena, Greece and China. For a time, however, the main residents were Irish building workers. It was said of the latter that, to begin with, they 'caused a considerable amount of trouble as they did at other hostels at a lesser extent; their conduct has however improved during recent months'.[111] They were not the only guests to cause trouble. When a party of 100 English dockers left after having stayed from 22nd to 31st January 1943, their rooms were found to be thoroughly verminous and pallets, pillows, blankets had to be cleansed at the disinfection plant at Bellahoustoun. It was decided to take 'no more dockers in the meantime'.[112] Other regular inhabitants of the Johnstone hostel were skilled workers from the REME plant at Linwood and the Royal Ordnance Factory in Bishopton.[113]

Shortly after the cessation of hostilities in Europe the Clydebank Education Authority asked for the return of Whitecrook hostel because of the scarcity of school premises in the town. However, the pressure for accommodation was also severe and it, therefore, took another year – until August 1946 – before it was possible to reconvert the premises and hand them back.[114]

The Lomond Road hostel, Balloch, continued to function as a working men's hostel through to 1947, when it was to be given over to the National Services Hostel Corporation who were to run it on behalf of the Ministry of Labour as a training centre for the building industry. Deafhillock hostel, Johnstone, was already being used for this purpose in 1946, although the men in residence here – ex-servicemen – went to training centres at Barrhead and Hillington on courses of six months' duration.[116]

Fairhill hostel, Hamilton, was similarly intended for the use of building trade trainees, but on the night of 25th August 1946, and on the following day, a number of families took the law into their own hands and invaded the premises. Sixty-three families (about 250 persons) moved into all the dormitory blocks. The open dormitories were without any cooking facilities and were considered to be extremely unsuitable for families; however 'in pursuance of government policy the squatters have been provided with water and electric light and every effort has been made to keep the drains in order and to prevent any public health nuisance'. At first the government made 'repeated efforts' to persuade the squatters to move out so that the buildings might be made ready for trainees, but this proved to be no simple matter.[116] Remarkably, officials and the squatters thereafter settled down together in the community, for while, on into 1948, the latter continued to live freely in the dormitory blocks with water and electricity provided, the main dining room and the two recreation rooms in the administration block were converted by the Ministry of Works into temporary office accommodation for the Inland Revenue (valuation department) and the new Ministry of National Insurance. Nothing, surely, could more vividly illustrate the tolerant, benign attitude taken to the squatters movement at this time of chronic housing scarcity. Since the camp had obviously ceased to be any kind of formal hostel the Association's interest in and responsibility for the premises effectively came to an end and the Hamilton Town Council agreed to take it under their control.[117]

In 1948, Hillhead hostel, Kirkintilloch was also handed over to the local Town Council. Some of the buildings were converted to dwellings while others were intended to become a community centre. Thus, through 1947-48, all of the Association's working men's hostels were handed over to the care of other public agencies.

As we have seen then, during the war the Association provided five evacuation camps for children and six hostels for working men. However, in March 1942 it was also asked by the Secretary of State to provide three family hostels, and these too deserve some attention.

The original request, in fact, specified five hostels for 'the temporary accommodation of families whose homes might be rendered uninhabitable as the result of enemy action'[118], but again, perhaps because the bombing attack on Scotland was not sustained in 1942, the number was reduced to three. The hostels were Lintwhite hostel, Bridge of Weir; Clober hostel, Milngavie; and Kingston hostel, Neilston; and they were built between June 1942 and the summer of 1943 – the last (Bridge of Weir) being completed on 15th August.[119]

They were very large establishments, each being designed to accommodate no less than 1,216 persons together with staff. (Two buildings at Milngavie could not be erected because of the existence of peat underneath the site, hence its capacity was reduced to 1,152.) Each hostel consisted originally of a kitchen and restaurant block, three staff blocks, sick bay, bath and wash house block, disinfecting hut and blanket store, reception office, warden's office, warden's house, and 38 married quarters or cubicle blocks (36 at Milngavie). The restaurant could serve 656 people at one sitting but perhaps of more interest are the married quarters blocks. Each of these included eight cubicles measuring 8 feet by 15 feet and furniture was provided to accommodate four persons per cubicle. Heating was by 'a slow combustion stove' and access to the cubicles was from a corridor running the length of the building. Lavatory facilities were located at one end of the corridor. Only cold water was available on tap, but hot water was provided by coal fired boilers with a draw-off cock.[120]

121 The Association strongly recommended to the Department of Health that all internal walls should be plastered, that a small circulating hot water system be installed in the married quarters blocks; that central heating should be substituted for the slow combustion stoves in these blocks; and that there should be additional bathing facilities. The Department replied to the effect that as the accommodation to be provided was of a very temporary nature, as the permissible expenditure per head was very restricted, and as the standard of accommodation should in no way exceed that of similar hostels then being erected in England, the Association's proposals could not be approved.'

The cost of construction was limited by the Treasury to £79,040 per hostel or £65 per person.[122]

By the time the hostels were completed the government seem to have had second thoughts as to the best way in which they might be used. After 1941 no major bombing campaign had developed against Scottish cities; hence the original possibility for which the hostels had been designed had mercifully not materialised. By the summer of 1943, there was some reason to hope that, with the war beginning to run strongly against Germany, the need to find accommodation for thousands of additional bombed out Scots might not arise. That there would be other uses for the hostels was clear, but for two of them the decision on their future was postponed and the Bridge of Weir and Neilston hostels were allowed to stand unused for several months while the war in Europe moved towards its climax.[123]

As far as the Clober hostel in Milngavie was concerned, the war damage of 1941 to Dunbartonshire had compounded an already serious housing shortage in that area and it was felt necessary to provide some relief as quickly as possible. However, since there was now some genuine prospect of an end to the war before too long, it was realised that it was appropriate to begin pursuing policies designed to deal with the transitional period leading to the full-scale resumption of house-building. In these circumstances the required standard of transitional accommodation would be to a higher level than that specified by the emergency provisions under which Clober and the other hostels had been designed.

Thus it was that although the Milngavie hostel was theoretically available for use on 31st May 1943, just 11 days later the Secretary of State asked the Association to adapt it immediately to provide transitional houses for families made homeless through enemy action.

Almost at once work commenced to convert the 36 married quarters into 108 houses of three and four apartments, at a cost of £205 and £265 respectively. Later the sick bay and other offices were also converted to dwellings so that by May 1944 the hostel had been adapted into 119 houses. The kitchen was turned into a communal cooking facility and the restaurant divided into a community centre and school rooms. While this work was being done the opportunity was also taken to erect two Nissen huts on the site which were then adjusted as an experiment to see if they could provide adequate prefabricated transitional housing. On 17th December 1943 the two Nissen houses and the conversions completed by that date were formally opened by Mr Johnston, the Secretary of State.[124]

For a time there was some talk of troops making use of the hostels at Neilston and Bridge of Weir, but nothing came of this, and their first occupation occurred in March 1944 when 600 Gibraltarian refugees were housed for 11 days.[125] This was not a happy experience, and when, in July a further 1,752 Gibraltarians were shared between the two hostels for a few days prior to repatriation, they left behind a trail of damage and took away with them almost anything that was portable, including crockery, cutlery, pillows and so on.[126]

Despite that unfortunate experience, it was in the role of providing for various victims of the war that each of these hostels were to prove most useful. At the end of September 1944, 38 people, who had been repatriated from German internment camps in Northern France, were accommodated at Bridge of Weir and for the rest of the year similar groups continued to arrive. Rehabilitation was undertaken by the hostel staff under the supervision of a medical officer from the Department of Health. Several were found employment in the locality while others gradually trickled off to stay with friends elsewhere, but by the spring of 1945, 90 repatriates were still in residence.[127]

As that climactic year advanced, however, so the inflow from Europe and the Far East increased. The annual report for 1946

remarked 'that the Bridge of Weir Hostel now cares for a larger number of repatriates than any other hostel ... in Britain'.
[128] The majority of the repatriates had been interned in Germany or occupied France, and in the Far East. Their physical condition on arrival was not good, and in some cases indeed it was very bad. Many of them had never been in Britain before, had no friends here, were without funds or clothing reserve, and could speak little or no English. Rest and feeding were necessary for rehabilitation, and with this in view double rations were allowed to repatriates for the first few weeks of their stay. A local doctor was appointed to attend their health and a nurse is available in the hostel. Medical officers of the Department of Health visited the hostel frequently and exercised a general supervision over the state of the hostel and the health of the inmates. The inmates were assisted by the hostel staff and the Department of Health to make contact with their friends and to find employment. Those without means and/or employment receive an allowance from the Public Assistance Authorities, out of which they make a token payment to the hostel for their board. Those in employment pay at a higher rate. At the request of the Department of Health and with their assistance a welfare officer was appointed in January to collaborate with the warden and the Department's officials in doing whatever is possible to arrange for the return of the repatriates to their own countries or their settlement in this country.

Gradually a considerable number were returned to such places as Belgium, Canada and the Channel Islands, but by March 1946 there were still 414 in residence, consisting of 172 men, 149 women, 55 boys and 38 girls. Bearing in mind the spartan standards to which the hostels had been constructed, the Association did everything possible to increase the comfort of the accommodation, by making internal modifications and by securing a better quality of furniture. In addition a library and other recreational facilities were provided and a small school was set up for the younger children. The local Bridge of Weir WVS rallied round, as ever, to distribute 'large quantities' of clothing and to help in many other ways.[129]

In the next year (1946-47) 376 of the repatriates left Bridge of Weir hostel, but a further 282 arrived from Europe, the Far East and Palestine, so that by March 1947 there were still 93 men, 121 women and 106 children in residence. Apparently, the general standard of health of residents improved greatly during the year, but it was eventually decided that the hostel should be run by the hospitals' branch of the Department of Health: hence in March 1947, it too passed out of the Association's hands.[130]

Following the traumatic visit of the Gibraltarians the Neilston hostel reverted to a care and maintenance basis for several months but in March 1945 it was opened up to receive refugees from Soroya Island in the north of Norway. A total of 452 people, of whom 169 were children under 15 years of age, arrived, accompanied by a small (mainly medical) Norwegian staff. Many of these people were in an extremely poor state of health and, again, despite language difficulties the local warden and his staff and the Glasgow WVS did everything they could think of to make the Norwegians comfortable.

On 12th April His Majesty the King of Norway and several of his Ministers visited the hostel and lunched with the refugees. The King expressed to the Association his warm appreciation of the way in which his people were being cared for. Later the Norwegian Government asked the British Government if they might take over the running and expense of the hostel while it was required by their refugees and this was agreed so that from May until the end of September the hostel was fully in the hands of the Norwegians. In the interim the standard of the accommodation was upgraded and a number of dormitories were converted to create a school and a nursery school.[131]

Forty years on it is still satisfying to learn of all the people mentioned in these pages sloughing off at least some of the grime and suffering of war in the free, clean sunlight of a peaceful Scottish summer.

When the Norwegians left, the Kingston hostel at Neilston returned once more to a care and maintenance basis while consideration was given as to its future. Eventually it was decided to experiment by converting one dormitory into a dwelling house and, if that proved successful, the intention was to alter the other buildings on similar lines to produce transitional housing, as had been done at Milngavie. However, this hostel was the second to fall 'victim' to the squatters movement of 1946.

On the night of 16th-17th August (a week before the invasion at Hamilton) 110 families, consisting of 350 people, poured in and took possession of the dormitories. Some of the equipment was in store and this was later removed. But the families did manage to appropriate some of the furniture. Again, it appears to have been a reasonably amicable affair with water and electrical supplies being maintained and the squatters happily providing receipts for the furniture in their possession. With the families using electric cookers in the former dormitories the wiring system was unequal to the load and apparently fused nightly for a time. However, no-one seems to have been unduly concerned and it is interesting to note that when the bulk of the valuable equipment and fittings had been removed to government stores, the residue was cheerfully auctioned off among the occupants.[132] Indeed, the attitude on both sides is revealed by the fact that when the Department of Health appointed a factor to levy rent in accordance with the number of rooms occupied by each family and to make a charge for electricity, no-one seems to have objected, and rents were duly paid to the warden to pass on to the factor.

When the hostel thereby passed out of the Association's control the intention was that it should be taken over by the County Council of Renfrew and properly converted into housing. The County Council wanted the Association to do the conversion work since it had, of course, already translated one dormitory into two satisfactory experimental houses, but, with the squatters in residence, the government were unwilling to give the Association the required permission.[133]

Thus it was that by 1947/48, with the exception of Clober, the Association's wartime camps and hostels had been handed on to other authorities, either through formal transactions carried out at the request of the Department of Health for Scotland, or under pressure from the informal intervention of squatters. Henceforth it was free to concentrate its attention exclusively on its main *raison d'être* – namely, the provision, maintenance and management of houses.

Reference has already been made to the conversion of the Clober hostel at Milngavie into transitional housing and, before turning to consider post-war planning, it is worth here giving some additional account of the Association's activities in regard to the transitional period since they exerted two important influences on the organisation's future development.

The first of these originated in July 1943 when the decision was made to convert the Milngavie hostel. Up to this point it had always been assumed that the selection of tenants and the factoring of Association houses would be left to the local authorities and this had been done in respect of the permanent houses completed before and during the war – the, what came to be called 'commissioners houses'. In the case of the Milngavie houses, however, the local authority could not manage the tenancies because the houses were intended, not for local people, but for families from Clydebank and its environs.[134] Moreover, by the nature of the Clober scheme, it was realised that management of the properties would present several novel and unusual difficulties. In these circumstances it was thought that the services of a trained woman property manager might be required and the general manager and secretary suggested to the council that the Department of Health for Scotland should be asked to second one of their employees, a Miss J.B. Pollock. Miss Pollock was then employed as a Welfare Officer, but it was known that she was a trained Octavia Hill house manager and, if the Department were agreeable, the intention was to ask her to manage the Clober development for the first six months.[135] To the satisfaction of the Association this arrangement was agreed.

In 1944, the Ministry of Fuel and Power asked the SSHA to take over the management of 700 houses intended for incoming miners and located in isolated parts of Ayrshire, Clackmannan, Lanarkshire, Midlothian, Stirlingshire and West Lothian. (Since Lord Traprain – Lord Balfour – was the Scottish Region Coal Controller at the time it may be reasonable to surmise that he was the originator of the idea.) 172 of these houses were permanent dwellings, but the other 528 were transitional houses which had been converted from Ministry of Works standard huts and which were only designed to have a useful life of ten years or so. The Association agreed to take them on readily enough, but on closer inspection, discovered that there were enormous problems associated with the task. In these pre-nationalisation days, although the mining industry was co-ordinated by the Ministry of Fuel and Power, the mines themselves were in the hands of individual colliery companies and many of the latter were in the habit of deducting the rents from their employees' wages. The system might have been reasonable in theory, but it was inefficient in practice. The companies were often slow to pass on information about strikes, illness, suspension and so on, factors which were likely to produce arrears of rent, and sometimes they did not even supply details of individual tenancies or whether or not men had moved on to other employment. As a result, for a time, it was virtually impossible to keep track of the factoring position. Moreover, the houses themselves, and the situation of tenants, were often in a lamentable state. The Ministry of Works huts/houses were very liable to condensation; gardens were unfenced wildernesses; many of the families had moved from tied mining cottages in other areas and had been able to bring with them only a few scraps of furniture; there was a great deal of homesickness, particularly among the wives who, of course, had followed their husbands as they moved to the new pits; and these developing mining communities were characterised, typically, by an almost complete absence of local social or community facilities. All in all, the management of these properties represented a fairly ghastly, if demanding, prospect.[136]

In these circumstances the Association turned once more to Miss Pollock and invited her to draw up a report, which was duly considered by Council on 25th August 1944. In her report Miss Pollock suggested appropriate arrangements for the management of the houses and advised the Association to appoint a trained woman housing manager and a trained assistant to establish an adequate professional housing management facility. The proposal was opposed by at least one prominent Council member who urged that the houses should be managed by the local authorities on behalf of the Association, but she was partially backed by the general manager who suggested that her ideas be adopted on a temporary basis and her secondment to the Association be extended for the time being. In the event, Council did not agree. Instead they accepted Miss Pollock's report in full, increased her salary and contrived to secure her services on a permanent basis.[137] Thus a truly formidable influence joined the Association and laid the foundation on which the housing management function was ultimately established. As will be shown later when events in the 1950s forced the SSHA to accept more responsibility for the management of its houses and tenants, it was able to cope with the crisis very largely as a result of the groundwork which had been done by Miss Pollock from the war years on.

In 1943 the Association was asked by the Department of Health for Scotland to erect 600 transitional houses of a similar Ministry of Works type. The task was accepted; 200 of the prefabricated 'Maycrete' dwellings were erected in Greenock and the remainder in sites in Dunbartonshire and Lanarkshire. Right from the beginning this was to prove a disastrous experience, with some of the prefabricated parts of the buildings being damaged in transit from the factory, with shortages of building workers having to be made good by use of unskilled Irish labourers, and with many delays being caused to the construction programme as a result of bad weather.[138] As things happened, the last of these 'Maycrete' houses was not erected until 1946, but long before then they were causing the Association a great deal of distress.

The Ministry of Works was entirely responsible for these buildings since it had supplied the original specification, the recommended adaptations, the constructional materials – concrete framework, 'Maycrete' walling units, roofing timbers and skirting, and windows – and had rejected the Association's suggestions in respect of flooring and external rendering. The Ministry over-ruled the Association's initial objections by insisting that it was experimenting with rendering and would provide definitive advice on this matter timeously. Moreover, when it was reported that similar buildings used in prisoner-of-war camps had not been waterproof, instead of cancelling or postponing the project, the Ministry and the Department of Health for Scotland both reacted by sending supervisors into the factories and onto the building sites in the belief that it was merely a question of good supervision.[139]

In use, the 'Maycrete' houses were a disaster. The fundamental problem was that the panels expanded and contracted in response to variations in temperature thereby destroying the effectiveness of almost any form of rendering. In addition, with predictable results, the Ministry of Works instructed that the pitch of the roofs be lowered in defiance of the roof manufacturer's recommendations. Eventually, the Department of Health accepted the Association's advice that the later houses be finished with brick panels, but it took several years before a sufficiently flexible rendering was devised to make the original houses reasonably weatherproof.[140]

Meanwhile, angry tenants, press and public could not be expected to distinguish between the Association and the government department which was actually responsible for these extremely poor buildings. To the fury and distress of Council, they were tormented by press complaints and by their critics in the Commons. In vain the Association responded promptly to tenants' calls for help, reduced rents while repairs were being carried out, experimented ceaselessly to find technical solutions, paid out compensation for damage to furniture, and publicly identified the source of responsibility. Eventually, the houses were made more or less serviceable, but not before the organisation had become thoroughly disillusioned with anything remotely connected with transitional housing.[141] (From 1950 on authority was given by the Department of Health for Scotland for these 'Maycrete' transitional houses to be demolished and replaced by permanent dwellings.[142])

Two consequences flowed from the Association's experience with the 'Maycrete' houses – one of short-term significance and the other of far more fundamental importance.

First, in December 1944 the Association was asked by the Secretary of State to consider taking over the entire responsibility for the erection of transitional housing in Scotland. It seems likely that the background to this proposal was connected with the general embargo which then existed on permanent new building and which was obviously thoroughly disliked by the local authorities. At the same time as the request was made, the Department of Health for Scotland issued a memorandum to local Councils indicating that transitional building should not be allowed to impede their permanent programmes, so it may be that in making his appeal to the Association the Minister was responding to pressure aimed at freeing town halls to concentrate on their main building efforts.[143]

A special meeting of Council was held to discuss the request and it was unanimously rejected. While the Association was willing, under certain conditions – that it was able to inspect, approve or reject the specifications of the house types involved, and that satisfactory arrangements were made in respect of labour – to build up to ten houses per day on any one area in small burghs and in the countryside, it 'could not undertake the responsibility for the erection of all the temporary houses in

Scotland'. It was felt that this job should be done by private building and civil engineering contractors and it is clear that Council – as with the Local Authorities – was keen to do nothing which would seriously interfere with its long-term building programme. Obviously too, with the 'Maycrete' houses tarnishing the Association's public reputation, while Council was willing to accept its share of the task of dealing with the immediate housing crisis, it was extremely suspicious of any suggestion that the Association should be involved to any major degree with the production of inferior houses.[144] In the event, the Association built no more transitional houses of any description and hence erected none of the famous, and much more successful, 'prefabs'.

The second consequence was far more enduring for the experience inculcated throughout the Association an absolute determination to insist on high standards of specification and site supervision and an inbuilt scepticism about prefabricated methods of construction. In the post-war period and much later, when industrialised building became fashionable, it was the Association's habitual practice to insert its own inspectors and supervisors into factories where prefabricated sections were being manufactured and to demand the highest levels of on-site control. As we shall see, the result was that designs and methods which, in other hands, produced fairly disastrous buildings, rarely had such evil consequences for the Association. Similarly, the need to devise effective technical solutions to unforeseen design flaws and to react speedily to tenants' complaints, was thoroughly learned, and this helped to develop a high level of professional responsiveness in every branch of the organisation.

Thus it was that although the Association's involvement with transitional housing was not great, the experience had the effect of originating the introduction and development of a housing management capacity, and of encouraging a determination throughout the organisation to adhere only to the highest standards of professional practice.

Turning to the question of post-war planning, as was described in the first chapter, the years of the Second World War were used by various government departments to engage in major re-thinking about many facets of life in the UK, and in preparing fundamental strategies which might be introduced on the return to peace. As far as housing in Scotland was concerned, the Association played a full part in this process, since it was then absolutely central to the government's future intentions.

In his Cabinet reconstruction of early 1941 Churchill appointed the greatly respected Labour MP Tom Johnston, to be Secretary of State for Scotland. On agreeing to take the post Johnston asked for the right to form a committee – a sort of Council of State – composed of all the living Secretaries for Scotland and which would plan for the kingdom's future. Churchill responded – 'That seems a sort of national government of all parties idea, just like our government here. All right, I'll look sympathetically upon anything about which Scotland is unanimous'.[145] Thus was born Johnston's 'Council on Post-War Problems', which, in addition to himself, included in its membership Ernest Brown, Sir John Colville, Sir Walter Elliot, Sir Archibald Sinclair and Lord Alness.

[146] Here was a mechanism which neatly brought together Labour, Conservative, Liberal and National Liberal, which turned to advantage the important posts at the Health and Air Ministries respectively held by Brown and Sinclair, and secured the maximum co-operation between the parties on proposals brought before it. Lastly – but perhaps this had all along been foremost in Johnston's mind – the authority of this Scottish 'Council on Post-War Problems' or 'Council of State', as it came to be called, and its known endorsement by the Prime Minister could be used as a sort of political jemmy to prise out of Whitehall the concessions that Scotland so sorely needed.

From September 1941 to February 1945 this committee met frequently to co-ordinate plans and dealt with a multitude of matters including hydro-electricity, the future of the herring industry, hill farming, the regionalisation of water supply, the unification of hospital services, industrial redevelopment, education reform and housing. As a result of these activities the grip of various Whitehall departments on Scottish Affairs was loosened and more and more came under the direct authority of the Scottish Office. In this way the momentum towards a separate housing policy for Scotland, which had been implicit in Elliot's pre-war programme – including the setting up of the SSHA – was maintained.

As early as March 1942 the SSHA first became involved when, for a short time, the Parliamentary Under-Secretary of State, Captain H.J. Scrymgeour-Wedderburn*, was appointed to the Council of Management. At his first meeting he told the Council of his discussions with the Secretary of State. The housing shortage in Scotland was already severe and would be much greater after the war, and it was, therefore, imperative that the Association make a major contribution to tackling the problem. Many inter-departmental committees were currently considering such matters as labour supply, materials, price controls, and so forth, and he asked the Association to help by submitting a memorandum for the guidance of the Secretary of State in formulating his plans.[147]

Prior discussions with the chairman had already led to the preparation of an outline memorandum and the detail was considered at a meeting of Council on 6th April. Thereafter a report was assembled and passed to Mr Johnston.[148] He must have been suitably impressed for on 29th June the Council of Management and senior officials were summoned to the Scottish Office for a full scale consultation with the Secretary of State and his staff. The minute of that meeting is revealing.

After welcoming everyone Mr Johnston reported on his discussions with local authorities and outlined what government was doing about such matters as labour and materials. He said –

[149] That he had decided to increase the personnel of the Scottish Housing Advisory Committee, to which many problems relating to post-war housing would be referred; that its terms of reference would be wide; and that the Association would have at least one representative on the new Committee. (William C. Davidson). The Secretary of State had been able to put before the Minister of Works and Planning and the Minister of Health information with regard to the constitution and functions of the Scottish Special Housing Association Limited and he thought it was

Henry James Scrymgeour-Wedderburn
Educated Winchester and Balliol College, Oxford. Succeeded his father as 11th Earl of Dundee, 1924 (claims admitted by House of Lords Committee of Privileges in 1953). Conservative MP for Renfrew, 1931-45. Parliamentary Under-Secretary of State for Scotland 1936-39, 1941-42. Minister Without Portfolio 1958-61. Minister of State for Foreign Affairs 1961-64.

probable that similar organisations would be established in England and Wales. With regard to post-war building, the houses requiring major repairs as a result of damage by enemy action (at present estimated at 63,000) would be given priority. The special requirements of men returning to civilian life after service with His Majesty's Forces and who had either married in the interval or now desired to be married, must be dealt with speedily. The Secretary of State regarded the Association as the government's building agents in Scotland and thought that, apart from any other service they might render, they would assist materially in preventing 'price ramps' in the building of houses after the war ...

The Secretary of State referred to the interesting and helpful report on post-war housing which the Association had recently forwarded to him, and he proceeded to discuss ... the recommendations contained in the summary attached to the report.

Location of Industry and Planning
The Secretary of State stated that he was entirely in agreement with the Association's view as to the need for the determination of government policy with regard to the location of industry and planning, as without such there would be great difficulty in preparing a long-term programme of house building.

Augmentation of Personnel of Building Industry
The government were taking steps to augment the personnel of the building industry, including the provision of technical education ... the Association stressed the need of short intensive courses of training on building schemes after the war to men demobilised from the Forces who were not previously engaged in the building industry, and to the importance of maintaining a proper balance among the various trades.

Control of Labour, Materials and Prices
The government were taking steps to control, after the war, building labour, materials and prices.

Prefabricated Timber Sections
The Secretary of State noted the information obtained by

the Association with regard to the prefabrication of timber sections in Scotland ... Enquiries ... had already been made ... (in) Canada, and the Secretary of State thought the Association's suggestions that enquiries ... be instituted ... (in) Sweden ... should be adopted.

Steel Houses
The Association's proposals that investigations and experiments be carried out with regard to steel houses would be carefully considered and further enquiry would be made by the Government Committees concerned.

Priority in Meeting Housing Needs
It would be remitted to the Scottish Housing Advisory Committee to consider what guidance might be given in meeting various housing needs and the advice with regard to post-war policy as to floor areas, number of rooms per house, density of houses per acre, etc.

Compulsory Acquisition of Land
The Association's recommendations that existing procedure should be simplified and shortened and that the Association be empowered compulsorily to acquire land for housing schemes on failure to reach agreement with the owners were discussed at length. The Secretary of State referred to the Government Committee under the chairmanship of Mr Justice Uthwatt which was considering the matter of procedure. Possible objections by local authorities ... were mentioned by the Secretary of State.

Water and Drainage Scheme: Roads and Services
The Secretary of State was in complete agreement with the views of the Association that water and drainage schemes should be provided well in advance of building operations, and that roads and services should be laid before building work commenced.

Housing of Aged Persons
It was stated that the Scottish Housing Advisory Committee will consider ... the housing of aged persons.

Provision of Furniture
The Secretary of State was wholeheartedly in agreement

with the Association's view that greater use should be made of the powers of local authorities to provide furniture and also up-to-date equipment, including refrigerators.

Private Enterprise
The Secretary of State referred to what he described as the appalling disparity between England and Scotland in the matter of building working-class houses by private enterprise, and stated that this matter would be fully examined with a view to private enterprise being encouraged to contribute its share of building in Scotland. *The Association's suggestions with regard to the encouragement of working-class people to own the houses in which they live would be carefully considered* (my italics).

Building Programme
There was discussion as to the period of the programme of post-war housing, but there was eventually general agreement that a ten years' programme should be adopted ... the view of the government was that the maximum number of houses should be built as rapidly as possible.

As can be seen, therefore, many of the key issues were being addressed from an early date in the war, and one can sense from these minutes that the Association, eager to get on with the job, had found in the Minister a kindred spirit.

At that meeting, the question of obtaining sites, preparing layouts and making experiments to surmount the problems which were bound to arise from shortages of materials, had also been discussed and the Association felt that a start should be made while the war was still in progress. Accordingly, in September, it was resolved to ask the government for permission to proceed to develop one or more sites where new techniques, materials, house designs and building methods could all be examined while the war was still going on. In this way the findings would be available for general use as soon as conditions permitted a major building programme to be initiated.[150] But it was not until 1944 that permission was given to proceed with this project, at Sighthill in Edinburgh, with the result that most of the houses there were actually built between 1946 and 1952, by which time they were too late to be as useful as was originally intended. Nevertheless, the Sighthill scheme is an extremely interesting one to which we shall return.

As 1942 ended, however, the Scottish Housing Advisory Committee were getting their investigations under way and invited the Association to submit evidence on such matters as design, interior planning, layout and standards of construction, and for the information of one of their sub-committees, included with their request was a general questionnaire on furniture.

The Association responded fully.[151] On types of dwelling, cottages of one and two storeys were most popular 'and should be used whenever consistent with good planning and amenity'. But terraced cottages, flats (deafening must be improved), and tenements (balcony service passages should be avoided) could all be satisfactory under particular circumstances.

In view of the contemporary development of sheltered housing it is interesting to note the Association's wartime attitude to housing for the elderly.

[152]   Hostels – these should be provided for elderly people. Units for single people should consist of living room, kitchenette/scullery, WC and coal cellar. An additional room (bedroom) should be provided for elderly married couples. Bathrooms should be provided for every four tenants.

While opinion varies, it appears that old people generally do not welcome the presence of a caretaker or a person of the 'help' type.

The hostels should be provided as part of a housing scheme and not erected on a separate site.

On standards of living space, the view was that the 'maximum overall area of houses should be increased to permit improvements in sizes of rooms, cupboards, etc'. General pre-war room sizes were acceptable but a greater overall area was particularly required to allow for built-in cupboards, and the appeal was made for more thoughtful internal layout. Detailed suggestions were made on internal planning. A few examples include –

Provide bathroom and WC in separate compartments. In two-storey cottages bathroom and WC upstairs and additional WC downstairs for use of children.

Where possible, kitchen should face north or east;

bedrooms east or south; and living room south or west.

Bedroom windows and doors should be placed with regard to furniture layout and more unbroken wall space should be planned for furniture.

Good planning should not be sacrificed for the sake of small economy in plumbing units.

WC should be fitted with spring to keep seat up when not in use (perhaps not such a clever idea – especially when one thinks of a small child's quiet contemplations being interrupted by sudden elevation).

Longer baths ... should be provided.

Consideration might be given to central heating in large schemes and also in hostels for elderly people.

Main cooking units should be gas or electric cooker, gas having a slight preference.

Electric washing machine desirable.

Refrigerator – very desirable. Provide refrigerator recess in constructing house.

And so it went on, with precise recommendations being made on every conceivable aspect of the internal arrangements which were thought to be appropriate. Similarly, on the standards of construction, a mass of advice was submitted – specifically on types of structure, sound proofing, weather proofing, wall, floor, and roof construction and finishing, and window types; and design recommendations were made both in respect of internal and external features. Once again, the appeal was made to be allowed to make experiments immediately in order to determine the best methods of circumventing shortages of certain materials and the certainty of a scarcity of skilled labour.

Attention was then turned to the general questions concerning the layout of estates and of the requirement for social and community facilities. For example –

Open spaces – bolder policy required. Large open spaces few in number, should be provided in place of small but numerous spaces. Playgrounds for smaller children should be provided in close proximity to houses.

... In large schemes far removed from a shopping centre, shops and a library should be provided and – if a scheme is large enough – a cinema ... Consultation with the Education Authority and the Church is desirable.

The provision of a garage and/or lock-ups for cars should be considered. This would probably prove to be an economic investment of capital.

The review then examined the question of furniture. When considered from the perspective of the contemporary sophisticated and prosperous consumer society, the notion that the house provider should also provide furniture may seem very strange, but it has to be remembered that, in 1943, memories of the chronic poverty of the inter-war years were still fresh and the Association was attempting to prescribe for a society in which timber and certain metals were extremely scarce and at a time when rigorous rationing was in force. In these circumstances, it was felt that purely private supply would mean the mass of the population simply having to do without.

As far as possible the Association recommended that features be built into the house design in such a way as to remove some of the need for furniture – eg fitted cupboards in the kitchen and bedrooms; fitted bookshelves, window seats, clothes drying facilities and so on. Elsewhere a list of movable furniture was recommended. Generally, the intention was that these items should either be sold to the tenant for cash, by hire purchase or simply hired out at an additional rent. Every care should be taken to avoid standardisation and it was argued that tenants should be able to make their own choices whenever possible.

All in all, it was a meticulous and thoughtful exercise and provides a most vivid insight into the ways in which attitudes were developing throughout these years. Most regrettably, in the hectic building after the war many of the most enlighted measures advanced by the Association were either forgotten or abandoned by various authorities and this was very much to the detriment of thousands of Scottish tenants.

With the benefit of hindsight it is not possible to argue that everything which was suggested in 1943 was entirely sound. But the flaws are rare. Most of the recommendations have easily withstood the test of time and one wonders what the framers of these documents must have felt when, in the early post-war years, their wise counsel was either ignored or rejected. Douglas Niven, writing of the products of the post-war era, describes them as being –

[153] Undersized and of poor quality; the majority contain

118

'built-in' defects, which now represent an increasing maintenance and a major cost problem for local authorities. Many of these houses were planned for peripheral city or town sites with indecent haste and without proper thought for layout or for community services.

And again –

[154] Long term investment potential, quality, maintenance and the provision of attendant social and commercial services were either ignored or given low priority in many housing programmes. It was somehow imagined that these services could be added at a later date. It was also believed that little harm would be caused by the lack of these facilities in new housing areas. The consequences of this misguided policy are now obvious to all concerned with housing problems in Scotland.

These criticisms are entirely valid and could easily be amplified a thousandfold. Importantly, however it is also clear that those responsible for the building policies of the late 1940s and 50s must carry the burden by themselves, for they were unarguably acting in defiance of the explicit advice which had been provided by the Association – and by others – during the war years.

About the same time as the Association submitted its evidence to the Scottish Housing Advisory Committee, it was also consulted by the Burt Committee which had been established by the government to examine alternative methods of house construction which might be used in the post-war building programme. In January 1943, Mr J.W. Laing, a member of the latter committee, inspected some of the poured cellular concrete (no-fines) houses which the Association had built and examined the shuttering which had been used.[155] Mr Laing was obviously impressed because the method was strongly recommended in the Burt Report in 1944 and the publicity given at that time resulted in many requests for information and advice in respect of the technique.[156]

Indeed, it is clear that the Association fully gained the confidence of the Burt Committee since its chairman, Sir George Burt, agreed that the Department of Health for Scotland and the Association should be given a free hand to experiment with demonstration house types which might be appropriate within the Scottish context. Thus the Sighthill experimental develop-

ment was sanctioned in April 1944 and initial plans were immediately drawn up to erect the following houses.[157]

One pair of no-fines concrete houses (8 inch walls).
One pair of 'foamed-slag' houses poured *in situ* (for which it is thought the Association's shuttering would also be suitable).
One pair of 'Gyproc' houses – similar to those erected in heavily bomb-damaged Coventry.
One pair of alternative steel-framed houses (Hill's Patent Glazing).
One pair of Weir steel houses.
One pair of 'Duplex' houses (later reconsidered).

These represented a first draft, but other houses which were also considered at that time were –

One pair of houses – foamed-slag, prefabricated blocks.

One pair of timber houses – prefabricated and imported from USA or Canada.

One pair of prefabricated brick houses.

One pair of steel-framed resin bonded plywood houses.

On succeeding months, many other houses were considered for the Sighthill scheme. The objectives behind the project were fundamentally to devise methods of house construction which would circumvent the chronic shortage of certain types of material – such as timber – and enable large numbers of workers who had had little training for the building industry to find employment in the forthcoming assault on the housing problem. In addition, however, the disastrous consequences of the recoil of industry from the dislocation caused by the First World War were well remembered. There was an absolute determination to ensure that history did not repeat itself. For example, throughout the present war the steel industry (and, therefore, the coal industry) had been fully stretched by the requirement for ships, tanks, military vehicles of all description, aircraft and so on and with the return to peace it was imperative to find some alternative outlet which would keep the furnaces and factories busy. In the same way the demand for concrete had expanded, while other industries – such as brickmaking – had contracted. In all of these circumstances, houses of steel or concrete were going to be essential if recession was to be avoided, but inevitably this involved the risk of a major and self-defeating reduction in the quality of houses. A key purpose of Sighthill – as with the Burt Committee's experiments elsewhere – was to ensure that sufficiently high standards of design were maintained.

As has been mentioned, there were subsequent delays to the project: nevertheless houses demonstrating twelve different systems of non-traditional construction were built by the Association between 1944 and 1952, and later a number of other houses were constructed on the site to demonstrate a variety of economic techniques, including space-saving design, economic use of softwood, and alternative methods of whole house heating. The last pair of houses were built as late as 1964 and were two timber dwellings erected on behalf of the Canadian Government.

The 69 houses on the Sighthill estate (two Weir 'Paragon' steel houses were demolished in 1966) eventually included 30 different house types, some of which are quite unique since they were never used elsewhere. Others were widely adopted both by the Assocation and local authorities. Once these houses had been built, it was obviously important to monitor their performance. When the Association was expanding rapidly in the 1940s and 50s Edinburgh, like other towns and cities, suffered from an acute housing shortage; hence to provide for staff and to ensure that the houses were constantly checked, these dwellings were originally allocated to employees. At the time of writing 26 have been sold to tenants and the 21 oldest houses are currently being modernised. Anyone remotely interested in post-war housing would be well advised to spend some time reflecting on the remarkable collection of houses in Sighthill Road and Sighthill Neuk.

In November 1943, Tom Johnston's ideas for the housing drive were maturing. He assured the House of Commons that comprehensive measures were in hand to meet Scotland's grave housing problem, that he was considering such matters as the expansion of the building industry, the acquisition of sites, alternative methods of construction and the provision of emergency housing accommodation. He added –

[158]
> We already have a national house-building agency in Scotland, the Scottish Special Housing Association. This Association can provide housing in any part of Scotland and I am at present planning for a large scale programme of building by the Association after the war.

In answer to a question, he confirmed that he would willingly extend the Association's statutory powers if necessary. Interestingly, and perhaps encouragingly from the Association's point of view, he had previously responded in the same terms to a similar question raised by the former ILP stalwart, David Kirkwood, MP.[159] Regrettably, however, it was too much to hope that Mr Kirkwood's ex-colleagues had also become convinced of the benefits which the Association could provide.

By May 1944, Johnston was ready to flesh out his plans into a realistic programme and Council were summoned to the Department of Health for Scotland to be given an outline of his intentions. These involved a massive increase in the Association's activities and, as a first step, he proposed significantly to

Tom Johnston, Secretary of State for Scotland 1942-45.

enhance the political and technical authority of the Council of Management. Lord Traprain had played little part throughout the war and was in any case fully occupied with the coal industry; James Welsh, MP had resigned on account of poor health. All the other members of the wartime Council were retained, but now, Sir Garnet Wilson, JP*, the Liberal Lord Provost of Dundee, was appointed as chairman. In addition, three experienced Labour local councillors, John C. Forman, JP*, John J. Robertson, JP*, and Thomas Paterson, JP* the first two of whom were Labour parliamentary candidates who were successfully returned at the 1945 General Election – were added to the Council, where they were joined by John Stirling, the Chief Architect from the Department of Health for Scotland.[160]

On 24th June, a letter reached the Association confirming these arrangements and indicating that, while Sir Garnet would be part-time chairman, Mr W.C. Davidson, who had served with distinction both on the Council of Management and on the Scottish Housing Advisory Committee, would be full-time vice-chairman, responsible for the day-to-day running of the organisation. Meanwhile, there would be nine other members of the Council of Management.[161]

On 31st July, the new Council assembled at the Association's offices – now at 11 Drumsheugh Gardens – where they were joined by the Secretary of State and Mr G.H. Henderson, the

Sir Garnet Wilson (1885-1975)
Dundee businessman and education expert. Vice-Chairman of the Advisory Council on Education in Scotland. Lord Provost of Dundee 1940-46. President University College, Dundee 1946-52. Member of Council, Queen's College 1953-67. Chairman Glenrothes Development Corporation 1952-60. Hon FEIS ˙1943; Knighted 1944; LLD St Andrews; Freeman of City of Dundee 1972.
John Calder Forman, JP (1884-1975)
Labour and Co-operative Party MP for the Springburn division of Glasgow 1945-64. Member of Glasgow City Council 1928-45.
John Jones Robertson, MP (1898-1955)
A Shetlander who went off to sea at the age of fourteen. Royal Navy 1914-18, being present at the Battle of Jutland. Navy's middleweight boxing champion. Subsequently became a fruit merchant in Edinburgh. Edinburgh Town Council 1938-45. Labour MP for Berwick and Haddington 1945-50 and East Lothian 1950-51. Joint Parliamentary Under-Secretary of State at the Scottish Office 1947-50.
Thomas Paterson, JP (1890?-1971)
Engine Driver. Labour member of Ayr Town Council 1937-71. Baillie and Freeman of the˙Royal Burgh of Ayr.

Secretary of the Department of Health for Scotland.

[162] Mr Johnston referred to the work which had been carried out by the Association during the war and to the Housing (Scotland) Bill at present before Parliament, which contained various provisions affecting the Association. He stated that, subject to the Bill becoming law, it was intended that the Association should build 100,000 houses within a period of 10 to 12 years after the conclusion of the European War: that the Association would build in the areas where the housing needs were greatest: and that so far as could be foreseen at present, it seemed that those areas would cover about one half of Scotland ... subsidies would be payable to the Association direct by the government, instead of through local authorities, as formerly, and loans would be available to the Association through the Secretary of State.

The Secretary of State then instructed the Association to recruit a competent staff adequate to meet the heavy demands which would be placed on them and, before leaving, paid tribute to several individuals, notably Alexander McKinna the acting chairman, for their sterling work throughout the war.

The interesting thing to note about Johnston's plan is not simply the sheet magnitude of the programme which was being allocated to the Asociation, but also its target area. *The areas where the housing needs were greatest* were undoubtedly in and around Glasgow and Lanarkshire and, to a lesser extent, in Dundee. Clearly, therefore, his intention was not to leave the old industrial heartlands to their local authorities, but to use the Association as an agent of major change in these localities.

The Housing Act of 1944 duly passed into law. At once thereafter, because of the critical nature of the immediate housing shortage, the Association was instructed to provide 10,000 houses which were to be erected during the transitional period, and a circular was sent out to local authorities asking them to co-operate in making land available. It should be understood that these were not intended to be temporary dwellings and, in the letter to local authorities with which the Association followed up the government's circular, it was explained that the houses would be of four or five apartments, the ratio depending on local choice, and that the intention was to build schemes of not less than 100 houses in urban districts

and not less than 50 in landward area.[163]

The Assocation set to work and a programme was immediately declared. The distribution – which was guided by the Secretary of State – gives an explicit illustration of where the emphasis was to be placed. Glasgow was offered 2,000 houses (20 per cent of the programme) and Dundee 700; Aberdeen, Clydebank and Greenock 600 each; Motherwell, Inverness and the County of Lanark 500; the counties of Midlothian and West Lothian 400; Coatbridge, Kilmarnock, Dumbarton, Ayr and Buckhaven and Methil 300; Arbroath, Hamilton and Stirling 200; Bathgate, Brechin, Hawick, Johnstone and seven other small burghs were each to have 100 houses as their first instalment.[164] In other words, only 1,100 houses were awarded to three counties and a similar number to small burghs. By contrast 7,800 were to be in the cities and large towns. Beyond doubt, the Association was being pointed towards the very heart of the problem.

Over the next few months the Association got down to the job, recruiting staff and pushing ahead with drafting site and layout plans. In some cases – as with Dundee, Clydebank, Motherwell, Coatbridge, Inverness, Kilmarnock and all the other small burghs and counties, the local authorities were quick to co-operate and for these areas the activity advanced rapidly. Elsewhere, there was a noticeable reluctance to identify sites.[165]

As the war in Europe came to an end, and brought in its wake notice of the demise of the National Government, the Association seemed to have every reason to look forward to the forthcoming general election with equanimity. The SSHA had been set up by a Tory Government and could expect to have its programme maintained if the Conservatives were successful. Equally, throughout the war it had been guided and directed by a Labour Secretary of State and the plan to which it was working was his. Johnston was retiring, but, with a Council dominated by Labour politicians, there was no reason to fear the return of Labour to power. Indeed, on 27th July Council happily intimated its congratulations to Messrs Forman and Robertson on their election to Parliament. However, those with longer memories must have had a doubt or two when the composition of the new government was announced and it was realised that the Parliamentary Joint Under-Secretary of State was to be the former ILP (now Labour) Member for the Gorbals Constituency of Glasgow, Mr George Buchanan, MP*.

Trouble was not long in coming. On 21st September Council met with Mr Buchanan at St Andrew's House and came away in distress. Apparently they were being accused of lack of progress, but they were not certain and complained of 'the vague and unspecified terms of the criticisms made by Mr Buchanan'.[166]

Faced with the Minister's evident hostility Council felt that it was necessary to clear the air quickly so that they could be certain that they were still expected to work to the plan drawn up under Johnston. Accordingly, a letter to Mr Buchanan was drafted, signed by the chairman and sent with the unanimous backing of Council on 11th October.

[167] As you were informed at the said meeting, the Council of Management, while not entirely satisfied with the progress which has been made, were unanimously of the opinion that the Association's efforts were not deserving of the general condemnatory statement made by you. The Council of Management recollect, with regret, that, although you were pressed to give reasons for the dissatisfaction which you

George Buchanan 1890-1955
Native of Gorbals, Glasgow. Glasgow City Council 1918-22. President of United Patternmakers' Union 1932-48. ILP Member for Gorbals 1922-48 and member of the 'Clydeside' Group. Joined Labour Party in 1939. In 1945 opted to become Joint Under-Secretary of State for Scotland in preference to Minister for National Insurance which Attlee offered. Minister for Pensions 1947. Chairman of National Assistance Board 1948-53.

expressed, you did not respond, but adhered to your general statement. It is an elementary principle that, where complaints are made, the party, or body, complained against should receive full specification of the complaint, in order that answers may be prepared. The Council of Management feel that they are entitled to nothing less on this occasion.

The Council of Management, comprised as it is of persons experienced in public affairs, consider that they are competent to judge the quality and extent of the work being done by the Association and that you must have made the statement referred to without having had the opportunity of making yourself completely familiar with the work of the Association and the difficulties which have confronted them.

The letter then went on to ask again for clear guidance as to the nature of the grounds for Mr Buchanan's dissatisfaction.

On 10th December Council were summoned to St Andrew's House – though noticeably neither Mr Forman nor Mr Robertson were present – to meet with Mr Westwood, the Secretary of State, and Mr Buchanan and to learn of the government's response.

The matter was handled politely enough, but the verdict was clear. The association was to be re-organised and was now to be directed towards 'the rural areas where labour supply was difficult'. It was to develop a strong direct labour force (it had been doing this as an act of policy for several months), and was to have its higher full-time staff strengthened. To facilitate these changes, while the Civil Service representatives on the Council, Mr Stirling, and Mr Rose and the vice-chairman, Mr Davidson, were to be retained, the Secretary of State required the immediate resignation of the chairman and his other colleagues. (Two, Mr Coutts Morrison and Mrs Monteith, stayed on for a few months while the evacuation camps were handed over, and second thoughts seemed to have prevailed in the case of Thomas Paterson.) Not even poor Mr McKinna, who had carried the burden through the war, was spared. They were invited to 'submit their resignations by next Friday', and to be out by the end of the month.[168] With them departed all Tom Johnston's best laid plans.

CHAPTER FOUR

1945 - 1955

As was noted in the first chapter, the estimate of Scotland's housing requirement made in 1944 was for 469,000 houses and it was reckoned that it would take something of the order of 19 years from the end of the war to achieve that target. It is against these estimates that one must set Tom Johnston's allocation to the Association of an objective of '100,000 houses within a period of from 10 to 12 years after the conclusion of the European war' concentrated in 'the areas where the housing needs were greatest', and which 'would cover about one half of Scotland'.[1] Clearly, therefore, if we assume that Johnston expected 200,000 houses or so to be built in the first 10 or 12 years of the programme (if 469,000 were to take 19 years or thereabouts, it would have been unrealistic to have expected much more, and in the event, these estimates were reasonably accurate since in the first 10 years 223,173 houses were built and the outcome over the 19 year period was 491,843) it is obvious that the Association was being asked to build about half of the houses and more than half so far as the major problem areas were concerned – *ie* pre-eminently in Glasgow and the old industrial heartlands of West Central Scotland and in Dundee.

Moreover, Johnston's intentions in respect of the SSHA should not be seen in isolation for, in his view, *regional* planning was required if there was to be a genuine long-term solution to Scotland's deep-seated social and economic ills. 'Heaven knows', he wrote later, 'there was great need for co-operation among local authorities for planning on a regional basis.'[2] During the war he commissioned the Clyde Valley Regional Plan which, although it was not published until 1946, was very much in tune with his philosophy. Under the leadership of Sir Patrick Abercrombie and Sir Robert Matthew the study team, composed largely of officials from the Department of Health for Scotland, investigated the physical, social, recreational and economic development possibilities of the entire Clyde region. In addition to calling for the creation of New Towns it pointed to the need to reduce drastically the density of Glasgow's population – three-quarters of a million people were huddled into three square miles around the city centre – to the imminent decline of both the Lanarkshire coalfield and the shipbuilding industry, to the need to relocate the steel industry towards the coast, and to the essential requirement for a Clydeside Regional Planning Authority to co-ordinate the immense restructuring tasks involved in social and economic recovery.

It is within the context of this regional approach that Johnston's intention for the SSHA should be considered. Having utilised the war years to explore and investigate the extent of the problem, and the way in which it could be expected to unfold in the post-war era, he and his advisers were in no doubt that the range and scale of operations extended well beyond the resources, means and frontiers of the local authorities of his day. Tragically, with his retirement and with the ending of the National Government, too many local authorities became once more arenas of, and vehicles for, the expression of party political ambitions; became theatres in which local political potentates could give expression to their personal and idealogicial aspirations. The immediate consequence was that the Clyde Valley Plan was shelved and not until the 1970s, with the reorganisation of local government, was a planning framework established which was equal to the task. In the interim, the price of this folly was exacted from the people of the area who were rehoused by the thousand in high density, peripheral and inner-city developments of, in most cases, dwellings of poor or inferior design and which, in any market where the choices of consumers might have been reflected, would surely have been rejected. Moreover, parts of Glasgow, Greenock and many of the neighbouring large towns were turned into urban and industrial wildernesses.

Why did it happen? Part of the answer is embedded deeply in the theory of local political power which had evolved within the ILP and subsequently within the Glasgow Labour Party. Writing of the inter-war years, Professor T.C. Smout describes the political attitudes which flowered under the tutelage of Sir Patrick Dollan, the leader of the Labour Group on Glasgow Corporation.

[3] It was Dollan ... party-machine man *par excellence* who really understood the Scottish working-class voter of the years after 1920. He manipulated an electorate frightened by the immense scale of unemployment and industrial collapse ... but nevertheless impressed by the practical energy of Wheatley in getting the Housing Act through in 1924 ... Labour in Scotland became synonymous with the defence of council housing, jobs in heavy industry, and sectarian schools; it had nothing whatever to do with participatory democracy, enthusiasm for socialism, or hope for the future.

After the war these views became the orthodoxy of the tight-knit faction which controlled policy. As Christopher Harvie says –

[4] Paradoxically, the victory of 1945 seemed to end Labour's golden age. Its personalities were dead or had retreated to the fringes ... In the 1950s there were probably no more than 500 regular Labour activists in the whole of Glasgow. This was not unwelcome to local councillors ... nor did it really disturb party organisers cast in the mould of Sir Patrick Dollan, Arthur Woodburn, and William Marshall, who concentrated on organisation and discipline at the expense of participation and ideas. The time of the wee hard men had come.

The central significance of council housing to the 'wee hard men' of local Labour politics in the period after 1945 was not a uniquely Scottish phenomenon, and it is important to keep the wider background in mind. But in few parts of the country was their position more rigorously defended. Douglas Niven sums up the outcome in the following words.

[5] Equally disturbing, though less fully appreciated, were the disastrous effects of many local authority housing policies in the post-war era. At the end of the Second World War politicians in many local authorities – especially in the west

of Scotland – believed that a complete programme of municipalisation of all privately rented housing was possible. Some even believed that all houses in a burgh or city should be owned by the local authority.

The result of this 'ridiculous notion', together with the continuation of rent controls, produced high rates and an absolute concentration of attention on new council building in what virtually amounted to a sustained assault on the private rented sector. In turn this meant continued decay and deterioration in many older but reasonable properties so that the high density new building proceeded cheek by jowl with the neglect and destruction of far too much of Glasgow and the other towns and cities of the region.

In short, then, many local Labour politicians regarded council housing fundamentally as the means by which the loyalty and support of working people would be secured in the long term. The quality of the houses, their standards of design and appearance, their utility as living spaces within which families and individuals could live and develop, and their physical relationship to services, amenities and to the wider civic environment – all of these were lesser matters and, as such, had to be subservient to the houses' essential function as political tools. Because the SSHA was seen as a threat to that end – as a threat to the sovereignty and autonomy of local politicians – it had to be excluded or confined.

Thus it was that George Buchanan rushed to deflect and curb the Association's activities. In 1953, Tom Johnston reflected somewhat ruefully on what had happened and it must be doubted if his regrets were primarily focused against his nominal political opponents of a lifetime.

[6]   Well, with the end of the National Government came also the end of our experiment in political co-operation for Scottish national ends. Into that experiment of the Council of State had gone four years of effort and in it I had sunk many of my own energies and hopes ... For a certainty there are considerable achievements in housing, in health, and in the right to work, which could be rapidly secured for this generation if they were taken outside the realm of party strife.

In the judgement of the author, the intervention of George Buchanan, and his Glasgow political paymasters, into the housing policies of the immediate post-war years was a disaster for the city and, indeed, for many other parts of Scotland. That, of course, is an opinion which others may care to dispute. What is certain, however, is that, as far as the Association was concerned, his impact was almost catastrophic.

As was explained, the immediate resignation of the senior members of Council had been demanded, but they eventually took their leave with rather more dignity two Council meetings later, on 31st January. At the intervening meeting at the end of December Sir Garnet Wilson recalled that the Secretary of State had said that he had 'nothing but praise for the work of the Association', and this may have been a fair reflection of the latter's innermost opinions, since he had been a junior minister under Johnston for much of the war. But Joseph Westwood was not the man to have stood up to Buchanan and his friends on an issue of this kind. Sir Garnet also went on to praise 'the splendid efficiency' of the Council of Management and of the team of officials which they had assembled, and concluded that 'no observer who studies the recent progress of the Association and the inherent difficulties of the time would come to any other conclusion than that they had shown both progress and speed in their operations.' Thereafter Mr McKinna, Mr Ronald and Mr Robertson, MP, departed with the 'hope that the Association would continue to prosper'.[7] At the January meeting the deputy chairman, William C. Davidson, speaking on behalf of all of the staff, expressed his 'very real regret' at the changes which were occasioning Sir Garnet's retirement. He praised the way in which the latter had dealt with the affairs of the Association. Mr Rose, the King's and Lord Treasurer's Remembrancer — the Treasury representative on Council — concurred with these remarks and stated 'that Sir Garnet had proved an ideal chairman and had always carried through the Association's business with the minimum of friction and a delightful geniality.'[8]

Clearly these men had had to go, since Buchanan was not prepared to tolerate an SSHA led by men who were capable of standing up to him in the manner expressed in their letter of the previous October. Interestingly, he made no criticism of the membership of the Council on the grounds that they had not been elected by democratic vote. (This was a charge which local authority critics of the Association frequently levied at that time.) On the contrary, he wanted a Council which would be quite unable to exert any kind of a challenge on policy matters, which is why he insisted that the chairman should be the chief executive and a full-time salaried official. From a purely management point of view, of course, that was an extremely dangerous proposition, because to whom was such a chairman accountable for the day to day running of the organisation? Unless the Minister was prepared to devote an inordinate amount of his attention to the Association, or the staff were to be fully integrated within the Civil Service – which was impossible in this case – the combining of the roles of chief executive and chairman was a recipe for trouble. It placed far too much authority, responsibility – and temptation – onto the shoulders of one individual.

As was mentioned previously, Mr Davidson and Thomas Paterson – a doughty Town Councillor, who was described to the author as 'the finest Housing Convener Ayr ever had; respected and admired by Labour and Tory alike' – and the government officers, Mr Rose and Mr Stirling, were retained on the Council, and they were shortly joined by Mr J. R. McIntosh, CBE, of Aberdeen. Then, in April Major Dalziel of Oxford was appointed to be full-time chairman.

Against the background of the chronic post-war housing shortage, George Buchanan could not, of course, dispense entirely with the services of the Association, although that might more closely have matched his views. Now, however, the second phase target of another 10,000 houses was directed increasingly towards the counties and burghs while Glasgow insisted that the Association's allocation to the city should be Weir steel houses or houses built by its own direct labour department. More generally the Association found itself hopelessly snagged up in shortages of men and materials as local authorities indulged in a frantic scramble for the scarce resources with which to process their housing programmes.

One of the problems which had been noted by the wartime investigation of the Scottish Housing Advisory Committee was the difficulty posed for local authorities by movements of the population as a result of industrial change. The pre-war emphasis on linking housing subsidy to slum clearance and to the relief of overcrowding had prevented 'housing authorities (from) building subsidised housing for work people transferred from other areas'.[9] This, of course, was not a problem to the SSHA which was intended to build where the need was greatest, and Johnston's hopes for the Association explain why no long-term measure had been introduced in the 1944 Housing (Scotland) Act to enable the local authorities to respond to the problem. As it was, in 1945, the Association had been given an early programme of one thousand houses for 'incoming miners' in Ayrshire, Dumfriesshire, Fife, Lanarkshire, Midlothian, Stirlingshire and West Lothian, and this activity now became more emphasised. Inevitably, however, under George Buchanan's influence, the Housing (Financial Provisions) (Scotland) Act of 1946, virtually doubled the subsidies to local authorities (from £13 0s 0d to £25 0s 0d for a five apartment house) and permitted them to follow an open 'general needs' building policy.[10] The initial consequence of this was a hopeless competition for resources and a general identification of building plans which had no chance of early fulfilment. Within two years huge programmes of construction had been earmarked all over the country which could not possibly be completed in the short term. The market for materials and labour had become grossly overloaded, and the pressure to resort to ill-considered methods of construction was almost irresistible. In other words, a difficult situation had been turned into something approaching an uncontrollable nightmare.

The Association, of course, had always been concerned with non-traditional methods of construction and, with the Sighthill demonstration site, it tried to sort out the wheat from the chaff, but with many manufacturing companies trying to get in on the prefabricated building act the risks of inferior products being adopted were obviously high. The firms with some experience of this kind of activity had some advantage and the Annual Report for 1946 noted that while the development of non-traditional house types was not yet sufficiently advanced for most of the producers to accept orders, Weir 'Paragon' Bungalows, Weir 'Quality' houses and Atholl houses (all steel), and Swedish timber houses and the Association's no-fines concrete houses were available – if in small numbers. On 27th November 1945, the Department of Health circulated local authorities giving them particulars of those non-traditional methods of construction which were most advanced and it was noted by the Association that only the Weir and Atholl houses and the

Association's no-fines method were nearing the stage where large-scale production could be contemplated. Interestingly, however, the 1,860 Association houses on which building was in progress at March 1946 were classified as follows:-

Traditional	776
Weir 'Paragon'	46
Orlit	2
Swedish timber	968
Association's no-fines	68
Total	1,860

At the same time the Association had agreed in principle to place contracts for 1,000 Weir 'Quality' houses and 500 Atholl Houses.[11]

The Association was never very enthusiastic about steel houses, fought endless battles with their manufacturers and, in fact, did not itself erect very many. Rather its preference was for the no-fines technique which it had pioneered and which it was to use with success down to modern times. Regrettably, however, right through the 1940s it was unable fully to utilise its knowledge and experience in this type of construction. With the wholesale expansion of local authority building the Association found itself compelled to use its direct labour force not so much for building no-fines houses – to which it was well-suited – as for site servicing (ie laying the drains, etc and preparing foundations) so that others might build less satisfactory houses.

The pressure exerted by the government at this time in favour of various prefabricated non-traditional techniques which might be used by the local authorities was intense and, at the request of the Ministry of Works, two additional small experimental sites were planned for Danderhall and Holytown. These estates, involving three different house types, were to be built to English standards to see if they would stand up to the Scottish climate. In addition the Department of the Chief Scientific Adviser was to co-ordinate a variety of experiments into tenants' 'ways of living' by incorporating within the designs variations in the interior layout and in methods of cooking and heating.[12] Similarly the Association was encouraged to provide site facilities in various parts of the country for manufacturers of prefabricated houses and throughout 1946, contracts were concluded for the erection of Orlit, BISF, Hills Pressweld, Whitsun Fairhurst, Brydon and Wimpey house types.

In June, the new chairman was summoned to meet Mr Buchanan and was berated for the Association's slow rate of progress. Council responded by initiating a further recruitment drive, both for head office staff and for on-site employees.[13] A full internal re-organisation had been set in train following the earlier changes in the composition of Council and it was intended to implement this later in the year.

Perhaps in response to the prodding from the Minister, Mr Dalziel produced a scheme to increase the pace of construction by linking the Association to the Orlit company. The latter firm indicated the wish to open two factories in Scotland, each with an output of 2,500 houses per year and the plan was for the Association to guarantee to take the total output of one factory, or, if the houses could not be erected immediately, to pay 90 per cent of the price when the units were available for delivery.[14] Since the houses were to be erected by direct labour it is difficult to see what advantage this scheme could have had over building by the Association's own no-fines technique. As it happened, the SSHA only erected a few Orlit houses in Ayr, Hamilton, Kilmarnock and at Garthdee in Aberdeen, and this was to prove to be a fortunate escape for, although they served well enough for many years, by the 1980s a fatal flaw had been discovered in the structure of these buildings. Deterioration in the concrete framework exposed the steel reinforcement in places to corrosion, and this necessitated complete demolition and replacement. But if Dalziel's plan had gone through, the Association could have been facing a contemporary disaster of major proportion rather than a minor problem.

Orlit houses at Ayr shortly before they were demolished in 1986.

In the event, the new full-time chairman's tenure of office was very short. In August 1946 five new members were admitted to Council – Mr A.G. McBain*, Mr J. McBoyle*, Rev W.C.V. Smith, Miss M.W. McLaughlin and Mr Grierson MacMillan*. At that point the Department of Health had given its general approval of the proposed new management structure.[15] But on 30th August – the second meeting which he had attended – Mr McBain intervened to intimate his intention of tabling amendments and asked that press advertisements should be deferred meantime.[16] At the meeting of 20th September he put forward his counter-proposals and drew attention to the excessive higher executive authority which was being placed in the hands of the chairman.[17] McBain's suspicions were now thoroughly roused and ten days later, as a result of his further investigations, Council met with the deputy chairman, Mr Davidson, in the chair to consider a resolution demanding the suspension of the chairman. This was unanimously carried[18] and a fortnight later, after discussions in the presence of lawyers, Mr Dalziel resigned on the grounds of ill-health. Perhaps indeed 'acute neuritis' had played a part in the matter, but undoubtedly the ill-considered determination of George Buchanan to reduce the chairmanship to an executive rather than a leading, over-seeing 'political' position was the root of the problem. That trouble had occurred sooner rather

A G McBain, Chairman of the Association 1946-51.

A.G. McBain (1895-   )

Member of the Institute of Chartered Accountants in Scotland. Chairman SSHA, 1946-51; director, Blytheswood Shipbuilders; board member, East Kilbride Development Corporation. Expert on taxation and a prolific writer on this and related subjects. In 1978 he was awarded the Papal Knighthood of St Gregory the Great and was the first Scottish non-Catholic to receive this honour in recognition of his services as financial advisor to the Catholic Church for more than half a century. He was responsible for the establishment of health insurance and retirement funds for priests and their housekeepers. A Glasgow man, much admired for his wit and character.

James McBoyle CBE

Depute County Clerk of Aberdeenshire 1929-34; County Clerk of the Stewartry of Kirkcudbright 1934-44; County Clerk and Treasurer of Midlothian 1944-61. Served on various government committees on local government finance and manpower. Hon Sec of the Society of County Clerks in Scotland 1940-50.

W. Grierson Macmillan

An Edinburgh tea merchant. Served on the Council until 1966, thus becoming the Council member with the longest record of service. Deputy Chairman 1964-66.

than later was to the advantage of the Association and its debt to Mr McBain was considerable. Incidentally, with the chairman's departure the proposed deal with the Orlit company was abandoned although the two things are not necessarily connected.[19]

What the Scottish Office thought of Council's decision to remove its chairman is not clear. (The minutes only refer to a meeting with the Secretary of State and Mr Buchanan, at which there was 'an exchange of views'.[20]) But the outcome was accepted as was the appointment of Mr McBain as interim chairman for three months, at the end of which time the position was to be reviewed in consultation with the Secretary of State.[21] Over the next few weeks the internal reorganisation was carried forward and many new appointments were made. In January, Council expressed its satsifaction with the way in which the task had been carried out and accordingly urged the Secretary of State to confirm Mr McBain's appointment for the next twelve months and to sanction an honorarium which took account of the fact that he would require to devote approximately one third of his time to Association business.[22] This arrangement was duly accepted and the Association never again repeated the experiment of a full-time executive chairman. (In fact Mr McBain served a full term of office.)

The twelve months after December 1945 almost certainly represent the nadir of the SSHA's fortunes. In that time the main part of its Council had been thrust from office; the plans for its central role in the post-war building programme had been strangled almost at birth; the new senior management with which it had been saddled had proved less than effective; and its rate of progress had become hopelessly snarled up in the mad log-jam for which the government's change of policy was partly responsible. Nevertheless, all was not loss in that year. For instance, George Ross had returned to take up the duties of secretary and finance officer, and another individual who was to give many years of distinguished service, David H. Halley, was appointed assistant secretary and solicitor. In addition, the search for larger and more suitable head office accommodation had proved fruitful, and numbers 15, 17 and 19 Palmerston Place were acquired, to be followed within the year by the purchase of the adjacent number 21. Above all, however, as far as the immediate future was concerned, by the end of the year the organisation was once more in the hands of a chairman who had already shown himself to be equal to the task.

As was mentioned, Mr McBain's first duty had been to carry through a reorganisation of the management structure and to secure additional senior staff of the required calibre. With a part-time chairman, there were obviously likely to be problems if the deputy chairmanship remained a full salaried appointment and William C. Davidson, therefore, agreed to resign his office and membership of Council to become the Association's land and property manager. Under the new arrangements a general manager was necessary to assume day-to-day control, and, with Mr John Lawrence, the well-known Glasgow builder, acting as consultant, a sub-committee of Council selected Mr S.A. Findlay, OBE, for the job. Great care was taken over the appointment, with two members of Council actually going to Poplar to see for themselves how successful Mr Findlay had been in his previous post.[23] In the event it was an excellent selection, as was the choice of Mr J. Austen Bent as chief technical officer and assistant general manager. The latter came to the Association from the Department of Health for Scotland and the Association agreed that he should continue to serve as a member of the Burt Committee.[24]

These appointments augured well for the future, but the Annual Report for the year to March 1947 could not disguise the slow progress which is illustrated by the following table.

[25]
Progress of post-war schemes as at 31·3·47

Sites nominated	21,038
Entry to site granted	15,608
Contracts placed	8,993
Completed	615

A year later the position had scarcely improved:

[26]
Progress of post-war schemes as at 31.3.48

Sites nominated	29,222
Entry to site granted	19,209
Contracts placed	11,619
Completed	2,714

At a meeting in March 1947 the new general manager had explained to Mr Buchanan that the proposed target of 6,879 houses allocated to the Association for the year ahead was hopelessly unrealistic since it would require a labour force of 11,000 men as compared to the 2,816 then employed.[27] Under the prevailing circumstances there was no possibility of the additional building workers being recruited. Indeed, the Association was having a hard enough time hanging onto existing labour in the face of the fierce competition for experienced men.[28] Similarly the position in respect of some materials – notably timber and steel – was also extremely difficult.

The disparity between the Association's planned programme and actual progress was a reflection of the general position prevailing throughout Scotland and it was obvious that the chaotic situation had to be brought under some kind of control. In October and November 1947 government circulars to the local authorities and to the Association instructed that only houses on which work had started by 24th October were to be continued if they were being built by traditional methods. Work on other houses for which approval had earlier been given was not to proceed until further notice, although special arrangements might be made in respect of non-traditional houses to prevent disruption to factory production.[29] In effect, this meant that the future programme was being suspended while an attempt was made to more strictly apportion resources between the various authorities. The report to the Council of Management at the end of March 1948 explained the situation thus. The slow progress –

[30] Was due mainly to erratic supply and prolonged shortages of a number of materials, including cement, timber, electric conduit, steel cast iron materials, plasterboard, hard wall plaster and glass. During the year special efforts were made by the Association to overcome these shortages by arranging, with the consent of contractors, for the transfer of materials from sites where they were not immediately required to sites where progress was being impeded for lack of them and some slight success was achieved by this means. It, however, was clear that the number of houses under contract in Scotland was far in excess of the number which could be completed in a reasonable time, having regard to the supply of labour and materials. It was

Myton Clyde houses.

141

thought by the government early in 1947 that . . . it was not unreasonable to expect the completion in Scotland in that year of 24,000 houses, of which the Association's share was 4,234 selected houses, but it soon became evident that this output could not be attained . . . It was not surprising, therefore, that in October 1947 the government announced that, except in the cases of houses wanted urgently for miners and agricultural workers and non-traditional houses for which work had been done in the factories, the erection should be postponed of houses which, though included in approved contracts, had not been begun. The government's policy of restricting the approval of fresh contracts to houses required in the interests of fuel and food production was re-affirmed.

The object was to reduce by the latter half of 1949 the total number of houses under construction at any one time to the number which it was estimated might be completed in 12 months. Incidentally, it is to be hoped that this realistic policy of avoiding the overloading of the market will result in reduced prices.

Interestingly, the same report records the various types of houses for which contracts had been placed in the post war programme, including the 2,714 completed at that date.[31]

	Houses
Traditional	4,021
Weir steel ('Paragon' and 'Quality')	2,511
Athol steel	1,342
BISF steel-framed	1,000
Hilcon steel-framed	138
Orlit concrete framed	358
Whitson Fairhurst concrete framed	654
Swedish timber	968
No-fines poured concrete (including Wimpey and Brydon types)	402
Keyhouse unibuilt	2
Foamed slag poured	2
Tarran-Clyde pre-cast concrete units	162
Hostel conversions	57
Total	11,617

Top left *The original timber houses at Carfin as they appear today.*

Left *A row of houses in the Garden village of Rosyth.*

Above *'Scottish Special', the SSHA anniversary rose.*

Above *The Queen in Calton in 1983.*

Top right *394 Gallowgate, an eighteenth-century tenement restored to its former glory.*

Right *Hutchesontown Glasgow.*

Top left *The re-development at Jedburgh which won international recognition by the award of the Europa Nostra Medal.*

Centre *Award winning restoration in old Dunbar.*

Left *The 'Coronation' houses at Dunkeld.*

Modern houses at Erskine and Dalry.

A sheltered development at Mintlaw, north of Aberdeen.

Another view of Erskine 'new community'.

Examples of new mixed developments which incorporate sheltered housing, at Clydebank and Kirkland Street, Glasgow.

A number plate at Bowling Green Street, Leith, of the type which won an award from the Saltire Society.

Top left *Rosebank Street, Dundee; another development which includes sheltered housing.*

Left *Ladywell Musselburgh.*

Sheltered developments in Glasgow, Dundee and Plean in Stirlingshire.

As this list indicates, the Association had been quite unable to concentrate its resources on the no-fines technique which it favoured for a semi-skilled labour force and the problem was further illustrated in the annual report for the year, which drew attention to the way in which the laying of main services – sewers, water, electricity and gas – was failing to keep pace with the rate of house construction. In some cases, oil cookers for temporary use had to be purchased and houses were let without electricity being available. 'Much difficulty in selecting sites for additional schemes has also been due to the lack of these main services, or some of them, and it is clear that substantial extensions will require to be provided in the next few years if housing is not to be delayed'.[32]

In October 1947 political changes occurred which must have been something of a relief. The Secretary of State, Joseph Westwood*, had 'proved a failure and was sacked'.[33] George Buchanan became Minister of Pensions for a few months, before leaving politics to take up the chairmanship of the new National Assistance Board. His replacement as Joint Parliamentary Under-Secretary of State with responsibility for housing was none other than Mr J.J. Robertson, MP, the former member of Council and he lost no time in coming to the Association's offices for wide-ranging exploratory discussions.[34] One can at once detect an easing in the relationship between the Association and government[35], but it was not within the Minister's power to restore complete order in the short-term, nor, of course, could he reverse the fundamental policy shift engendered by Buchanan in 1945.

During the year to March 1949, the pace of construction did quicken, with 3,305 houses being completed – an increase of about 1,100 on the previous year – but there was general frustration in the knowledge that the Association was capable of doing far more. Shortages of plasterers, joiners, and painters were noted although the supply of most materials was beginning to improve. In particular the Association was disgruntled about the use to which its direct labour force was being put. [36]   The main activity of the organisation during the year has been site-servicing and constructing foundations for steel houses, but two schemes of house-building, each of 100

*Westwood's health may not have been good at this time and he died within a few months of being replaced.

houses, on which all the work except the plumber and electrical work is being done by direct labour were commenced. Other schemes of house building by direct labour were in contemplation at the end of the year and it is hoped to extend such work substantially as soon as opportunity offers. Meantime, practically all of the Association's site servicing work is being done by direct labour, and includes in many cases the provision of sewers for local authorities.

In the following year no significant additions were made to the Association's programme, which was still far greater than could be justified by the rate at which houses were actually being completed. However, the breakdown of the programme indicated in the Annual Report at March 1950 is interesting in that it illustrates something of the way in which the emphasis had been shifted from 1945.[37]

General needs	23,129
Miners	10,536
Forestry workers	533
Managers	94
Ministry of Supply	60
Lighthouse keepers	47
Miscellaneous	38
Total	34,437

Of that total, only 10,239 of the houses had actually been completed and the houses for 'incoming miners' were taking up an increasing share of the activity. (In 1950-51, houses for miners made up almost 50 per cent of the completions for the year – see Appendix B.) Moreover, when the detailed returns are analysed it is clear that the thrust of the effort had been directed to burghs, small towns and to the countryside – notably in the latter case, in the form of houses for the Forestry Commission and for the Northern Lighthouse Board. Capital had been spent on 14,875 houses in 136 different localities. Some estates, such as Rankinston (8 houses) and New Dailly (12 houses) were very small, but the average size works out at approximately 194 houses, with the majority being less than 100. The major developments had been in Clydebank – Livingstone Street (614), Coatbridge (524), Aberdeen (330), Ayr (200 and 192), Kilmarnock (636), Greenock (400), Kirkcaldy (350,

32 and 54) and Tullibody (360). By contrast the only estates of note in Glasgow were 100 houses at Balornock, 104 at Cadder Road and 194 at Rosshall. A large development of 548 dwellings was also now under way at Toryglen, but it cannot conceivably be argued that the Association had been directed to the 'areas of greatest need' in the years immediately after the war.[38]

Swedish Timber houses for Forestry Commission workers.

A lighthouse keeper's house at Cantick Head, Orkney.

The Toryglen development is particularly interesting, not only because it illustrates something of the relationship which then prevailed between the Association and the city, but also because it gives a clear demonstration of the way in which the Corporation was pressurising the Association to abandon its preferred types of building.

Back in March 1945 Edinburgh Corporation's Housing Committee had asked the Association to construct, at its Sighthill experimental site, a block of flats of from six to eight storeys in height. This proposal was discussed fully with the Department of Health and Tom Johnston was consulted on the matter. As we saw earlier the Association had told the Scottish Housing Advisory Committee of its preference for cottage-type dwellings, but had indicated that flats could be appropriate under certain circumstances, and Johnston agreed with that view, indicating that there might be a place for flats in some of the more populous parts of the country. However, he also agreed that they should be left to the attention of the local authorities concerned and advised that the Association should not devote any of its resources to multi-storey flats. Accordingly the Association rejected Edinburgh's request.[39]

In the years immediately following the return to peace, although Glasgow was allocated more than 4,000 houses in the Association's initial programmes, the Corporation's reluctance to approve Association plans or to permit starts to be made was marked. However, a few months after Robertson's arrival at the Department of Health an agreement was tentatively reached for the erection of the first 350 dwellings at Toryglen. But the

Traditional houses built for incoming miners at Prestonpans.

plans, which were laid down by the City Engineer, Robert Bruce, were not greatly to the Council's liking, since he insisted on the use of multi-storey flats of up to ten storeys in height. The Association's planning and research staff were set to work to prepare type plans and Council debated the matter in April 1948. There was strong opposition, but the assistant general manager pointed out that if a decision were made, as a matter of policy, against the erection of multi-storey flats, this would result in the virtual cessation of all of the Association's activities in respect of Glasgow. He also stated his intention to ensure that a variety of types of dwelling would be constructed to provide for a balanced community and that the opportunity would be taken to provide buildings of some architectural merit. In the face of these arguments, and notwithstanding further objections from individual members, it was concluded that there was no real alternative to an agreement to build multi-storey flats, although the detailed plans would be closely scrutinised before final sanction was given.[40] In July 1949 the general site layout plans were approved by the Corporation[41] and the matter was further discussed with Mr Robertson in October of that year, when the difficulty of obtaining continuity of work in the Glasgow area was also aired. The Association explained its policy of frequent meetings with representatives of the Corporation in an attempt to promote harmony, and Robertson agreed to do what he could to obtain an additional allocation.[42] True to his word, two months later a further 250 houses for Toryglen were approved on condition that work on the first batch was fully under way by March 1950. But this agreement was not without strings. In order to avoid delay, while the Association was to continue with its own plans for the four and five apartment cottage houses, they would have to agree to build four and five storey flats to plans prepared by the Corporation, and, in the future development of the site, multi-storey flats capable of delivering the densities required by the Corporation's town planning scheme. When this arrangement was discussed in Council several members drew attention to the many matters of detail which would require careful consideration, but it was decided to recruit additional architectural staff and to give close scrutiny to the plans as and when they appeared.[43]

In January 1950, there was a general discussion about local

authority interest in multi-storey flats and the decision was made to inspect some developments in English cities, although it was recognised that buildings there might not be appropriate to Scottish conditions.[44] Accordingly, a delegation of members of Council and senior officers went to London on the 23rd and 24th of the month and had an 'interesting and informative' tour of inspection of various buildings. At the subsequent Council meeting Mr Bent reported some mellowing on the part of Glasgow Corporation, but said that their housing director still felt that it would be necessary on the grounds of density, to provide multi-storey flats in Toryglen. In the debate that followed –

[45]

It was the view of the Council that multi-storey flats had certain inherent disadvantages which rendered them less desirable as a family dwelling than the normal two-storey house, and they came to the conclusion that such flats should not be erected, unless it was impossible otherwise to achieve the density fixed by Glasgow Corporation. It was agreed, therefore, that Glasgow Corporation should be advised of the Council's views, and should be informed also of the likelihood of high rents being necessary for multi-storey flats, in order that the Corporation, if it so decided, might advise the Association that it was the Corporation's desire that multi-storey flats should be provided.

Meanwhile, it was also agreed to initiate a full scale study by officials to determine the best ways of providing this type of accommodation, should it prove absolutely necessary.

By April it was clear that the multi-storey blocks were required and Council examined a report on the proposed design and the relationship of the blocks to the surrounding community. Detailed consideration was thereafter given to such matters as structural forms, access, lifts, number of flats per floor, the provision of a club room on the ground floor which could be converted to other purposes in the light of experience, the absolute necessity of estate and caretaker's offices on the ground floor, laundering facilities, central heating methods, water carriage systems, the need for a 'house of rest' on the site which could be used for Church services, communal wireless aerials, and the need to earmark space for tenants' garages.[46]

If the Association was not happy about being pushed into

building flats, it was equally – if not more – disgruntled with the quality of many of the non-traditional house types which it was being virtually forced to construct. For example, in March 1950, after a lengthy and angry discussion of the problems which were being caused to tenants and to the Association as a result of the poorly designed and constructed Orlit and Myton Clyde houses, the chairman demanded to know what scope was allowed to adjust the plans of new non-traditional houses which the Association was asked to build. In response, Mr Bent explained the procedures by which such houses were approved by various government departments and committees and indicated that 'under existing conditions, it was only within very narrow limits that the Association was in a position to secure any amendments to the construction of non-traditional houses approved by the Department of Health'.[47]

Nevertheless the Association had already demonstrated that there were limits to its tolerance. In April 1948, attempts by the Weir Housing Corporation and the Ministry of Works to rectify the intensive condensation which 'had appeared in practically all "Quality" house schemes' were dismissed as 'being largely experimental in nature and there was no certainty that they would provide a permanent cure'. In consequence of its dissatisfaction, Council informed the Department of Health that the Association was unable to accept any allocation of Weir 'Quality' houses for the miners' third programme. It had been given no choice with earlier programmes, and was aware of the difficulty of finding suitable alternatives to the Weir house, but considered that the defects were 'sufficiently serious to justify the refusal of further allocations'.[48] Weir responded by agreeing to fit pitched timber roofs to the 550 'Quality' houses in the outstanding programme and, with a view to the future, to make arrangements to change to the non-fines concrete form of construction if the Association would provide a site for some prototype blocks. This was agreed (at Dysart), subject to details of design and price being satisfactory, but it was by no means the last occasion in which the Weir steel houses would give rise to dispute.[49] This incident triggered a wider dialogue with the Department of Health on the question of non-traditional houses in general and the Association pointed out that they were not only unsatisfactory, but also expensive.[50] A year later the Association returned to this question drawing the Department's

attention to parallel quotations for three estates which indicated
that the prices of prefabricated non-traditional houses 'were
substantially in excess of those for the traditional houses' by
whatever means the buildings were costed.[51] Later the Department laid down that it was necessary for some of the
companies and organisations which had been formed to deliver
non-traditional houses to be kept in being and that, therefore,
the Association and local authorities would be expected to
include a proportion of such dwellings in programme even
although their extra expense was acknowledged.[52]

The whole question of non-traditional houses was deeply
frustrating to the Association. As we have seen, one of its
original functions had been to specialise in methods of building
which would make a minimal call on traditional skilled labour
and it had, in particular, developed a preference for timber
houses and for the 'no-fines concrete technique' which was
particularly suited to construction by direct labour. In the
immediate post-war era, some Swedish timber houses had been
obtained but these could not match the lovely pre-war red cedar
Canadian houses and, in any case, in the current state of the
economy, the mass importation of the necessary supplies of
timber was out of the question. More readily available would
have been no-fines construction, and studies in 1946 had shown
that houses of this type to be built by James Miller and Partners
for the Association at Newtongrange had been cheaper by £100
per house than the lowest offer for buildings constructed by
traditional methods.[53] The mad-cap policies pursued after 1945

had, however, pushed this perfectly satisfactory method of building into the background, partly by forcing the Association's own labour force into becoming largely concerned with laying drains, water pipes and foundations for other house builders. As has been mentioned, the Annual Report for 1949 explained that 'the main activity of the organisation during the year has been site servicing and constructing foundations for steel houses ... Practically all of the Association's site servicing work is being done by direct labour, and includes in many cases the provision of sewers for local authorities.'[54]

As the 1940s drew to a close the economic state of the country seemed very poor and on 24th October 1949, Mr Attlee told the House of Commons of the need to reduce inflationary pressures. The Secretary of State followed this up by writing to the Association at the request of the Prime Minister to explain that, while it was not intended that there would be any reduction in the numbers of houses to be built by the local authorities and the SSHA (with a General Election pending a reduction was almost impossible) savings would have to be made over a wide range of public and private activities. For this reason more houses of three-apartment size were to be built, and the Association was invited to suggest such other economies as might be available for consideration by a committee of Ministers.[55] A few weeks earlier Mr Robertson had told Council of the need to reduce imports of timber by introducing alternative methods of construction.[56]

In September 1950 the Association gave both written and oral evidence to the Scottish Housing Advisory Sub-Committee on design and workmanship of non-traditional houses and was praised for being helpful and reliable. This had given officials the opportunity to challenge the cost and effectiveness of several of the house types then being built.[57] A few weeks later Council gloomily noted the latest upward movement in prices. 'Prices of non-ferrous metals, bituminous products, cast-iron and galvanised goods, cement and other materials had increased and it seemed likely that an increase could be expected in the price of timber. In addition, impending increases in the cost of rubber and oils would probably increase transport charges, which in turn might affect prices generally. Furthermore, deliveries were becoming slow ...'[58]

In April the Association submitted to the government its

suggestions for lower cost three-and four-apartment houses and was informed that inter-departmental discussions were in progress aimed at devising a policy on the relationship between standards of accommodation and costs. 'The general manager reported that ... proposals for the provision of houses incorporating reduced standards were to be considered by the appropriate Ministers at an early date' and that the Association might be asked to erect some prototype houses to the suggested specification.[59] In fact, when these specimen houses were erected later in the year at Sighthill and Toryglen, they were built not to the Association's ideas, but to plans produced by the Department of Health's own architects. However, on the eve of the Election in October 1951, Mr Tom Fraser, MP, the outgoing Parliamentary Under-Secretary of State, 'expressed his gratitude to the Association' for its efforts towards reducing costs 'with as little interference to existing standards as possible'.[60]

Meanwhile the Association had also been directing attention back to no-fines construction. In May of that year Mr Bent told Council that, provided there was careful consideration of structural details and strict site supervision, the method was 'one of the best alternatives to the use of brick', which was why various authorities in Scotland and England were coming to recognise its worth. The Association was about to make a start on a substantial scheme of no-fines houses at Mains of Fintry, in Dundee.[61]

When the election of October 1951 brought the Conservatives back to office, the new Parliamentary Under-Secretary of State, Commander Galbraith, MP, lost no time in bringing Sir George Henderson and other officials from the Department of Health for a full-scale meeting with the Association to discuss the twin needs of reducing costs and increasing the rate of production. Mr Galbraith's first thoughts seemed to be towards a return to the timber houses of the late 1930s, but, although the Association was enthusiastic enough, the problem of importation made this not a particularly practical suggestion. However, the Minister indicated his intention to inspect the low cost houses erected at Sighthill and Toryglen within the next few days and these might prove useful. He asked for detailed guidance on various costs throughout the building industry. The general manager then drew attention to the no-fines technique and explained that a 25-man squad, of which 50 per cent were unskilled workers, could pour 10 houses per week and that there was no reason why this progress rate could not be speeded up by improved methods and equipment. He 'expressed the opinion that there was great scope for still further improvement in the technique of building by such methods, which would result in more houses being built without the use of additional skilled labour.' By contrast, the Association also pointed to the excessive thinness of some of the walls of the timber houses currently being erected and Mr Galbraith said that the timber had 'now been increased from five-eighths to seven-eighths'. In summing up he stated that 'while the government were against any reduction in standards of construction, it was felt that every economy in the use of space within the houses could be justified on the grounds of reduced costs. He added that it was impossible at this stage to revise the plan.'[62]

Over the next year the Association conducted many experiments on costs of construction. Two Weir timber houses were erected at Sighthill – there were objections to the elevation[63] – as were six houses and two flats, in various forms of construction, aimed at securing maximum economies in the use of timber.[64] Similarly costs of no-fines houses constructed by direct labour were carefully monitored and the cost of a four-apartment house erected in a scheme of 100 houses at Prestonpans was shown to be £1,395, which 'compared favourably' with costs for other house types.[65]

Gradually the emphasis of the direct labour organisation began to swing back to house construction. In the year to March 1951, it had built 276 houses; the following year, the number was 756; and a year later 1,366 were built in this fashion. At the same time it should be noted that, in 1953, whereas direct labour was being used to build on 13 schemes (2,586 houses) it was still supplying site servicing to no less than 64 schemes. Roughly 2,000 men were in the direct labour force in any one month.[66] From 1951-52 to 1954-55 the Association was building at a total rate of approximately 5,000 houses per annum, (see Appendix B), and the total head of labour employed on Association work was of the order of 5,600 men.[67]

It is clear, therefore, that over these years the Association turned once more to its favoured no-fines method, but this was not an entirely straightforward business and, as we shall see, it did give rise to some problems.

In the first place, the method was obviously at its most economic in substantial schemes were the capital costs of steel shutters were spread over a reasonable number of houses and where men could move swiftly from one task to another. Where fewer houses were required, perhaps in rural communities or burghs, the method was not really appropriate. As the chairman explained to Commander Galbraith in October 1952, 'some alternative non-traditional method was required for the small authorities whose needs were often for a small number of houses on each of several scattered sites.'[68] In particular, the chairman was keen to find a method which could fully utilise the services of small-scale contractors in the rural areas, since their activities were currently restricted by the shortage of traditional materials.[69] Council noted the good reactions of the members of the public who had visited the low-cost houses at Sighthill[70] and gave close consideration to such non-traditional houses as Blackburn No-fines, O'Sullivan On-Site, Bellstone, Easi Form, Lawrence and the 'Reema' House which might also possibly help to provide an answer.[71]

However, the day of the post-war prefabricated non-traditional house was nearing its end. In the summer of 1951 the Association had carried out a detailed inspection of all the Weir 'Quality' houses in its possession and had discovered that the exterior paint was coming off in more than 500 of the houses and that two-thirds of the stock of Weir buildings were defective in one way or another.[72] A little later so concerned were Council at the state of these houses that payments were withheld from the company pending clarification of the responsibility for making good the defects.[73] Over the next year or so specialist surveys were conducted both by the company and the Association. This involved removing steel sections and subjecting them to metallurgical tests to see if the potential life of the houses could be estimated. 'Dr Howie, who had been instructed by the Association, was not confident that the houses would last 60 years, while Mr Arnott, who was an employee of Messrs G. & J. Weir, had expressed the view that, given certain conditions, the houses could be expected to have a useful life of "something like a century"'.[74] (As things have turned out, suitably and extensively modernised, most of the Weir 'Quality'

– now Weir 'Phoenix' – houses have survived and are reasonably satisfactory. By contrast when the Weir 'Paragons' – erected immediately after the war – were surveyed in the 1970s with a view to modernisation, most were found to be in such poor condition that they simply had to be demolished.) Eventually, after the Treasury had been brought into protracted negotiations, the Association and the Weir Housing Corporation agreed to split, on a fifty-fifty basis, the estimated cost of £121,170 of repairing all the houses. The work itself involved patching in places and complete re-harling at a fixed price of £75 per house.[75]

This experience, of course, had not improved anyone's disposition towards steel houses and by the spring of 1953 there was great concern at the increasingly uncompetitive cost of prefabricated houses generally. In March a meeting was held with Sir George Henderson, the Secretary of the Department of Health, at which the Association's worries were expressed: he was told that, meantime, high tenders were simply being refused.[76] In the following month the matter was taken up with Commander Galbraith, who agreed that unreasonable tenders could continue to be rejected and if the problem persisted, he would consider what, if any, action was required. By the time of the regular autumn meeting in October the relative competitiveness of no-fines construction by direct labour was unanswerable. Attention was drawn to publicity which had recently been given to the cheapness of a no-fines house which was being independently sponsored, and it was pointed out that the Association houses were in fact £137 cheaper and that a further reduction in costs would be effected soon. The Minister instructed the Association to concentrate on its own methods of no-fines construction, but reminded Council of the many interests in the building industry which had to be reconciled and, in order to prevent friction, asked that the proportion of work done by direct labour be kept to the present levels.[77] Interestingly, at the same meeting, he congratulated the Association on building 5,182 houses in the past year out of a total of 31,000 completed in Scotland and, thereby, becoming the largest new house provider in the Kingdom.

From then on, therefore, the Association came to rely more and more on no-fines, particularly when its own labour force was involved and where the standard of site supervision could be maintained at the highest level. That this was essential was demonstrated on one occasion at Toryglen where the no-fines walling for flats being erected by a contractor on behalf of the Association was condemned by the technical staff. Some of the blocks were ordered to be demolished and the Association insisted that the contractor accept full responsibility for the remainder for ten years after completion.[78]

In his booklet *The No-Fines Story*, Ron Macintosh gives the flavour of the period. Referring to the need to find satisfactory substitutes for roughcast on the outside and wet plaster in the inside because of the acute shortage of skilled craftsmen in the trades concerned with these tasks, he explains how

[79]   Bob Shiach, the Association's chief engineer, and I thought up a steel shutter that was to do two things in one; give a perfectly straight wall, but with the external finish already in position. The internal shutter panel was . . . perforated steel plate welded to a light steel frame; but the external shutter was of solid steel. These panels were mounted with connecting bolts between, passing through steel sleeves as spacers. The bolts were specially designed so that after the 'no-fines' wall was poured and set, the solid steel shutter could be jacked out 1½ inches to 2 inches, leaving a cavity into which an external skin of sand and cement would be poured. Early in 1952, the experimental shutter was delivered to Greenfield Depot, having been manufactured by Fred Braby and Company Limited, at their Petershill Road Works, Glasgow. A panel was poured, complete with external finish, quite successfully. Attempts were made to patent this invention, but were ultimately dropped. There were obvious difficulties, however, when it came to consideration of doing this on a much larger scale – maintaining exact alignment of the finish, avoiding uncoated pockets and dealing with the retraction movement of the outer shutters at corners. On the other hand, the perforated plate inner shutter gave such a beautifully straight wall, that in itself it seemed to solve the problem of applying finishes. And so we dropped the complexities, developed the perforated steel plate shutter as we know it today, adding gates to enable pouring below the windowsills.

. . . The first set was tried out early in 1953 on a small

cottage site at Pumpherston, Midlothian. Some modifications were necessary, particularly for ease of handling, but the basic design was sound and the results satisfactory. This was, in fact, a great breakthrough. The new shutters fulfilled all our hopes. They gave a far truer wall surface and the perforations provided the means for fixing brackets and inserts in exact required position to carry window frames and other components to be cast in the wall. The perforations also gave light to see how well the no-fines was being distributed in the shutters, and gave access for podging the no-fines into difficult positions. Later on it was found that they were far more adaptable than was at first thought, so that with a very limited number of basic panel sizes almost any house design could be built with them. The forecast of long life was also realised, as shutters made in those early days (were) still in use almost twenty years later after resheeting with new perforated plate. Thus shutters costs per house had been slashed.

From this, the Association spread its wings . . .

And therein lay the problem. For a constructional method which had originated as a means of rapidly erecting cottage type houses proved itself to be readily adaptable for the purposes of building three- and four-storey blocks of flats, and even multi-storey buildings of up to ten storeys in height. The latter were, as we shall see, not unreasonable, but the former were enthusiastically seized upon by those authorities which aspired to high density developments. The first of the three storey blocks were erected at Arden in Glasgow and, thereafter, similar buildings were provided in Dundee.

The development of the four-storey blocks had an interesting consequence. With a three-storey structure the shutters were simply erected to their full height, but for four-storeys it was decided that a precast concrete floor was required between the second and third storeys to give additional strength. Since the Association was not in the business of producing precast units, Concrete (Scotland) Limited, of Falkirk were approached and asked to develop an appropriate floor. 'Thus was born the Bison Wide-Slab, used subsequently nationwide.'[80] Obviously, the Association was not responsible for what the company did subsequently with the idea, but with hindsight this was not the best use to which the technique could have been put, at least so far as domestic dwellings are concerned. As it is, all that can be said in mitigation of the Association's involvement with blocks of this kind is that, by that time, Glasgow's plight had become very severe and, as Mr MacIntosh says, the method enabled 'rapid production to meet the very urgent need for houses'.

We shall return to the use of no-fines in multi-storey construction in the next chapter, but meanwhile it is appropriate to note the width of the Association's operations now that it was striking its peak rates of construction.

In April 1954, it was noted that in the financial year to the end of March a building rate of just over 99 houses per week had been achieved in a programme which broke down as follows.[81]

Programme	Houses
General Needs	3,693
Miners'	1,059
Forestry Commission	137
Local Authorities	189
Lighthouse Board	12
Admiralty	10
Royal Ordinance Police	6
Ministry of Supply	18
Ministry of Works	12
Ministry of Transport	2
Hospital Board	4
Total	5,142

The number being constructed for local authorities is interesting. In the main these were for small councils with few resources of their own. But at this time there was also a tendency for local authorities to invite the Association to tender for some contracts in the knowledge that, if it became known that a bid was to be submitted by the Association's direct labour department, this had the effect of squeezing other tenders. In fact, of course, as the Minister had made clear, the amount of work which the direct labour force was permitted to take on was fairly carefully restricted.

As the Association's building activity resumed after the war, so also, obviously, the number of houses to be managed increased. The question of rent policy, particularly after the intervention of Mr Buchanan, posed some problems. As the annual report for 1947 explained –

[82]   In the first place, the Association are expected to secure such rents as will enable them to operate as nearly as possible within the ordinary Exchequer subsidies, plus the equivalent of the corresponding rate contributions, which are applicable to local authority schemes. Secondly, the Association are obliged to consult local authorities in regard to the rents to be charged and ordinarily to accept as tenants those families whom the local authorities nominate. Thirdly, the Association's houses, unlike those of local authorities, come within the scope of the Rent Restrictions Acts and rents, once fixed cannot be increased.

Under these circumstances the Association did not have the flexibility which was open to local authorities. It had no rate fund to draw on, it could not select tenants who could afford to pay and, if it got the calculation wrong, it could not vary rents in the light of experience. Initially, this caused great difficulty. On the one hand, the Treasury, recognising that the houses were no longer simply for working-class people, 'would take exception if a tenant in good financial circumstance were allowed to occupy a house which, in addition to being subsidised under the normal subsidy and rate contribution arrangements, was ... being further subsidised by a deficit contribution from the Treasury.'[83] And on the other hand, Mr Buchanan would not agree to rent levels which would avoid a deficit, nor did he want rents to be fixed for the country as a whole. Moreover, while 'Mr Buchanan had agreed to the introduction of a rent rebate scheme, (he) was of the opinion that no rebates scheme should be applied in any area where the local authority are against such a scheme, notably in the case of Glasgow, and that schemes of local authorities should be used where these are in existence.'[84]

But that, of course, was not the end of the matter and around the time of Mr McBain's appointment as chairman there were months of negotiations, and often acrimonious exchanges, involving opinions from, variously, the Treasury, the Department of Health and many local authorities.

Eventually, in 1948, approval was given for the rents of post-war houses to be fixed in the range £35 to £39 per annum in the cities and £29 to £35 elsewhere for houses of three, four and five apartments. One problem with that, of course, was that rents for pre-war houses were held at a substantially lower figure because of the operation of the Rent Restrictions Act. The Association operated a rebate scheme by setting up a fund equivalent to £2 per house, out of which relief was granted in those areas where the local authority authorised such a scheme. In the event this meant that it was applied in seven out of thirty-eight local authority areas where the Association had houses and the report to Council that year noted that –

[85] The annual average rent of the 2,455 houses in the 1944 Act schemes was £32 9s and relief was at an average rate of £1 5s 7d per house per annum. The number of tenants who received relief was 319, of whom 194 were in Motherwell and 99 in Coatbridge, out of 402 and 188 tenants in these burghs respectively. The average annual rent of the 402 houses in Motherwell was £32 13s 7d and relief was at the rate of £5 6s per house per annum. The average annual rent of the 188 houses at Coatbridge was £33 and relief was at the rate of £5 8s per house per annum.

The high incidence of rebates in Motherwell and Coatbridge was thought to be because of 'the relative poverty of the Association's tenants in these burghs', and perhaps also because of the way the local authorities concerned selected tenants 'in accordance with housing need' and the spirit which they encouraged tenants to apply for relief.

As has been mentioned the determination of rent levels had been a cumbersome and difficult business and the outcome left Association rents significantly higher than the rents operated by many local authorities, but, almost as awkwardly, lower than those applied in other parts of the country. The result was a stream of protests from various local authorities and one of the first things that Mr Robertson had to do on his arrival at the Department of Health was to meet a delegation organised as the 'Clydebank Conference of Local Authorities' and reject their appeals in respect of Association rents.[86] In the event, however, five local authorities – West Lothian, Ayr County, Clydebank, Airdrie and Bo'ness – 'refused to factor Association houses on the ground that the Association's rents would cause them embarrassment.'[87]

In fact, at the outset of this process, when it had seemed likely that the Association would have to implement rents sufficient to avoid any deficit, combined with a large scale rebate scheme for low income tenants, it was recognised that the high rents might lead to a refusal to co-operate on the part of many authorities. Under these circumstances the Association examined the possibility of rapidly expanding its own housing management capacity. A report from Miss Pollock was called for and, as early as June 1946, she suggested not only appropriate systems of management, but that a scheme be established for training students under the guidance of the Society of Women Housing Managers. This was generally approved by Council.[88]

By 1949, with some local authorities withdrawing from factoring, it was clear that new arrangements would be required, and a Council sub-committee was established to work out the details. As a result it was finally concluded that the Association policy was to allow local authorities to manage the houses where they wished to do so, but otherwise to use direct factoring. For this to be done economically it was recognised that occasionally it would be necessary to take over some houses where the authority was perfectly willing to be involved, if these were close to an inadequate number of houses in the territory of an unhelpful authority. Accordingly, a regional factoring structure was established based on Motherwell, Ayrshire, Dunbartonshire and West Stirlingshire, East Stirlingshire, West Lothian, Bo'ness and Fishcross, Fife and Midlothian and Broxburn. When this arrangement was reached, Council also noted with approval that Miss Pollock had been co-opted onto the appropriate committee of the Scottish Housing Advisory Committee.[89]

By 1950, the situation had changed still further so that the annual report for March of that year summed up the situation thus:[90]

Of the ... 11,301 houses erected in 53 local authority areas, 8,283 houses in 42 areas were factored by the local authorities and 3,018 in 11 areas by the Association staff operating from head office and three sub-offices. Eight of these 11 local authorities declined to factor the Association houses, involving 2,988 houses.

Of the 1,500 Agency houses, 602 were factored by local

authorities and 898 by the Association staff.

The whole question of rents, and the Association's response to the efforts of some authorities to exert pressure on it, led to a considerable strain in the relationship between the Association and some sections of the Labour Party. In January 1950 it was noted that several Trade Councils had urged the Secretary of State to transfer all Association houses to the local authorities.[91] Later Council also discussed some hostile comment which had been made at the Institute of Housing Conference at Rothesay on 24th February, and considered a resolution tabled at the Scottish Trade Union Congress by the Amalgamated Engineering Union, to the effect that 'the Association should be no longer a house-owning organisation and that all houses it (had) built should pass to the ownership of the local authority.'[92] Then Motherwell Town Council asked the government to be allowed to purchase all Association houses in the town at a price to be fixed by the district valuer. The Department of Health response to this was to forward the request to the Treasury in the expectation that it would thereafter be passed to the Ministers concerned for a decision on policy. In fact, a preliminary meeting had been arranged with the chief valuer to determine the likely basis of transfer. The Council of Management reacted with some vigour and informed the Department that 'the Association's functions had always been to build and own houses and that, as there appeared to be no reason to change these functions, Council was of the opinion that the houses in Motherwell should not be sold to the Town Council.'[93] Nevertheless, Motherwell kept up the pressure, sending a delegation to the Department of Health in October to press their case. At the same time Council noted a report that the Scottish Labour Party Conference had passed a resolution demanding that Association rents should be held in line with the rents of local authority houses.[94]

In April 1951, the chairman and general manager were summoned to London to meet with the Scottish Parliamentary Labour Group. Prior to the meeting the chairman, with the approval of Council, indicated his intention of informing the Group that Association rents could not be reduced. One Council member, the Rev W.C.V. Smith, voiced his concern that some tenants who were badly housed, were known to be refusing SSHA houses because of the high rents, but he agreed that this involved wider matters than the Association's rent policy and indicated his general support for the Council's position.[95] Subsequently the chairman reported on the meeting with the Labour Group at which 'very full and helpful discussions had taken place.'[96] In October it was learned that Coatbridge Burgh Council had joined the campaign to take over Association houses and, when this was discussed, Mr Paterson expressed the opinion that 'there was a feeling in some quarters that, in time, the Association might become a central housing authority and that local authorities would be denuded of their housing functions'. Mr Fraser, the Joint Parliamentary Under-Secretary of State, explained to the same meeting that consideration of the Association's future would have to wait until after the general election.[97]

What would have happened if Labour had won the election of October 1951 can, of course, now only be a matter of conjecture. However, there is no doubt that the hostility directed towards the Association was pretty intense in some areas. With the Conservatives in power, the Association's efforts turned more towards the cities and provoked the following outburst, which was reported in the Scotsman of 24th November 1954.

[98] 'The Scottish Special Housing Association is dying. They are on the way out. Their work is finished, so why should we prolong the death agony?' asked Councillor A.D. Jameson at yesterday's meeting of Edinburgh Corporation Housing Committee.

He was maintaining that the site preparation work for 204 houses – which the Association proposed to build for the Corporation at Telford Road and Niddrie Mill – should be done by private contractors who were 'looking for work'.

…(He went on) 'They have been building houses for small burghs in rural districts, where these burghs do not have money to finance houses themselves. Now these rural districts are built up so the Association are coming into the towns to keep themselves alive. This Association is dying. It is disgraceful that it should still carry on.'

A number of members spoke in support of the Association. Councillor J.C. Brown said 'Whether or not we like this set-up, they can provide us very successfully with houses for this scheme. It is in no way interfering with our own housing programme. It is in addition to it. Surely we must take advantage of it for our own people.'

Councillor Jameson's motion ... was defeated by.ten votes to five.

Councillor Jameson's views may stand as representative of some of the attitudes of the time, but it is odd that the year in which he believed the Association to be 'dying' was one of the peak years of building activity and was the year when the 'General Needs' programme reached its absolute high point of 4,019 completed houses.

Throughout much of the period under discussion there had been few changes in the composition of the Council Management. However, in July 1951, Mr McBain intimated his intention to resign at the end of the year. He wished to devote more time to his personal affairs while expressing the hope that he

Part of the re-development at Dunkeld completed for Perth County Council to mark the Coronation in 1953.

could continue to serve on Council as an ordinary member.[99] (This he did for a further year.) At his last meeting with Council before the General Election, the Minister, Tom Fraser, paid tribute 'to the outstanding service which the chairman had rendered since he took office in 1946, when the Association was going through difficult times. As a result of the chairman's efforts, the Association's activities had prospered, and he heard nothing but praise from other members of the Council of Management and from officials of the Department of Health of the work which he had done.' Mr. Fraser stated that 'he had great pleasure in conveying to the chairman his high commendation and sincere thanks for the excellent services which he had rendered.'[100]

The aftermath of the change of government in 1951 was not quite as traumatic as had been the case in 1945. But when the Association intimated its choice of Mr Paterson – by now chairman of the Scottish Housing Advisory Committee – to succeed Mr McBain,[101] this suggestion was declined and they were informed that the position would no longer carry an honorarium. 'Council agreed unanimously to minute their view that they had not received the consideration and courtesy to be expected.'[102]

Obviously feathers were somewhat ruffled, but the government had found a worthy successor to Mr McBain in the person of Sir Ronald J. Thomson*, and notice of his appointment was given in February 1952. Otherwise there were no immediate changes and subsequent adjustments were made under the normal procedures and even then were confined to two retirements and two additions over the next two years. (Council members retire after three years, but at the discretion of the Secretary of State, they may be re-elected.)

Culling over the minutes of these days, one is struck by the harmonious way in which Council generally operated, with very few issues having to be put to the vote. (This is still true.) One exception, however, is worthy of comment.

1953 of course, was Coronation Year, and the Association decided to mark the occasion by collaborating with Perth

Sir Ronald J. Thomson (1895-1978)
Border Regiment 1914-17 (wounded 1917). Elected to Peeblesshire County Council in 1922 serving as Convener from 1931-58. President of the Association of County Councils in Scotland 1948-50.

County Council and the National Trust for Scotland in restoring and preserving a group of houses of special architectural or historic interest, and by planting trees throughout housing schemes up and down the country. As far as the first project was concerned, the houses identified were some cottages in the village square at Dunkeld, but the Treasury, somewhat meanly, rejected the suggestion since the village was not in 'an area of greatest need'. Nevertheless, a more limited restoration was done by the Association acting as straightforward agents for the County Council.[103]

The tree-planting project also went ahead, but the problem arose over the inscription proposed for the metal plaque to be located near the trees. The suggested words were 'Planted to commemorate the Coronation of HM Queen Elizabeth II, 1953'.[104]

In the course of discussion on the wording of the inscription the Council were unanimous that the description of Her Majesty as 'Queen Elizabeth II' was correct but some members expressed the view that, because of recent disturbances, it would be expedient to omit the numeral. Because of differing views on this matter among members of Council, the chairman called for a motion and amendment. Mr McIntosh, seconded by Mr Smith, thereafter moved that the numeral be omitted from the inscription and Mr Paterson, seconded by Mr Rose, moved as an amendment that the numeral be retained. On the vote being taken, five Members voted for the amendment and four for the motion, two Members abstaining from voting. The chairman declared the amendment carried.

Their dilemma is understandable for, in 1953, there was no question debated with more heat throughout the length and breadth of Scotland.

CHAPTER FIVE

1955-1979

By the mid-1950s the worst of the immediate post-war housing crisis was over, at least as far as the smaller towns and rural areas were concerned. Early in 1955 the Association completed its thirty thousandth house – a long way short of Tom Johnston's intentions for the first decade of peace, but still a substantial contribution. A little earlier Department of Health Circular No 82-1954 signalled the formal end to the phase by announcing that, as from 1st June 1955, central control of non-traditional house building would cease and that local authorities could henceforth select designs in direct consultation with the various contractors and promoters.[1] This freedom was backed up by the production of government handbooks on house design and layout for the guidance of Housing Committees. To the Association the change made little difference since, as we have seen, it was already concentrating on its own no-fines technique and it continued to consult closely with the Department's technical staff whenever designs which had not already been approved were under discussion. In other words, it was still implicit that, as the central government agent in Scotland, the Association should always try to adhere to the best available practice and act as something of a model for the local authorities. But if the change did not, therefore, have much effect on the Association, it did indicate that the government were no longer concerned to keep the prefabricated house builders in business and were content that some authorities would now wish to proceed at a rather more leisurely – and cautious – pace.

Nevertheless, the problem in some of the cities – in parts of Edinburgh, in Dundee, and, above all in Glasgow – was still very severe. In the case of the latter city, the freezing of the Clyde Valley Plan after the war and the determination of the Corporation to hang on to its citizens, and to resolve its own problems, had merely intensified the situation so that 'Glasgow's congestion in 1956 was unparalleled in the United Kingdom'.[2] Unfortunately, from the point of view of the city planners of the day, they had found their plans to be caught in the vice of the economic facts of life of the period. To redevelop the city in the way they had in mind required the creation of high density communities on relatively small areas of land, and that in turn meant large blocks of flats. But, as has been shown in the previous chapter, such was the scramble for building resources in the first ten years of peace that there was frequent scarcity of materials and labour and, consequently, almost continuous upward pressure on prices. In addition, the building industry was not well versed in the techniques of constructing high flats, with the inevitable result that structures of the kind which the Corporation wished to employ were extremely expensive. As the Council of Management had pointed out in 1950 in respect of the proposed multi-storey flats at Toryglen, the expense involved was almost bound to require the levying of high rents. And therein lay the rub, for the Corporation were absolutely committed to a low rent policy supported by a substantial local subsidy and the city's rates were already significantly higher than in comparable cities elsewhere in the UK.[3] It was in the face of such financial considerations that plans to build the multi-storey blocks at Toryglen had been temporarily suspended.

In August 1953 the Clyde Valley Advisory Committee urged that Cumbernauld New Town should be established immediately to relieve some of the pressure on the city and this was, in fact, done two years later. However, it was bound to be several years before this development was in a state to make an impact on the problem and it was estimated that by 1959 all building space in Glasgow would be completely used up.[4]

In October 1954, the general problem was discussed at a meeting between the Council of Management and the Minister, Commander Galbraith. He was concerned at the continuing loss of good agricultural land to building and indicated that it was 'imperative to build multi-storey flats on central sites. If the Association, as had been suggested, were able to build multi-storey flats in no-fines construction at reasonable cost, this would be a considerable contribution to the problem.' He asked that the project at Toryglen 'be pressed on urgently.'[5]

Earlier in that month discussions had been held with Glasgow's Housing Committee and the latter 'while welcoming the Association's approach to the problem of multi-storey flats' were unwilling to give formal approval to the project until they were fully satisfied about the financial implications for tenants. When the plans were examined it was noted that the cost per flat would be £1,610 if 300 or more flats were built and £1,700 per flat in the case of one prototype block.[6] (Two years earlier the cost of a four-apartment no-fines cottage had been estimated at £1,395.[7])

Since it was obvious that much of the future building programme would be in connection with the cities, and would be dependent on high density building, the Association had swallowed at least some of its objections to housing of this type. Technical staff for many months had been striving to deliver some solution which might be regarded as acceptable. To set this in context, after the peak years from 1952 to 1955, it seemed certain that the building programme would be progressively strangled unless some means could be devised which would enable the Association to make inroads within the generally unco-operative cities. For example, at the meeting with the Minister mentioned above, the chairman told him 'that there was some disquiet among Association staff arising out of the delay in providing an allocation for the ... programme and asked whether an assurance could be given to the staff regarding the life of the Association.' An encouraging statement was immediately forthcoming, but the incident illustrates some of the pressure which staff felt themselves to be under. If flats were what the politicians wanted, then flats would have to be provided.

In May 1953, the general manager, the chief technical officer and the building manager had gone to Holland and to Germany to see what lessons were to be learned.[8] Holland had been, as far as we knew, the birthplace of no-fines, whilst Germany since the war had been using the masses of rubble in their bombed cities by crushing it down to provide aggregate for rebuilding, using the no-fines method.

... We flew via Amsterdam to Stuttgart, where the major project visited, then in its early stages, was the Max Käde House, a students' hostel, nineteen storeys high (three below ground), the upper thirteen of which were to be in no-fines concrete using crushed bricks. Its designers, the late Professor Deininger, consulting engineer, and Herr Ludwig Kresse, were later employed by the Association to advise it on the design of its ten storey blocks of flats. From Stuttgart we went to Mannheim, where the 'Ladies' House', a most impressive ten storey block of single-person flats was inspected together with low rise schemes.

Professor Deininger and Herr Kresse, the Association's German consultants, examining a model of the Max Kâde house.

On Monday we went by train to Dordrecht, where we met Mr Greve, who, as chief housing architect at The Hague, had developed the system 'Korrelbeton' (no-fines) in the years 1919 to 1920 with the aim of building dwellings with unskilled labour. Here and at The Hague, we saw the Dutch method of building in no-fines concrete, from two to four storeys. We were also shown cottages built at Scheveningen in 1921 using a refuse destructor clinker as aggregate. We saw a variety of shuttering methods, heard many opinions as to the qualities and potentialities of no-fines concrete and returned on the Tuesday much inspired by what we had seen.

On that visit a lot of useful information was acquired and, as was mentioned, Professor Deininger and his colleague were appointed as the Association's consultants. However, a mobile laboratory was also obtained and a research assistant, Colin Muir, was able to provide precise information about the strengths which could be obtained from different types of stone or from mixtures of different proportions of stone and cement and water-cement ratios. In addition, various employees made their contributions as, for example, when Mr Allan, a joiner, was awarded £10 in recognition of a suggestion which produced a useful modification to the shuttering.[9] Finally a mass of information was obtained from English authorities about things such as the running costs of lifts and the management of flats.[10]

Thus it was that a detailed plan was drafted to erect the ten-storey blocks of flats at Toryglen and the problem of costs was relieved in December 1954 when the Department of Health for Scotland informed the Association that an additional subsidy of £10 10s per house above the ground floor would be payable in respect of the flats.[11] Subsequently, the plans were approved by the Dean of Guild Court,[12] Glasgow Corporation Planning Committee and by the Building Research Station, and permission was given to begin erecting two prototype blocks in August 1955.[13] These 60 two-bedroomed houses, with laundry and stores in the basement, were duly completed early in 1957 at a final cost of £1,818 per house.[14] From an architectural point of view, they are considerably more interesting than many of the later blocks since they are L-shaped and are capped by an oversailing flat roof.

At this time, there was a great deal of interest generally in

the Association's ability to build cottages, low-rise and multi-storey blocks of flats in no-fines and, at an exhibition of building plant held in Glasgow in June 1955, something of the technique was demonstrated.[15] Following the exhibition requests for information came from as far afield as Western Australia, and the Council agreed to make advice available to Australia or to any other Commonwealth country which was interested.[16] A little later Thomas Paterson, acting in the absence of the chairman, escorted a deputy Prime Minister and a delegation from the USSR on a visit to inspect the low-rise blocks of no-fines flats being constructed at Arden.[17]

By 1955 the problem of obtaining sites in Glasgow was seriously impeding the Association's programme and while high flats in the inner city might be one way ahead, it was suggested in July of that year that the realistic alternative was to build in areas outwith the city, but still for tenants to be nominated by Glasgow Corporation. It was agreed to take this idea up with the Minister.[18]

At the meeting in October, Commander Galbraith – now Lord Strathclyde, and newly promoted to Minister of State at the Scottish Office – again asked the Association to complete the two prototype blocks at Toryglen 'as quickly as possible' before turning to the general situation in Glasgow. He was aware that the Association had been authorised by his Department to build something of the order of 2,696 houses in the city under the current programme, but that there were, as yet, no available sites. The idea of erecting these houses elsewhere for the use of Glasgow tenants was under consideration and the Clyde Valley Planning Advisory Committee had been asked for an urgent report on the whole problem. Until that report was forthcoming no great progress could be made.[19]

In the new year negotiations on the matter continued, with Glasgow Corporation declining to transfer any of its own sites, but suggesting that the Association might be able to build within the city if it were willing to employ the Corporation's direct labour organisation. This was not a particularly helpful proposal since the practice was not permitted under the legislation then applied to municipal direct labour.[20] Next, Glasgow agreed to provide land for a further 850 houses at Toryglen and two additional sites in the following year, but urged the Association to build part of the city's allocation of houses at Cumbernauld. (This idea would have been welcome enough to the Association, for it had tried repeatedly to persuade the government to allow it to build the New Town.[21] But the response had been that the government were unwilling to amend the legislation to designate the Association as a Development Corporation.[22] In fact the Association did assist Cumbernauld with site servicing and its direct labour organisation erected 208 terraced houses, 96 maisonettes, 169 garages and a sub-station within the New Town.[23]) Finally, in September, the government informed the Association that, as part of the current review of housing subsidies, its role in the provision of houses in Scotland had been revised. Henceforth it was to (a) provide houses for local authorities which could prove economic hardship; and (b) provide houses as part of the Glasgow 'Overspill' arrangements.[24] This would be the subject of legislation in 1957.

On the day in which Council learned of the arrangements for the opening ceremony for the first of the Toryglen flats, they also heard with regret that their consultant engineer, Professor Deininger, had died. However, it was now clear that with these flats, together with the revised subsidy arrangements, the Association had produced the sort of economic solution for which the cities had been waiting. The Corporations of Edinburgh, Dundee, Clydebank and even Perth approached the

The first no-fines high rise flats in process of construction at Toryglen.

Association and asked for similar multi-storey blocks while Glasgow also wanted more, including another two on the same site at Toryglen.[25]

These suggestions were not without their problems since, in 1954, the Minister had instructed the Association to restrict its direct labour organisation to approximately 1,300 houses in any one year and, on that occasion, had declined to allow it to build 500 no-fines houses for Midlothian.[26] However, negotiations with the various authorities continued with the Association submitting competitive tenders to build on an agency basis.

At the, by now, annual meeting with the Minister in October

1957, no-fines multi-storey building was inevitably a topic of discussion and Mr J. Nixon Browne, the Under-Secretary of State, 'considered that the Association was showing the way in this connection' saying that 'the Secretary of State had asked him to convey to the Council of Management his personal gratification and satisfaction with the progress which the Association had made'.[27]

This then was the beginning of the high-rise era in Scotland and, having made a start, the pressure to go higher and yet higher was almost irresistible.

The Glasgow Overspill Programme commenced rather slowly, as was perhaps inevitable since many of the towns and burghs whose co-operation was required were understandably somewhat cautious about receiving a large influx of Glaswegians for whom there might or might not be local employment. Essentially, the scheme was for the SSHA to supply fifty per cent of the houses, but the planned parallel outward movement of industry was obviously going to be harder to effect. A list of local authorities which might be prepared to co-operate was compiled by the Department of Health and in December 1957 the Association was authorised to commence negotiations.[28] The initial agreements were with Kirkintilloch, Haddington and Johnstone and by the following August officials were able to report that 2,300 houses of the General Needs Programme for Glasgow had been earmarked in the form of Overspill housing, with sites for the balance of 832 houses still to be identified.

A year later the Minister was still enthusiastic for Overspill and told the Council that, while another New Town was not ruled out, the possibilities of Overspill would have to be exhausted before it became a serious consideration.[29]

Nevertheless, by 1959 it was clear that the programme was developing only slowly and that the problem was the unwillingness of industry to move.

Theoretically, the initial target for Overspill was to transfer approximately 3,000 families from the city a year, but in the event in only one year (1964) was that figure reached and, in any case the great majority of the migrants went to the New Towns, 'with houses and jobs waiting'.[30] However, as is shown at Appendix B, over the full life of the construction programme from 1959 to 1982 the SSHA erected almost 10,000 houses in many parts of the country. The most successful elements in the programme, when judged in terms of its original purpose – *ie* to assist the movement of people out from Glasgow – were probably the developments within commuting distance of the city, and one wonders what proportion of the other houses were actually let to former residents of the city. But, as we shall see, some excellent building was done under the scheme, although it did tend to become somewhat overshadowed by the later and rather more soundly based 'Economic Expansion' Programme. The peak building year for Overspill was 1963, when just over 1,000 houses were completed: in January of that

year the programme was noted as follows – Irvine 700 houses (with a further 268 if demand picked up), Johnstone 560 houses, Kirkintilloch 300 houses (again with 150 more to come), Grangemouth 350 houses, Whitburn 277 houses, Arbroath 300 houses, Stewarton 150 houses, Dunbar 50 houses, Bonnyrigg and Lasswade 50 houses, Stevenston 25 houses, Peebles 10 houses, Renfrew County 1,050 houses (the latter was for a proposed development outwith the boundaries of Johnstone and was intended to support the opening of the new car factory at Linwood), Bathgate 150 houses, Hamilton 200 houses (some to replace prefabs) and Fort William 100 houses (with another 100 for local needs). Some indication of the way in which this programme was to become progressively bogged down is evidenced by the fact that by the date of this report – with almost twenty years of Overspill to run – more than half of the number of houses eventually completed had already been identified.

31   The Association's present programme of Overspill houses for Glasgow totals 5,047 houses. Of these, 2,569 are included in schemes where house erection is either completed or in progress and 1,106 of these have been completed. The Scottish Development Department's authority has been received to proceed with a further 1,373 houses for which planning is proceeding.

837 houses are held in abeyance pending the local authority making progress with their own Overspill

Opposite *The re-development of medieval Culross.*

houses and 268 at Irvine are held in abeyance on the instructions of the Scottish Development Department.

Mention of the 50 Overspill houses for Dunbar draws attention to another interesting facet of the life of the Association. Perhaps because, as an organisation, it was fundamentally preoccupied with the provision of what might be termed 'ordinary' housing, there was almost invariably considerable enthusiasm whenever the opportunity arose to tackle something which was a bit unusual, particularly if it involved the chance of making a contribution of genuine architectural merit. For example, in March 1958, the Council was delighted to learn that the cottages which had been completed for Perth County Council in Dunkeld in 1953 to mark the Coronation had attracted an award from the Saltire Society.[32] Similarly in 1957, the Association was very proud to be appointed architects and agents for three small developments in the ancient mercantile Royal Burgh of Culross, and enormous care was taken to produce work which was worthy of the lovely setting of the medieval town. In 1960 the Culross Development was opened by the Secretary of State, John Maclay, (Viscount Muirshiel) in a ceremony which also commemorated the erection of the Association's fifty thousandth house.[33] Later the Association's sensitive treatment of Culross was to attract another Saltire Award (see Appendix L) and building or restoration within an ancient environment became a form of activity which was seized with relish whenever the infrequent opportunity occurred.

In the case of Dunbar the approach, though equally interesting, was somewhat different. In the autumn of 1958 the Association agreed to co-operate with Professor Sir Robert Matthew of Edinburgh University by appointing him as architect for a small development which he was to design and supervise as a live project for his students. Thirty houses at Pinkie Braes in Musselburgh were completed in this way and that estate was opened by Sir Edward Appleton, the Principal of the University, in May 1961.[34] When the Dunbar Overspill proposal for 50 houses came under discussion, the Town Council requested that they be provided in the form of a central redevelopment, and the Association considered that this would be a suitable second challenge for Sir Robert and his students. The result was a collection of rather modernistic buildings, but again, in 1966, it received a commendation from the Saltire

Society.[35] Today it provides a rather odd – and not particularly flattering – point of comparison with some of the very recent redevelopment work which the Association has done in inner Dunbar.

At the end of the 1950s the subject which most firmly thrust the Association into the public eye and, indeed, which produced the most far-reaching changes in the nature of the organisation was the rent question. The background to this was the muddled relationship between rent and rates which then existed in Scotland whereby the rates were fixed in accordance with the rent level attached to a property and were payable partly by the occupier and partly by the owner. In these circumstances, private landlords, with their rents controlled, were in an almost impossible situation, being quite unable to recoup the rate burden by raising rents. Moreover, although local authorities were not subject to the Rent Restriction Acts, the connection between rent level and rateable values made it impossible simply to increase rents without also increasing rates. The upshot of this was that (as was pointed out in the annual report of the Department of Health for Scotland in 1952) whereas the average rent of a council house had risen from £18 17s 7d in 1938 to £23 16s 1d in 1951 (an increase of 20 per cent), in the same period the cost of building material had increased by 200 per cent and the growth of earnings in the building industry was 130 per cent. Similarly, the average annual rent of a pre-war council house rose from £21 2s 6d in 1949 to £23 8s 2d in 1956, an 11 per cent increase, at a time when the general index of retail prices had grown by 38 per cent. Clearly the economic basis of rented housing in Scotland was progressively losing touch with reality.

It was in an effort to resolve the problem that the government introduced first the Housing (Repairs and Rents) (Scotland) Act, 1954 which allowed owners of controlled houses to increase rents by two-fifths on condition that the properties were in good order; and second, the Valuation and Rating (Scotland) Act 1956, which separated rateable values from actual rents and abolished owners' rates. When this was done the ridiculously low real levels to which many local authority rents had sunk was clearly revealed, for the average council rent in 1957 was shown to be a mere 5s 6d per week.

The government issued a circular in June, 1956, pointing out

that whereas in 1938 rent had accounted for 10.5 per cent of average earnings, by 1955 the proportion was only 4.5 per cent. Accordingly authorities were urged to review their rent levels on the basis that –

a subsidies ought not to be given to those who do not need them:

b no one in genuine need of a house should be asked to pay more rent than he can reasonably afford.

From then on the government repeatedly exorted local authorities to put their rent levels on a more realistic footing and this marked the start of a period of considerable tension between central and local government.[36]

The main problem, of course, was that too great a proportion of the housing budget was having to be borne by ratepayers and, in addition to objecting to this in principle, it was the government's view that high rates were damaging Scotland's ability to sustain a healthy economy. A government circular to local authorities in 1962 stated the case. 'A policy of keeping rents artificially low is unfair to rate payers with low incomes who are not in council houses and is prejudicial to the long-term interests of the area and indeed the country as a whole.'[37] A little earlier the Secretary of State told MPs 'Experience shows that the low rent tradition ... stamps an area as industrially and socially old-fashioned, so that new industry tends to hesitate before seeking new investment and providing new employment in such areas.'[38] Writing of this period John

Gibson concluded that council rents 'were often much too low to the detriment of the town or county council's ability to embark on other services or on work which should have gone hand in hand with new housing, as, say, the building of community centres and other amenities.'[39]

Inevitably the Association found itself caught up in the conflict which erupted between the government and local authorities. Early in 1957 the process of formulating a new rent policy was begun with proposals for increased rents being drafted and submitted to the Department of Health for approval. The intention was to reach an average rent of £35 per annum and to introduce a rent rebate scheme.[40] (The previous rent rebate scheme had become virtually irrelevant and the annual report of March 1957 noted that, with applicants receiving National Assistance grants, only two tenants had received rent relief amounting to £6. The same report noted that of the 84 local authorities in whose areas the Association owned houses, 46 were charging higher rents than the Association's standard rents.[41]) The Department were cautious, generally approving the suggested scheme, but indicating a wish to hold the maximum increase to 7s 7d per week and urging a flexible view of the rent rebate proposal so that it might be modified in the light of experience.[42] However, the policy was approved in December and communicated to the public and local authorities early in January 1958[43] with the intention of implementation in the following October. Essentially the standard rents became £33, £36 and £39 for three-, four- and 5-apartment houses respectively, but since new rents were not in any case to exceed old rents by more than 7s 6d per week, and since the Association were instructed to implement local authority rents where the latter were higher, there were bound still to be variations in Association rents between different parts of the country.[44]

When the news of the proposed rent charges broke there was uproar with protests flooding in from local authorities and tenants' groups all over the country.[45] Many deputations demanded to meet the Council of Management and when one such arrived from Glasgow Corporation they were sympathetically received, but politely rebuffed. Sir Ronald Thomson, the chairman, stated the Association case as follows. Rents had not previously been increased, but the Association's commitments

had grown substantially.

⁴⁶ ... This was due to the large number of houses built by the Association and it had to be kept in mind that the average cost to the Association of each house was 30s per week and even the rents as now proposed would still leave approximately half of that figure to be met by the Treasury.

The chairman also explained that the Association was entirely government financed and that there was no comparable body in England. In all its deliberations on rent the Association had to keep in mind the ruling principle that rents had to be fixed within ranges approved by the Secretary of State in agreement with the Treasury, having regard to the fact that taking their operations over Scotland as a whole the Association were expected to work within the Exchequer subsidies available ... Until 1954 the Association's houses had been subject to rent control but since de-control was introduced the Association had been giving prolonged consideration to the rent question.

The chairman reiterated that there was no body comparable to the Association in England and unless the Association took a realistic view of rents it was possible that Parliament might decide not to continue giving Scotland the benefit of the Association's operations. In determining what the realistic view of rent might mean, the chairman instanced the figures for rent and rates in some English cities ... While it was admitted that the rates in England were lower than the rates in Glasgow, it was nevertheless apparent that the total outgoings of a tenant in Glasgow on the basis of the Association's proposals compared favourably with those of tenants in some English cities. For instance, the *total* outgoings of a tenant of a three-apartment house in Birmingham were 35s 5d per week, in Carlisle, 28s 6d per week and in Coventry, 37s 3d per week, as compared with 30s 7d in Glasgow under the Association's proposal and 21s under the Corporation's present rent policy.

As regards the rebate scheme, the chairman stated that the Association considered that the scheme would prevent hardship and would provide relief for people who were not so well off. In addition if there were a decrease in actual earnings through a reduction in overtime the rent rebate scheme would undoubtedly be helpful to the tenants affected.

(As a matter of interest, following successive comments by the auditor on Glasgow Housing Accounts for 1955, 1956 and 1957, and a complaint to the Secretary of State from a Glasgow councillor, a formal enquiry was held under the chairmanship of Mr C.J.D. Shaw, QC, – later Lord Kilbrandon – into the city's failure to review rents under the Housing (Scotland) Act, 1950. The report found that the Corporation had failed to discharge its statutory duties, and in 1959 city rents were increased from an average of 5s 2d per week to 8s 5d [47]).

Glasgow's appeal was, therefore, rejected, as were the protests from many other sources. However, in the face of this onslaught, the Council did waver. When the various relevant papers were passed to the Department of Health for consideration, it was suggested that, while Council were fully behind the new rent proposals in principle, in order to deflect some of the trouble it might be better to postpone implementation until 1961, which would be the year of the introduction of newly revalued rates.[48] The Secretary of State agreed that there was some danger of rent strikes and industrial unrest, but he was satisfied that the scheme was fair and reasonable and felt that the Association should adhere to the planned timetable.[49]

For one member of Council, James McBoyle, the county clerk of Midlothian, the rent changes imposed an impossible burden. His County Council was opposed to the Association's proposals and he himself had objected to them, particularly on the ground that when the Association had first been established it had been obliged to fix rents in negotiation with individual local authorities. On this occasion, it was intending simply to impose the new rent level. Moreover since Midlothian were intent on fighting the new scheme he clearly felt there to be a conflict of interest and resigned.[50]

As 1958 advanced and the date of implementation grew closer so the dispute widened and in July Council noted the position as follows –

[51]
1   46 local authorities factoring 16,069 houses, had agreed to co-operate.

2   Glasgow Corporation, who were responsible for 3,872 houses, had agreed to issue notices (of the new rents to

184

tenants) but not to continue factoring.

3 Two authorities, embracing 622 houses, had refused to issue notices, but were prepared to continue factoring.

4 Three authorities, embracing 906 houses, had refused to issue notices, but had reached no definite decision regarding factorage.

5 Twelve authorities, embracing, 5,418 houses, had refused to issue notices and had terminated their factoring arrangements.

6 Inverness, in respect of 702 houses, had reached no decision on notices or factorage.

Interestingly, in August, attention was drawn to the fact that some authorities were complaining that the Association's rents would still be too low[52], but more generally it was the opponents of the increase which made the running and notice was given of a rent strike when some tenants' associations organised the return of substantial numbers of unsigned missives.[53]

In October Mr Nixon Browne, the Under-Secretary of State, told Council that they 'were fulfilling a national duty in introducing the new rent scheme, including the rebate scheme. He assured the Council of Management that Ministers were wholeheartedly behind the Association in the matter and would give all possible support.'[54] Council may have needed this assurance for, in addition to the general chorus of abuse, the Association was now locked in a legal battle. Nominally it was Midlothian which had taken action, but in fact West Lothian, Ayrshire and Lanarkshire had joined the first named county in obtaining Counsel's opinion prior to raising the action.[55] In the event, on appeal to the Court of Session, the Association's position in respect of its general right to increase rent for post-war houses was upheld; but in the judgement it was noted that, in relation to the older 'Commissioners' houses', negotiation with the local authorities probably was a pre-requisite. Aware of this possibility, the Association had not yet applied the new rents to these houses.[56]

Gradually, in the new year things began to settle down again, but the rent strike in some areas caused general concern. Broadly, the policy was only to take legal action against tenants who were in arrears to the extent of £10 or more[57] and, as was explained to Mr John Taylor, MP, – who had expressed the concern of the Parliamentary Labour Group at the amount of arrears which were accumulating against some tenants – tenants who indicated a real desire to pay their debts were treated as sympathetically and leniently as possible.[58] Nevertheless, on seven occasions actions in the Sheriff· Court were contested by tenants' associations, and one case was appealed to the Court of Session. Again the findings were in favour of the SSHA, with tenants being held liable for the new rents and accrued arrears.

Obviously, however, where local authority rents were low many tenants felt that the new SSHA charges were extremely unfair. For example, as late as April 1960, Council noted that sixteen tenants in Association houses factored by local authorities were still withholding rents, and that the same was true for no less than 1,254 tenants in houses under Association management, the majority being in Glasgow.[59] Not until October 1960 could Council note, no doubt with relief, that the last of the tenants had given up the struggle.[60]

An interesting footnote to this episode, though one which was presumably much less publicised, is connected with the fact that some local councils regarded the new Association rents as being still far too low. As was mentioned, the Department of Health wanted the Association to match local authority rents in these cases, but when it was realised that Ayr Burgh rents were £39, £57 and £64 for two-, three-, and four-apartment houses respectively, this was considered to be too much. Council wanted to hold rents there to a maximum of £45 per annum[61] and when the Department objected, the chairman and Mr Paterson demanded to see the Minister. Their appeal, however, was not successful.[62]

In October 1960 Lord Craigton, the Minister of State, summed up the government's position. 'He wished to express thanks in particular to the Council of Management for their success in introducing the new level of rents ... (Council's) determined but fair actions had assured complete success and the government was very grateful. The future was undecided although it was clear that rents in some areas could not be allowed to remain at their present levels, but the Association had led the way in 1958 and it was now considered desirable to allow the new valuations in 1961 to take effect before reaching further conclusions.'[63] (When rents were increased to a new average of £52 per annum in 1962, there was virtually no trouble, although on this occasion, the change was implemented through detailed negotiations with individual local authorities.[64])

The whole episode produced a fundamental transformation in the way in which the Association managed its houses. As we saw earlier, events at the end of the war and a dispute with a few local authorities over rent-fixing in the years around 1950 and had forced the Association to establish a housing management function under the leadership of Miss Pollock. From time to time some members of Council had wished to extend direct management, but the view had generally been that, in the interest of promoting good relationships, it was better to allow local authorities which wished to do so to continue to factor the houses in their areas. In consequence, the annual report at March 1958 noted that 'of the 41,330 houses owned by the Association, 31,008 were managed by the local authorities and the remaining 10,322 in 25 local authority areas by the Association's staff operating from head office and three sub-offices.'[65]

Throughout the rent dispute of 1958-59 several local authorities attempted to pressurise the Association by declining to continue with factorage. In these cases the Association policy was simply to extend its own management services, with the result that by March 1960 the position had been transformed. 'Of the 47,380 houses owned by the Association, 19,607 were managed by the local authorities, 46 by private factors, and the remaining 27,727 in 37 local authority areas by the Association's staff operating from head office and six sub-offices situated in Aberdeen, Cumnock, Dumbarton, Glasgow, Kirkcaldy and Motherwell. Rather less than half of the Association's houses are now factored by the local authorities as agents for the Association for which the local authority are paid commission, plus outlays on stationery, stamps, etc.'[66] One suspects that, in reality, this development was not unwelcome, since when some local authorities, for example Dunbarton County Council, recanted their original decision and asked to resume management, their offers were rejected.[67]

A few months before the rent quarrel started, the Council of Management had noted with pleasure Miss Pollock's appointment to the office of President of the Society of Housing Managers at the Society's annual conference in London in June

1957. This was felt to be well merited since the Association was extremely proud of their management procedures for which she was largely responsible.[68]

Space precludes a detailed account of the various changes in personnel throughout these years but some of the more signficant movements were as follows. As we have seen, Mr McBoyle departed over the rent question, and he was preceded a few months earlier by the Rev W.C.V. Smith, who resigned to take up a charge in Toronto.[69] Earlier in 1954, two interesting additions to Council had been Provost Mrs Ewart of Hamilton and Sir Alexander Brebner, the former, in particular, proving to be a formidable and useful contributor. A year later the Secretary, Mr Ross, who had served from 1937 to 1939, and again from 1945, retired. At his last meeting the chairman expressed Council's 'debt of gratitude to him for the loyalty and hard work which he had given to the Association ... It was abundantly clear that without Mr Ross's keenness the Association would not have been able to occupy the position in housing affairs which it undoubtedly did.'[70] David Halley was promoted to become the new secretary and solicitor. In 1958 Austen Bent left to become Director of Housing to the City of Manchester[71] and was succeeded as chief technical officer by the capable and shrewd Harold E. Buteux.

An interesting incident, which shows something of the relationship which had developed between the Association and the Department of Health for Scotland occurred when, in announcing his retirement, the Department's deputy secretary, Mr Craig Mitchell, asked to meet with the Council of Management.[72] When he was introduced at the meeting of 2nd June 1959, the chairman commented that Mr Mitchell had been concerned with the Association right from its inception and 'had proved to be at all times most sympathetic and helpful. His ever-ready co-operation, courtesy and tactful appreciation of the Association's problems had been a continuous source of help ... Thomas Paterson added that he was sure 'local authorities generally would echo the chairman's sentiments ... Craig Mitchell would be greatly missed in St Andrew's House for his willing and expert guidance on housing matters.' In reply, Mr Mitchell spoke of the 'happy relationships which had existed between the Council of Management and its officials and himself and his colleagues in the Department of Health ...

He would always remember with pleasure and appreciation his cordial relationship with the Association.'[73] In these days civil servants were carefully draped in anonymity and shielded from the public view, and it is, therefore, all the more important to record something of the contemporary assessment of the contribution made by men of Craig Mitchell's stamp.

In 1960, Colonel Sir James Miller* replaced Sir Alexander Brebner and the following winter saw the departure of one of the Association's truly outstanding Council members – Thomas Paterson of Ayr. Throughout the 1950s there was no great attempt to interfere with the political bias of the Council – as, indeed, is evidenced by Provost Mrs Ewart's appointment and the retention of men like Mr Paterson, who were certainly not Conservative in outlook – and this tolerance of various (usually unstated) shades of political opinion was (and is) a great source of strength to the Association. In November 1960, the government insisted that independent management consultants should conduct an organisation and methods survey of the direct labour department – an operation which was necessitated by the somewhat indifferent performance of direct labour at that time[74], but a review practice which was typically resented by trade unionists. When the O. & M. survey was announced Mr Paterson and Provost Ewart gave notice of their intention to resign.[75]

Council were horrified and instructed the chairman to write formally to both members urging them to withdraw their resignations. Mrs Ewart agreed to do so, but Mr Paterson, perhaps more stubborn, more determined or simply tired after a very long innings, refused to budge, while writing to convey 'the pleasure which he had enjoyed in working with the chairman, the members of Council, and the officers.' At the meeting of January 1961, the chairman confirmed the decision to his colleagues and spoke of the very active part which Mr Paterson had taken 'in the affairs of the Association since he was first elected in 1944 and his views, arising as they did from a long experience in housing matters, had always commanded respect. Mr Paterson's contribution to the Association's achieve-

Col Sir James Miller MC TD DL
Served with the Royal Artillery throughout First World War. Member of Berwickshire County Council and Convener 1949-61. President of the Association of County Councils of Scotland 1956-58. Knighted 1958.

ments over the years had been outstanding and it was with the greatest of regret that the Council received Mr Paterson's resignation.[76] In the annual report he was paid a unique tribute, for on the first page was included the following statement.

[77] Mr Thomas Paterson, JP, resigned from the Council of Management in January 1961 after seventeen years' continuous service. His resignation was accepted with regret and the Council recorded in their minutes their appreciation of the service of the highest order which Mr Paterson had given.

In fact, Mr Paterson did not precede his chairman by very long for, in September 1962, Sir Ronald Thomson resigned and, once again, it was a question of principle. This time the dispute was over the methods to be applied to the determination of the salaries of the three senior officers – the general manager, secretary and chief technical officer. Council had proposed to link their salaries to those accorded to their counterparts in the employment of Glasgow Corporation but this had been rejected by the Scottish Office in favour of a connection with the lower scales applied to the senior officers of New Towns. From April to September there were several meetings on this matter, including a confrontation between the chairman and the Secretary of State, John S. MacLay. When his advice was rejected and since, as he saw it, he had failed to protect his staff, Sir Ronald, in keeping with the gentlemanly code of honour to which he subscribed – and which in our more cynical age, often seems to have sadly faded from public life – informed the Minister that he could no longer continue to serve. His resignation was received with very real regret by colleagues and staff alike and, in particular, Mr Crow said 'it had given him personally the greatest possible pleasure to serve under Sir Ronald and his waygoing would be a great loss to the Association.' Others joined in the chorus of tributes, speaking of their 'admiration for the unfailing excellence with which Sir Ronald had carried out his duties as chairman.'[78]

In October 1961, the weight of the burden of the duties of chairman had been recognised by the appointment of Colonel Sir James Miller as deputy chairman, and Sir James now succeeded to the senior office with Mr W. Grierson McMillan becoming his deputy.[79]

Perhaps depressed by Sir Ronald's departure, the general manager, Mr S.A. Findlay, announced his intention to retire at the end of March 1964[80] but some difficulty occurred in finding an ideal replacement and he agreed to stay on for a further three years.[81] However, his health was not good and he withdrew in May 1965, again with many tributes. As the Association's chief executive from the end of the war he had presided over its growth and development from a small organisation possessing 2,000 houses to one which, by that date, had contributed 60,000 houses to the resolution of Scotland's housing problem. The chairman commented that 'Mr. Findlay's success had, however, progressed beyond the confines of the Association's operations and the high esteem in which he was held in professional circles was evidenced by the senior offices he had held in the Engineers' Guild, the Institution of Civil Engineers and the Building Research Station.'[82] His successor was Mr L.W.S. Cross.

With the 1959 general election out of the way, and confirming the Conservatives in power with an increased majority, attention once more returned to the problems of Glasgow, and of finding a method of enabling the Association to operate within the city in a manner acceptable to the various parties concerned. Early in March 1960 the Department of Health sounded out the Association as to its willingness to be involved in a major central redevelopment and gave some information on the nature and scale of the operations which were likely to be necessary.[83] By November the details were available and showed a programme of 3,500 houses to be built at Maryhill Barracks (Wyndford), Hutchesontown/Gorbals Area D (Note: not the Hutchesontown Area E, which was entirely the responsibility of Glasgow Corporation) and Broomhill, and these were intended to be completed in annual instalments of 1,000 houses which would enable all three schemes to proceed simultaneously.[84] In each case, at the insistence of the local authority, the developments were to be constructed to provide extremely high population densities. At Wyndford, for example, the specified density was of 61 houses per acre on a 30-acre site and, in the event, 1,898 flats were built there over the next seven years. Harold Buteux, the new chief technical officer, was thus given an early chance to show his mettle as the Association strove to meet the objectives in a way which would provide a decent means of living for the tenants who were eventually to live in such a tightly packed community. He drew attention to the need for good spatial planning and architecture. His design provided for about half the flats in the form of three- and four-storey blocks of flats and maisonettes and the remainder in tall or very tall buildings. Generally, the layout was an open planning arrangement forming a series of interpenetrating squares and a variety of architectural finishes was introduced to give each square or enclosure its own individual appearance. The result was, by the standards of the day, a most successful development from which, in time, the Association was to learn a great many lessons.

To build estates of this nature, of course, it was necessary to go well beyond the ten-storey no-fines blocks which had been erected at Toryglen and later at Dryburgh in Dundee. (When the first block at Dryburgh was opened in January 1960, Council noted that no less than 25,000 people had come to inspect the flats, which gives an indication of the level of interest which then existed in buildings of this type.[85]) As early as December 1958, an agreement in principle for two fifteen-storey blocks (112 flats) to be erected at Foxbar in Paisley had been completed. At that time discussions with the Association's German consultants had arrived at the conclusion that the limit of height for construction in load-bearing no-fines concrete was probably twelve storeys: hence it was necessary to examine alternative techniques, particularly if the Association's own labour force was to be involved.[86]

A few months later the Department of Health invited the Association to join with it in forming a Joint Development Group for multi-storey buildings 'which would be charged with the duty of detailed examination and research allied to practical building experience in connection with the erection of multi-storey flats and maisonettes which were expected to form a large proportion of the houses to be provided over the next ten years ... The work of the Group would include consideration of the actual design and construction of high density housing which would give a practical demonstration of standards of design and construction and give opportunities for the study of particular design problems, cost factors, etc.'[87]

Naturally the Association welcomed the chance to co-operate with the Department's own technical experts in this way.

Eventually, the Development Group produced a slab block, eight-storeys high, containing forty-eight maisonette dwellings to be erected at Fortrose Street in Glasgow. Council objected to the cost[88] and the designs were subsequently altered to produce one additional storey and five more maisonettes, giving a cost of about £3,000 per flat exclusive of landscaping.[89]The Group then turned its attention to planning a twenty-acre development at Anderston Cross, but when the Fortrose Street scheme was opened in 1964 its completion also marked the Association's five thousandth house within the city.[90]

Side by side with the activities of the Joint Group, the Association's own studies proceeded and were given added impetus by the announcement of the three high density developments in the Glasgow programme. To assist the Association's own technical staff an independent consultant engineer, Mr W.B. Zinn, was appointed to advise on the fifteen-storey blocks which were to be erected on the basis of *in situ* construction[91] and Mark IV multi-storey blocks of no less than twenty-six storeys, the latter being specifically intended for Glasgow.

By this time, however, consideration was also being given to prefabricated or 'industrialised' methods of building high flats and Mr Buteux submitted a detailed report on the techniques employed by Messrs Raymond Camus & Co of Paris. The appraisal drew attention to many of the questions which would have to be resolved before the system could be adopted for use in Scotland. Council congratulated the officials on the quality of the report and, although Mr Paterson reminded his colleagues of the problems experienced with prefabricated houses built in the post-war years and urged that particular attention be paid to the demands of the Scottish weather, it was agreed that the report be passed to the Department of Health and considered further by the Joint Development Group.[92] More was soon heard of the 'Camus' system for it was taken up by Messrs Holland, Hannan and Cubitts, who indicated an intention to establish a factory in Scotland provided they could be given a guaranteed annual programme of 400 houses for two years. The firm proposed to erect the first 800 houses themselves in order to gain experience of the relationship between factory and site. Thereafter other contractors would be able to purchase units. The first 800 houses would be supplied at a guaranteed price and the subsequent negotiated prices were predicted to be substantially lower than the current prices of comparable houses. With the approval of the Department this scheme was tentatively accepted[93], but it was later blocked by the Treasury.[94]

When the 'Camus' system was under consideration Mr Buteux demonstrated it with reference to drawings and models of the proposed developments for Hutchesontown/Gorbals Area D and Broomhill. Skilful model-building was something which the chief technical officer had encouraged and Council, delighted with the results, suggested that they should be exhibited for the benefit of MPs, local authority representatives and members of the public. A few months later the Association was invited to organise the UK exhibition to be displayed at the Paris Conference of the International Federation of Housing and Planning held in September 1962.[95] This was enormously successful[96] and, on its return to this country, the exhibition

Sir Ronald Thomson, Sir John Greig Dunbar and Harold Buteaux discuss the model display on exhibition at the College of Art in Edinburgh.

was displayed in the Hall of Sculpture at the College of Art in Edinburgh, the opening ceremony being performed by the Lord Provost, Sir John Greig Dunbar, who was shortly himself to become a Member of the Council of Management.[97] Interestingly, Glasgow Corporation – still apparently prickly in its attitude to the Association – declined to have the exhibition mounted for public display within the City. Nevertheless, the British Council had no such qualms and, at their expense, the exhibition was taken to Nigeria for display at a Conference at Ibadan on 'Organisation and Town Planning in Nigeria and Elsewhere in Africa.'[98] This too was evidently a great success.[99]

The next stage in the development of the high rise, industrialised, building era is marked by the publication of the Emmerson Report, a *Survey of Problems Before Construction Industries* prepared for the Ministry of Works by Sir Harold Emmerson. The Association had submitted notes to Sir Harold on productivity and these had formed the basis of later discussions with him. What emerged was basically the classic industrialist's outlook of the period, for at that time, almost throughout British industry, the way ahead was perceived to be through mergers and consortia. It was the age when big was considered to be beautiful, and in the meetings with the newly designated Scottish Development Department which followed the need to form a consortium which could process large-scale projects was accepted. What part, if any, the Association would take in this remained to be seen, but meanwhile permission was granted for a pilot industrialised project to be undertaken at Wyndford.[100]

A little later the Department convened a meeting of local authorities with the intention of forming a study group for industrialised building and a paper was submitted by Mr Buteux for consideration by the group at its first meeting in September 1962.[101] One of the principal concerns was with the undeniably excessive cost of building multi-storey flats and after this was discussed in an exchange of views with the Treasury, the chief technical officer was cross-examined by Council on the possibilities of tackling the density problem in Glasgow by other methods. Regrettably there was no instant alternative if the city's requirements were to be met: however, he was eager to consider the matter further.[102] At the same meeting Mr Buteux reported on negotiations which had been opened with Concrete

(Scotland) Limited in regard to their system of wall-frame construction of high flats, a method which would leave the finishing trades to be dealt with by direct labour or by specialist contractors. An advantage of wall-frame construction was held to be that a large development was apparently not required to enable a prototype scheme to be built. Arrangements had been made to inspect the factory and a partially erected building, and tests were to be conducted to ensure that the type of walling and jointing were adequate to withstand the Scottish climate. If the system proved satisfactory a prototype could be erected without delay so that the results could be made available for early consideration by the consortium of local authorities.[103]

Interestingly, a few days later, the Association's German no-fines consultant, now the delightfully named Herr Pfefferkorn, carried out a detailed inspection of the Association's ten-storey blocks at Toryglen and in Dundee, and reported the structures to have met their requirements in full and that the experiment of building ten-storey blocks of flats in no-fines concrete had been successful.[104] There had, of course, been some teething troubles with the earliest buildings at Toryglen, and accordingly a continuous monitoring programme was in hand.

In April, 1963, the chief technical officer returned once more to wall-frame industrialised building, and produced proposals for ten eight-storey Mark X blocks of flats comprising a total of 310 dwellings to be erected at Wyndford and Carron Street. Each block was to contain 16 two-apartment and 15 three-apartment flats, and the report was supported by an exhibition of models and drawings. The contract was to be fulfilled by the Direct Labour Organisation with Concrete (Scotland) Limited acting as sub-contractors and being responsible for the whole structural carcassing which would be produced at their factory. Part of the report contained a detailed analysis to produce comparative cost profiles as shown below.

1 Average cost per flat of Mark X built by
   industrialised methods   £2,960
*2 Average cost per flat of similar blocks
    built in traditional methods with brick facing £2,998

* For technical reasons it was not possible to use brick
  cladding above 15 storeys

3 Average cost of flat of similar block built
   by traditional methods with concrete
   panel facing   £3,320

It was also anticipated that erection by industrialised methods would be speedier and, therefore, it was agreed to seek the Department's approval to proceed.[105] In the event seven Mark X blocks were erected at Wyndford and three at Carron Street (see Appendix C). By June the required permission had been received to start with this project and at the same time it was noted that negotiations were in hand with Gilbert Ash Limited for the construction of four Mark VI 24-storey blocks at Hutchesontown/Gorbals Area D.[106]

To set these developments in context, however, it should be noted that in July of that year it was concluded that no less than 80 per cent of the Association's programme, both at the time and in future, was unlikely to be suitable for building high by industrialised methods. Even at the peak of this phase, therefore, the SSHA's main preoccupation was with cottages or with other low rise buildings. Partly for this reason Mr Buteux's mind was ceaselessly being deployed to finding methods of achieving high densities without the excessive use of high flats.[107] He thereafter submitted models for the information of the Council showing how the external walls of new types could be poured in no-fines concrete and the interior finishing speeded up by means of standardisation and prefabrication. A model layout was shown indicating the provisions for the segregation of pedestrian and vehicular traffic with provision for open car parking on the basis of one car space for each house with one additional car space for every two houses for visitors. In the utilisation of such a layout it would be necessary to provide houses in three storeys in order to achieve the densities of between 70 and 80 persons per acre which were sometimes required.

In this case Council agreed to the erection of six houses of the proposed three-storey type as an experiment after which a further report was to be submitted. No matter how much it went against the grain, it was thinking of this kind that was eventually to render liveable inner city redevelopments on the scale of Wyndford as well as high density schemes elsewhere.

Taking one month as a random example of the Association's

building activities at this time, the Direct Labour Organisation's immediate programme in September 1963 was as follows.[108]

House Building Jobs Completed but not Finalised

Dundee, Foggyley	120 no-fines 10-storey flats.
Dundee, Foggyley	94 no-fines houses.
Johnston Castle	280 no-fines houses.
Carron Street	180 no-fines houses.
Irvine	334 no-fines houses and garages.
Auchterderran	113 no-fines houses.
Paisley	112 15-storey flats.
Langlands Road	112 15-storey flats.
Eastriggs	55 no-fines houses.
Port Glasgow	64 traditional houses and garages.
Airdrie	58 no-fines houses and garages.
Johnston Castle	38 no-fines houses.

House Building – Jobs In-Progress

Clydebank	392 15-storey flats.
Irvine	98 no-fines houses.
Wyndford	280 15-storey flats.
Fortrose Street	61 8-storey flats and garages.
Toryglen	112 15-storey flats.
Linwood	226 no-fines houses.
Kirkintilloch	120 no-fines houses.
Linwood	84 no-fines houses.
Linwood	445 no-fines houses.
Total	3,378

A further 517 houses were being built by private contractors, giving a total of 3,895 houses in progress. In addition, 302 houses were shortly to commence, sites had been obtained for 4,396 houses for which plans were in various stages of preparation, and 798 houses were programmed, but sites for these had not yet been obtained. At that date the number of men employed on Association work was as indicated below.

On Capital Work

Contractors	1,233
Association DLO	1,186
DLO Depot	39
Total	2,458

On Maintenance

| DLO | 274 |
| Grand total | 2,732 |

In the following month Lord Craigton, the Minister of State, congratulated the Council and commented on the government's 'great reliance on the Association in connection with housing operations in Scotland ... The redevelopment of certain areas in Glasgow was one of the biggest enterprises in Great Britain at the present time and the Association's share in that enterprise gave cause for the greatest satisfaction.'[109]

A little later Council noted the formation of a consortium of local authorities and other bodies 'to promote the adoption of system building for multi-storey construction and of standardised building components and specifications etc.'[110] and, after meetings of the steering committee, it was announced that the group would be known as the Scottish Local Authorities Special Housing Group or, more commonly SLASH.[111] Essentially, the purpose of SLASH was to conduct research into system building and into the rationalisation and standardisation of techniques and components. To accomplish these tasks it was to draw on the Scottish office of the National Building Agency and the Association's own Research Group suitably strengthened and enhanced.[112] In the event, SLASH functioned for many years, not being formally dissolved until as late as 1985, but its main activities were obviously in the mid-1960s.

In July 1964, following a report on progress with the Mark X eight-storey blocks at Wyndford, it was agreed to make the site available for examination by local authorities, government departments and professional bodies. A month later Glasgow Corporation, evidently impressed, asked if they might use the Association's architects and type plans in other developments to be performed by the same contractors and this was readily

Princess Margaret visiting the Wyndford Estate in May 1963. Mr Finlay, the General Manager, is standing at the back.

approved on a commercial basis.[113] At the same time both Cumbernauld and Glenrothes Development Corporations asked if the Association's Direct Labour Organisation would erect some of Mr Buteux's no-fines low rise dwellings, and Council agreed that twenty prototypes might be constructed, with a view to tendering for involvement in the main contracts which were expected to follow.[114] By October Council were learning with pleasure of the large number of visitors who had inspected the buildings at Wyndford and the many favourable comments, particularly on the high standard of internal finish which had been achieved by the Association's own labour force.

In that same month attention now turned to the Tracoba multi-storey system which was being proposed by Gilbert Ash Limited and permission was given for the chief technical officer and other senior officials to proceed to France to inspect buildings of the type. At the same time it was noted that of the fourteen contractors who had been invited to tender for the Mark IV 26-storey flats intended for Wyndford, only five companies had shown an interest and only two had actually submitted tenders. Eventually the contract for this job was awarded to Laing Construction Limited.[115]

Another item considered by Council at that time concerned the SDD/Association Joint Housing Development Group's proposals for the first phase of 116 houses for the Anderston Cross Development which the Group was to carry out as part of the Association's programme in Glasgow. A joint tender from the Direct Labour Organisation and Concrete (Scotland) Limited won this contract, although it was recognised that building by traditional means might be cheaper. Since part of the object was research the additional cost was considered to be acceptable.[116] Interestingly, a year later it was learned that the Group's Fortrose Street scheme had been awarded a Saltire Society commendation.[117] (One of the Department's architects responsible for the development is the Association's present director of technical services, John Fullarton.)

Late 1964, of course, saw the return of Labour to office and the implications for the Association of the change of political direction will be considered shortly. However, in order to follow the high-rise building phase to its conclusion, it should be mentioned here that the general policy thrust of the new government was sharply to increase the Association's program-

me, but to do so in a manner which once again, tended to direct it away from Glasgow. Although there was certainly no immediate movement away from high-density high rise system building, over the next few years the bulk of the activity within the city was connected with the completion of dwellings already in programme and with agency work carried out on behalf of the Corporation.

The Joint Group's Anderston Cross project was mainly for low-rise high density building, but elsewhere, largely at the government's insistence, the Tracoba system was increasingly used. 789 flats were to be prodouced in 18- and 8-storey blocks on five sites in Glasgow by this method, and the tender concluded with Gilbert Ash Limited estimated the cost at £4,919 (later £4,971) per flat, exclusive of garage accommodation, play areas and landscaping, which would require an additional £900 per house.[118] Clearly costs were beginning to escalate sharply and the Association was far from certain that the end product would be an improvement. In consequence, the negotiations with the company became bogged down, but when the concerns about reduced standards were taken to the Minister he replied

[119]   that the government did not want houses erected 'on the cheap' but had to hold a balance between cost and the urgent need for houses and that with regard to the

A scenic view of Hutchesontown, Gorbals.

particular industrialised system referred to, in view of the protracted negotiations, the urgent need for the 800 houses involved and the financial restrictions at present operating, the Association should proceed with the 800 houses even although, like members of the Council of Management, the Minister himself was not happy with the unavoidable reduction in standards.

When the first Tracoba blocks were completed in 1969 it seemed that the Association's early fears had been fully justified for, when buildings at Broomhill, Gorget Avenue and Wester Common were inspected, in addition to exterior rust staining of panels, severe honeycombing of some concrete panels was detected. The Association refused to accept the blocks at Wester Common and Gorget Avenue until major remedial measures were taken and similar work was also carried out at Broomhill.[120] (Subsequently, there, have been no very great problems with the buildings.)

Before then, however, Nemesis had visited the high-rise builders, and the episode emerges from the Council papers in the most ironic manner. On 2nd July 1968, Mr Buteux drew Council's attention to a photograph of a Tracoba block in Algiers which had been damaged by a terrorist bomb. The picture showed that the damage had been contained within the immediate area of the explosion and that there had been no form of collapse, and this seemed to give confirmation of the essential strength and stability of the structure.[121] Exactly one month later Council were receiving a report on the partial collapse of a block of flats at Ronan Point at Newham in London together with the preliminary results of the Ronan Point Inquiry being conducted by Imperial College on behalf of the Ministry of Housing and Local Government.[122]

The Association's immediate response to this disaster was to require the technical staff and consultant engineer to set in hand an inspection of all the high rise buildings in its possession.[123] Later, and with the guidance of an SDD Circular on the matter, a more careful investigation was conducted[124] while the plans of the buildings then under construction were reconsidered.[125] Some strengthening work was carried out[126], but generally the Association's blocks were found to conform to the enhanced specifications and standards set out in the government circular. Traditionally Ronan Point is held to mark the beginning of the end of the high rise era but it should be remarked in passing that the last building of the kind to be erected by the Association was in fact ordered more than a year earlier although it was not actually completed until 1973. Probably this was a coincidence linked to the new direction towards which the Association was now being guided.

With the setting up of the Scottish Development Department in 1962 the thrust of government industrial policy in Scotland began to swing towards the fostering of areas where economic growth was considered to be likely and in 1963 Council discussed with the Minister the White Paper *A Programme for Development and Growth in Central Scotland*. The Minister explained that there would be demand for houses to support industrial development in the designated growth areas.[127] Broadly, the Government's White Paper anticipated an eventual requirement for some 20,000 to 30,000 houses a year and indicated that these were to be provided by the New Towns where appropriate and, elsewhere, by the Association. Some of the local authorities were not too keen on this proposal and a few months later the Association noted that it had been excluded from various meetings and discussions on the subject.[128] Nevertheless, within a few weeks an indication was given of initial annual instalments of about 2,000 houses in respect of identified growth points.[129]

After the General Election of late 1964, the new Joint Parliamentary Under-Secretary of State, Dr Dickson Mabon, was quick to carry out a tour of inspection of the Association's building operations in Glasgow and elsewhere in the west of Scotland, and within a matter of days notice was received of an immediate additional 'General Needs' Programme of 2,400 houses to be commenced in 1965/66, although precise details were not yet available. On the same day, Council noted a new Overspill programme of 500 houses for Cumnock and a first instalment of 50 'Growth Areas' houses to be erected near Cowdenbeath.[130] In July of 1965 another unusual addition was made to the programme when the County Council of Dunbarton declined to build houses in connection with the development of the Royal Navy's base at Faslane. The government decided to resolve the problem by designating the locality as a 'Growth Area' and authorised the Association to provide the houses, a families club, a shop and other buildings for the

NOTE: Two 9 storey blocks were completed in the late 1970s as the final phase of the Anderston Cross development, but these were small by comparison with the structures of the 1960s.

Ministry of Works on an agency basis.[131]

In the winter of 1965/66 Council discussed two significant White Papers, *The Scottish Housing Programme 1965-70*[132] and *The Scottish Economy 1965-70* and learned that detailed discussions were in train as to the emerging programme.[133]

By March further information was available and, although exact details were still sketchy, it was noted that the number of new houses started in each year was to increase progressively so that by 1970 work would have begun on no less than 20,000 houses in various parts of the country. The Department's circular No 5 of 4th February had drawn local authorities' attention to the scale of the Association's intended operations under the terms of the White Paper and urged them to give their full co-operation.[134] In May, the detail of the plan emerged. The 'Growth Areas' notion had developed into a full scale 'Economic Expansion' programme of 5,000 houses per annum covering the five years to 1970 and this, taken together with 1,000 houses per year to be built on agency terms for various authorities, meant that the Association were being asked to build at an annual rate of 6,000 houses.[135]

Not even in the hectic period of the early 1950s had building rates of this order been achieved and, in the event, although completions did jump from 1,835 in 1964/65 to 4,212 in 1970/71 (see Appendix B) the targeted speed was never reached for various reasons, but principally because of later government efforts to curb inflation and because the anticipated rates of economic growth were simply not achieved, hence demand for new houses in the growth areas expanded more slowly than had been hoped. Meanwhile, however, the Association turned to consider how best to increase the volume of construction.

Council decided that a rule of thumb would be to attempt to complete approximately half of the building by direct labour, and that negotiations should be opened with Messrs George Wimpey & Company Limited in respect of a large portion of the remaining part of the Association's own programme. The company was to be invited to tender for this work on the basis of building to the Association's house designs. For agency work in Glasgow the Corporation's approval was to be sought in relation to various industrialised systems then in use, but traditional brick construction would be adopted where appropriate although it was expected that these would be 'isolated cases'. While the various discussions were going on application was made to the SDD for permission to spend an additional £400,000 in re-equipping the Direct Labour Organisation.[136]

The Department was not over enthusiastic about such a large proportion of the work being done by the Association's own labour force and the problem began now to be increasingly influenced by the government's introduction of Selective Employment Tax. Essentially this tax was a payroll tax which was intended to discriminate in favour of certain industries and certain types of employment. All employers were liable to pay the tax, but firms in particular industries or localities had the money refunded or were given an additional premium as a bonus. In the case of the building industry the tax operated to the advantage of the users of concrete and against brick-builders – presumably in an attempt to increase the employment of unskilled labour, but perhaps as a deliberate means of discriminating in favour of the municipal builders, who tended to rely more on concrete than the private building companies, the latter obviously depending on traditional crafts and bricks and mortar. It was a most odd and ill-considered departure, but it certainly stimulated a fresh surge of questionable building by urban local authorities throughout the UK. However, from the Association's point of view, the effects were not disadvantageous, since its no-fines technique was favoured by the tax[137]. But to avoid excessive use of direct labour, by March 1968, six contracts had been concluded with Wimpey for 682 houses with a further 3,035 on eleven schemes to follow; negotiations were in hand with Alexander Hall & Son Limited for 247 houses at East Calder[138] with the intention that similar contracts would be concluded later; and ultimately five independent firms were engaged in this manner.[139] In each case the companies built the houses to Association designs using the no-fines technique which by, 1968, had been formally recognised by the Department as an industrialised building system.

By this stage designs of no-fines houses had, of course, become very sophisticated, and largely under the guidance of Harold Buteux, the accumulated experience to date had been brought together in the form of the staff *Architects Handbook Three*, which included a range of adaptable house types, and by the establishment of a library of Standard Details.

[140] The Library started as an amalgam of all construction details and components used by the SSHA over the years in its low rise houses. By having all this material instantly at hand, the technical department had control over all the work done; architects' designs, materials problems, practical difficulties of building in modern materials such as pre-cast concrete. It proved to be a very flexible approach. The range of house types could be added to easily and new ideas were developed for corner blocks, wider pends – whatever was needed for more adaptable living, or for the circumstances of any particular site.

On 31st March 1966, for example, new designs included, or shortly to be included, were listed as follows.[141]

    a Patio single storey houses;
    b Split level houses;
    c Detached houses and variations for terraced and semi-detached;
    d Three-storey point blocks of flats;
    e Three-storey houses.

The government's overall objective was now to have the local authorities, the Association, New Towns, private developers and housing associations building at a combined annual rate of 50,000 houses by 1970 and, as in the immediate post-war period, this produced an almighty scramble for available land. As early as 1967, the report was commenting; 'the more the overall housing programme for Scotland as a whole progresses the more difficult will the acquisition of sites become and more of the sites will tend to be problem sites, difficult to develop.'[142]

In order to assist with planning the Association was given its long coveted powers of compulsory purchase under the terms of the Housing (Scotland) Act 1966. In October of that year the Minister emphasised that the Association, as an instrument of the Secretary of State, should not in any way fail to achieve the full programme envisaged.[143]

A few months later the new Joint Parliamentary Secretary of State, Lord Hughes, discussed the government's target of 50,000 houses per annum, '10 per cent of which were to be erected by the Association.' If the Association could meet their target figure this would be an excellent example to others. In

Association's Planned Housing Programme for Five Years Ending 1970

Year ending 31st December	1966	1967	1968	1969	1970
Starts	1,120 (Actual)	2,800	4,800	5,000	5,000
Completions	2,289 (Actual)	2,000	3,500	4,400	5,000

Planned Agency Programme

Year ending 31st December	1966	1967	1968	1969	1970
Starts	348 (Actual)	700	200	500	1,000
Completions	322 (Actual)	500	500	100	500

The comparable tables for March 1970 show the eventual outcome of the five-year plan.[146]

Actual Housing Programme for Five Years Ending 1970

Year ending 31st December	1966	1967	1968	1969	1970
Starts	1,120	2,194	2,875	2,952	3,287
Completions	2,296	2,184	2,048	2,779	3,540

Actual Agency Programme

Year ending 31st December	1966	1967	1968	1969	1970
Starts	348	696	416	850	253
Completions	315	535	635	409	612

reply the chairman said that in 1968-69 the Association expected to complete 4,000 houses and, with agency work included, this would give a total output in excess of the 5,000 target. In the following year it was hoped that 5,000 houses in the Association's own programme would be completed.[144] At that stage the predicted programme was as shown above.[145]

As can be seen, the agency activities were pretty well maintained over these years and were comfortably ahead of target up to the 'Starts' of 1970 – the year in which the Conservatives returned to power. This perhaps is a measure of the cost advantage which no-fines bestowed on the Association under the current tax arrangements and it is interesting that, as early as 1967, Council were agreeing not only to make the drawings and technical details available to the New Towns and some local authorities, but were actually supplying contractors such as Hall, Cruden and Wimpey with no-fines know-how, drawings and bills of quantities so that they could 'obtain further contracts from Scottish local authorities, provided suitable aknowledgement to the Association is made, and that no charge (in respect of these services) be levied.'[147] All of this co-operation was in an attempt to increase the overall rate of production, keep costs of components and materials in check, and assist the contractors, whose traditional modes of operation were at a disadvantage because of SET.

By comparison, although the Association's own programme did expand to 1970, it never reached the hoped-for rates of construction. The annual report for the year to March 1969 explained the problem in an underlined comment in which it referred to 'the considerable number of schemes in the very last stages of design and appraisal (approval) which have had to be postponed or phased back because the original timing and extent of the need for houses appeared to be either very optimistic or quite wrong.'[148] The point is almost exactly repeated, again in an underlined note, in the report for the following year[149], and it is clear that, while somewhat embarrassed at the failure to reach the target, the Association was bluntly emphasising that the problem was a failure of demand to reach the levels at which the government had aimed. In other words, while the economic expansion idea was fundamentally sound, the sustained rates of economic growth had not materialised.

Nevertheless, despite the fact that it proceeded at a slower rate than was at first anticipated, the economic expansion programme dominated a large part of the Association's new building activities throughout the late 1960s and 1970s and ultimately produced almost 20,000 houses in various parts of Scotland. Moreover, since some of the people moving to new growth industries were in a higher income bracket than most of the Association's traditional tenants, it represented something of a move up-market. In fact, that comment is perhaps less than precisely accurate, since by this era the standards required by society were generally becoming higher than had formerly been the case and it may be that improved houses and estates would have been developed at this time in any case. Be that as it may, the fact is that there was an optimism about this programme, perhaps best reflected in its title, and the Association seems to have responded to it by producing progressively more attractive houses, estates and communities.

To begin with the details were worked out by a Houses for Industry Committee drawn from various government departments and the SSHA and, after considering the Committee's recommendations, the SDD supplied the Association with its programme of houses for the selected localities. Initially many of the developments were in central Scotland and, indeed, there seems occasionally to have been something of an overlap with Overspill as in the case, for example, of the development at Linwood in connection with the Rootes car factory.[150] In instances of this kind Overspill houses which happened to be in the right area were sometimes allocated to tenants applying under the terms of economic expansion. Other examples from this period are the houses at Fort William which were built to support the pulp and paper mill, and the houses erected in various parts of Dunbartonshire to provide for Royal Navy personnel and civilian staff associated with Faslane.

Much of the discussion in this chapter has dealt with the Association's activities in respect of new building, and that is a fair reflection of the emphasis to which policy in these years was directed. Nevertheless, it would be a mistake to ignore the work which went on to maintain and modernise the existing stock of houses.

In June 1959 Council agreed to assist the Scottish National Housing Company in its plans for a five-year modernisation programme for its houses at Rosyth by including the company's requirements within the bulk purchase of materials.[151] However, it is clear that both of the SNH Companies were in deep financial trouble and, in February 1963, it was learned that the Secretary of State was prepared to advance the Association the funds to acquire the assets of the two companies. After discussion 'The Council of Management agreed that an offer of £650,000 be submitted to the First Scottish National Company for the purchase of the 1,872 houses at Rosyth, together with the offices and people there and that an offer of £1,083,300 be made to the Second Scottish National Company for the 2,549 houses in Scotland, together with the offices and depot at Shettleston.'[152]

The houses were duly taken over on 31st March, but it was quickly realised that they were in an extremely poor state of repair. As early as June rewiring work revealed that many of the Rosyth houses were riddled with woodworm and that large scale rehabilitation was necessary. In the first year alone almost £150,000 had to be spent on improvements at Rosyth[153] and over the next five years major repairs had to be carried out on the former stock of both companies, involving a total expenditure in the region of £625,000.[154]

The general notion of rehabilitating older houses seems, typically, to have been slow to develop, at least in terms of using the Association to discharge such a function. However, in May 1962 the SSHA were approached by Rutherglen Town Council and asked to improve, on an agency basis, 48 houses in a four-storey tenement block. The idea was put to the SDD and when approval in principle was received, a specialised group was established within the technical section, to provide the expertise for the conversion of old buildings.[155]

Gradually activity of this kind expanded and when, shortly after the general election of 1964, the new Minister, Dr Dickson Mabon, visited the Association's schemes he inspected conversion work being carried out at Paisley, Barrhead and Port Glasgow.[156] Thereafter work of this kind gradually increased and the report of 31st March 1968 was able to speak in terms of a 'large-scale programme of modernising older properties.' The accounts for that year showed progress as indicated in the relevant table:[157]

Almost all this activity was done on agency terms for other authorities, but in 1970 permission was given for the Association to capitalise some of the work on its own stock and there was also the intention that it could itself acquire older properties for full scale modernisation. £250,000 was earmarked for expenditure in this way in 1969-70 with £650,000 being the intended future annual spend in the form of loans repayable over thirty years. The first properties to be so purchased were in Arbroath (72 houses) and Forfar (26 houses). Some indication of the general growth of rehabilitation activity is given by comparing the figures for 1970 with those for 1968.[158]

Given the extent of the Association's new building programme at this time it would be easy to assume that modernisation was regarded as a secondary activity, but this would be a

Rehabilitation Programme 1968

	Total Houses	Estimated Cost £	Houses Completed	Houses In Progress	Houses Soon to be Started
Conversions	1,784	1,361,174	1,175	21	588
Internal rehabilitation	2,886	257,570	1,836	24	1,026
External rehabilitation	6,222	1,391,113	3,732	1,099	1,391
Site improvement	2,242	390,000	136	–	2,106

Rehabilitation Programme 1970

	Total Houses	Esitmated Cost £	Houses Completed	Houses In Progress	Houses Soon to be Started
Conversions	1,848	1,639,889	1,481	233	134
Internal rehabilitation	15,237	1,076,570	10,175	2,038	3,024
External rehabilitation	18,057	1,977,904	11,160	4,949	1,948
Site improvement	79	1,803,157	42	16	21

Conversions: usually involve
(1) Converting a number of old sub-standard tenement flats into a smaller number of new flats up to modern standards,
(2) Bringing older houses up to modern standards of space and equipment by, for example, making a small bedroom into a bathroom.
Internal rehabilitation: consists of rewiring, replacing heating installations, new bathrooms and kitchen equipment and providing close doors.
External rehabilitation: Involve re-roofing, renewing cladding, gutters, downpipes and porches.
Site improvements: consist of providing better fencing, more landscaping, children's play areas, car parking and garages.

mistake. In fact, since the offices at Palmerston Place look out at the back to Manor Place and across to the magnificent Georgian houses of Edinburgh's New Town, it is not surprising that the neglect of some of the older buildings of Scotland's cities and burghs was deplored by many members of staff and rehabilitation work was accepted with enthusiasm. In a paper entitled *Homes for One Hundred Years or More* Harold Buteux rejected the general demolish and build policies which had dominated thinking in the post-war years.

[159] There are over-riding factors such as how frequently we as a nation can afford to renew totally our housing stock; certainly not as often as every sixty years (the normal amortisation period). It is doubtful whether even America, with its enormous resources, could afford to renew its total housing stock in that time. Usually it takes at least a year

to decant and demolish a housing area and two years to rebuild. If the whole of our housing stock were to be out of commission for rebuilding once every sixty years,. this would mean that one-twentieth of our domestic environment would always be in the process of demolition and reconstruction ... We have learned at an appalling cost in human sociological terms that modernisation is often more acceptable than total renewal.

The Association's skills at repair were put to an unwelcome but important use in 1968, when the tremendous gale of 15th January left a swathe of stripped roofs and damaged buildings across the central belt of Scotland. Many of the SSHA's own houses were affected and, in some cases, the damage was quite extensive. A few tenants had to be temporarily rehoused while repairs were being carried out and the Association co-operated with local authorities who were similarly afflicted. For example, in February Council noted that nine Association houses had been lent to Dunbarton County Council to temporarily rehouse tenants and that the County Council had responded by making six of its houses available to the Association for the same purpose. At the same time it was learned that many tenants whose houses had had to be repaired were appealing for financial help for redecoration expenses, but while Council sympathised, it was felt that liability had to be repudiated if the Association's obligations in law were to be protected.[160]

Nevertheless, the damage to Association property was relatively minor when contrasted with the experience of Glasgow and, to a lesser extent, Stirling, where the roofs of some of the older tenements in particular had been severely affected. Naturally, the Association at once responded to the appeals for help and its own labour force was set to work, while a Council member, Sir John Greig Dunbar, obtained the services of Messrs Sir Robert McAlpine & Sons Limited to provide sub-contracting services to the DLO for some of the tasks.[161]

For much of 1968 many men were involved in making good the damage and David Halley describes the episode thus –
[162] The damage was so extensive that it was decided to dispense with scaffolding from the ground up to the roof repairs – erection and dismantling of which would be expensive and time-consuming. The building department introduced a system of bolting aluminium ladders in pairs

across the roof, from which eaves platforms could be suspended and from which the construction team could operate. Sadly, before the technique was fully developed, two workers lost their lives in falls. Another employee was awarded the Glasgow Corporation Medal for Bravery for having saved a fellow worker from a similar fate. In an endeavour to speed up the work, ways of waterproofing the roof without removing the remaining slates were devised.

In May the chairman reported on his tour of inspection of the Glasgow sites 'where the Association's workmen were carrying out the dangerous and difficult task of roof repairs with commendable ability'. Mention was also made of the curious scaffolding arrangements which were apparently attracting the interest of various authorities throughout the UK.[163] In July attention was drawn to the public tribute paid by Stirling County Council to the Association[164] and in October the Minister, Lord Hughes, added his thanks for 'the magnificent work being carried out by the Association's DLO on the repair of storm damage in Glasgow and Stirling.'[165]

Everyone who experienced the great gale of January 1968 will remember the incident well, and many of the landmarks of Scotland's recent past have a similar habit of popping out of the Council minutes, reports or other Association papers. For example, a much less spectacular but significant event is noted

Repair to storm damage carried out on Glasgow tenements in 1968. Note the hanging scaffolding.

Above and opposite *A sequence illustrating no-fines construction at Queensferry. These houses were also interesting in that they were the first built in Scotland to metric standards.*

on 10th March 1958, when Dumbarton Town Council decided to make a 'smoke-control order' for an area which included SSHA houses at Bellsmyre. This was the first occasion in which the Clean Air Act of 1956 – arguably the single most important piece of post-war legislation in terms of its effect in enhancing the quality of life of millions of urban dwellers in the UK – first made its presence felt on the Association. In this case the question concerned how the costs of modifying fires should be apportioned between the Association and the local authority.[166]

Similarly, in January 1967, the Association was asked to submit evidence to the Royal Commission on Local Government Reform in Scotland (out of which eventually emerged the main lines of the Regional and District structure of local government which came into existence in 1974.)[167] A factual statement of the present management arrangements was conveyed to the Commission, but that was regarded as insufficient and a further request came seeking views as to how local government housing arrangements ought to be modified. A submission was duly prepared which advocated regional housing authorities, but when this was discussed in Council ex-Provost Mrs Ewart and Mr Monteath objected, feeling that the Association should not adopt political postures and that the suggested structure 'would result in many of the housing functions enjoyed by local authorities at the present time being taken from them'. Nevertheless, with some minor amendments, the memorandum was submitted, although Mrs Ewart asked that her dissent be recorded.[168] (In the event, housing remained a District function after reorganisation so the Association view did not prevail, but it is interesting to note that Command Paper No 4583 on the *Reform of Local Government in Scotland* did suggest greater use of the Association in support of regional strategy.[169])

Again, in 1968, the metrication movement made itself felt and the Association responded by designing and building 18 houses to metric specifications on its economic expansion site at South Queensferry.[170] In due course, on 21st November 1969, the chairman of the Metrication Board, Lord Ritchie Calder, opened the 'first metric houses in Scotland.'[171] Over the next few years a wide range of new house types were designed to metric standards and, noting that this task was largely completed, the annual report of 1972 commented: 'these suites of houses continue the policy of having a range of standard house types with standard details capable of a wide range of permutations: this allows adaptation to meet individual site characteristics.'[172]

Other matters which emerge from the minutes are much less likely to jog memories but they are, in some ways, even more interesting, since they say something of the recognition accorded to the contributions made by individuals and of the gentle good manners with which the business of the Association was usually discharged.

For example, in May 1970 Council's attention was drawn to the impending retirement of Mr E.E. Gamley, the manager of the Haymarket branch of Clydesdale Bank. Since Mr Gamley had for many years looked after the Association's account, the chairman was instructed to write to him to express its appreciation and good wishes.[173]

A year earlier Council noted with delight that Mr Macintosh, the construction manager, had been awarded an OBE in the New Year's Honours List[174] (an event perhaps not unconnected with the sterling work which his department had carried out in repairing the storm damage of the previous winter), and they were also proud later in the year when Harold Buteux was accorded a similar honour.[175]

By 1971, of course, many of the members of staff who had joined at the end of the war were about to celebrate 25 years of service with the Association and Council decided to mark the occasion by inviting all those concerned to a lunch at which each would be presented with a commemorative scroll.[176] As such things have a habit of doing, this lunch eventually became an annual event with members of staff retiring after long service also being honoured.

Another interesting little incident mentioned in June 1972 concerns the gallant action of a member of staff based at the Falkirk office. Miss Shirley Mitchell 'had shown remarkable initiative in capturing a person who had stolen money from the office.' Shirley, in fact, had followed the man concerned onto a bus, got the driver to lock the doors, and summoned the police. Council unanimously commended Miss Mitchell's action and invited her to a lunch at which she was presented with a suitable gift.[177]

Over these years there were, of course, many other more

formal events. In February 1965 the Secretary of State opened the Association's sixty thousandth house at Eglinton, Irvine[178], and on 9th February 1968 he opened an Association house at Wyndford which had been identified as the millionth house erected in Scotland since the end of the First World War.[179] Later, in September 1969, Mr Ross attended another ceremony, this time to mark the completion of the Association's seventy thousandth house, which must have given him some satisfaction since it was in his own constituency of Kilmarnock.[180] In addition, by this period, the excellence of many of the Association's developments was being recognised by a variety of awards. For instance, in the same month it was noted that a Saltire Society award had been accorded to Wyndford as well as a commendation to a small development at Cove and Kilcreggan.[181]

Once again, apology has to be made for the failure to give a fuller account of the various changes in personnel throughout these years but if justice were done to everyone who contributed the result would be a hopelessly unwieldy and overlong book. However, some of the more notable changes were as follows.

Sir Ronald Thomson was succeeded as chairman by Colonel Sir James Miller. When Labour returned to office at the end of

An award winning overspill development at Cove and Kilgreggan.

1964 there was no immediate major reshuffle of Council, but after the 1966 general election had confirmed the Wilson Government in office with an enhanced majority, changes did follow. In 1965 William S. Gray joined the Council, and a year later, when Sir James was not re-nominated by the Secretary of State, Mr Gray succeeded to the chair. Initially there were a few reservations about this appointment, for some members of Council felt that Mr MacMillan, the deputy chairman, who had been on the Council for twenty years, mostly acting on an unpaid basis, should have been nominated for the post.' However, Council had no real option but to respect the Secretary of State's choice.[182]

Nevertheless, Mr Gray soon proved himself to be a vigorous and flamboyant chairman who gave an energetic lead at a time of rapid expansion in the Association's activities and he worked assiduously to improve the relationship between the Association and the many local authorities with which it had to deal. For example, it was largely at his initiative that the word Limited was dropped from the SSHA's title[183] since many local authorities and tenant associations apparently took the word 'to mean that the SSHA was a profit-making commercial body'.[184] It was also at Mr Gray's volition that the cloak of relative anonimity which, as a quasi-government body, the Association had traditionally worn was dropped. In 1967, a public relations department was established to keep the press and public informed about the organisation's activities and to create a house journal for the benefit of staff. In fact *Housing Special* rapidly became a highly professional publication winning successively in 1975, 1976 and 1977 the award of the Association of Industrial Editors.[185]

Another of Mr Gray's ventures was less successful and this concerned the attempt to secure more modern and efficient head office accommodation. The Palmerston Place office complex is little more than a warren of converted tenement houses and whereas it is conveniently located from the point of view of local staff and its modest appearance is not unbecoming, it is certainly not calculated to inspire the highest level of organisational or administrative efficiency or to make any very impressive impact on the visitor. Throughout his term of office, therefore, Mr Gray attempted to procure a move to more up-to-date premises and various locations were considered throughout Edinburgh where a new office block might be erected.[186] The government were not unsympathetic[187] and for a time it appeared as if the move might be made to Livingston New Town[188], but gradually the effort foundered, partly because of lack of enthusiasm on the part of staff and ultimately because of the sheer cost involved. (Interestingly, a move to new purpose-built accommodation was examined again in 1983 but once more the cost was considered to be prohibitive.)

Of the other Council members, perhaps the most formidable was Mrs Ewart and she became deputy chairman in 1969. When, in 1971 she eventually retired after 17 years of continuous service there were many tributes, not least from the chairman, who spoke of 'his regret at losing her wealth of experience' and of the 'great help to him' which she had been in sharing the burden of senior office. David Halley also spoke on behalf of the officials and expressed their 'thanks for the encouragement and understanding she had shown over the years'.[189]

From the early 1960s the Association enjoyed a period of sustained continuity in its senior officers. One departure must be mentioned, however, since it concerned the retirement of the redoubtable Miss Jean Pollock, the chief housing manager. When, in 1969, she finally stood down after 25 years of service to the Association, there was much gratitude for the way in which she had developed the housing management section from virtually nothing until it had become 'responsible directly or indirectly for... some 67,000 houses'. The chairman referred to her membership of the Scottish Housing Advisory Committee, to her past presidency of the former Society of Women Housing Managers, and to the recognition which had been accorded to her work when she was awarded the MBE in 1962. 'Miss Pollock was known throughout the length and breadth of Scotland, not only in official circles but indeed by very many tenants, and she had proved herself a valuable and faithful officer of the Association.'[190]

The expressions of goodwill were echoed on all sides and it should be recorded that she is remembered with awe and affection by many of the longer serving members of staff who are still with the Association. One such recounted to the author Miss Pollock's delightful habit of 'never, but never, allowing anyone from the chairman to the office clerk to have the last word,' and there is no doubt that the tradition of humane, caring and efficient standards of housing management to which the Association adheres is in great part Miss Pollock's legacy. But perhaps the best tribute to her service was accorded a few days before her retirement when Council considered SDD Circular No 11, dated 6th February 1969, entitled *Housing Management in Scotland*. Having examined a report on the standards and guidelines set out in the Circular, Council noted 'that so far as the Association's housing management organisation was concerned it already met the recommendations'.[191] Miss Pollock had set the standard.

Jean Pollock.

Interestingly two of her original three assistants, Mrs J. Aldington and Mrs E. Macdonald, continued to serve as area housing managers but they have since retired. The new chief housing manager, Len Ferguson, came to the Association from East Kilbride Development Corporation, but even he represented something of a continuation of Miss Pollock's influence since much of his early training had been with the SSHA.

In the 1970s the orientation of the economic expansion programme began gradually to swing towards the north-east in support of the growing North Sea oil and gas industries. Initially the Houses for Industry Committee suggested a programme of 14,000 houses in that connection to be built between 1973 and 1977,[192] but the new Conservative Government was more cautious, and although the future programme was not substantially cut-back, it did proceed on more modest lines. There is on file a record of one most interesting meeting where Council discussed the programme point by point with the Under-Secretary of State for Development, George Younger, and it gives an indication of how carefully government were attempting to measure the likely growth of demand all over Scotland. At that meeting, for example, it was acknowledged that the volume of agency work for the local authorities was bound to diminish sharply and careful consideration was given to the likely requirement for Stonehouse New Town which it was thought might largely be built by the Association.[193] Eventually, in 1974, the Houses for Industry Committee was abolished[194] and a few months later Council noted the changing direction of Scottish economic planning represented by the establishment of the Scottish Development Agency.[195]

In fact, building large numbers of houses in the north-east of

Scotland as the oil industry expanded was no straighforward matter. In December 1973, the chairman drew the Minister's attention 'to the intolerable level of land prices which he thought were directly related to the planning situation brought about by the planning authorities not earmarking sufficient areas for housing development'. He specifically exampled 'the high price being asked for land at Westhill, Skene, to which also was attached onerous conditions regarding roads, etc'. The Minister responded that 'the need of North Sea oil developments was such that he would be prepared to agree to the high acquisition cost.'[196] Indeed, at that time, such was the pressure on the Association to provide houses in the face of chronically high land prices that, for the first time, it resorted to buying up some private developments. 'The chairman, referring to building in Easter Ross, stated that the Association had approached private builders with a view to purchasing some of their houses' and explained that the purchase of 75 of these had been approved. 'The Minister ... confirmed that the Department would be willing to issue any necessary authorisation.'[197] As a result, between 1974 and 1979 some 676 houses, typically in the north-east, were acquired in this manner, although, of course, far more houses were built under normal arrangements.

Not all economic expansion activity of the 1970s was related to oil or gas and, for example, one development which is worthy of mention was at Tweedbank, between Galashiels and Melrose. The area was acknowledged as one of relative decline and the object here was to reverse the drift of the population away from the Borders. The plans for Tweedbank, in fact, took almost a decade to mature, but work eventually began in 1973 as a joint venture between the SSHA, Roxburgh County Council, the Scottish Industrial Estates Corporation (now part of the SDA) and some private developers.

[198] The ten-year delay probably brought architectural benefits to Tweedbank, since its aims and achievements are clearly of a higher quality than some earlier housing developments. The setting is determinedly rural, within a bend on the River Tweed, and is dominated by a park, playing fields and by Gun Knowe Loch which was created with the aid of MSC labour and which has become the home of much birdlife. Three main groups of housing are separated by the parkland, the houses themselves generally being

harled with pitched roofs of a traditional type. The design avoids ... the challenge of large scale classical townscape found in many of our eighteenth and nineteenth century towns. The attempt was to relate instead to some of the qualities of scale, space and variety in the picturesque tradition of informal village growth over a long period. The result is, in fact, a large, idealised, car-based village consistent with its location just a few miles from Darnick Tower, Melrose Abbey and Abbotsford, carefully disguising the fact that it is yet another development constructed in no-fines concrete, and that the picturesque layout was controlled by the requirements of that method of construction.

By the 1970s no-fines had become a sophisticated building method, ideally suited to operations on a greenfield site. It was, therefore, not altogether surprising that, in 1976, phase 1 of Tweedbank received yet another Saltire Society Award. On the same day that this news reached Council it was learned that the North Barr (phase 2) development at Erskine had been similarly honoured.[199]

Erskine was in fact, an Overspill project which became to some extent blended with the needs of economic expansion.

Part of the overspill development at Tweedbank.

The original plan envisaged a new township of 30,000 people which would be constructed on the south shore of the Clyde and to the north of Paisley. The Association relished the prospect of being at the heart of a venture of this scale since, as has been mentioned, from the late 1940s whenever a New Town was under consideration, it had pleaded with successive governments to be designated as a Development Corporation so that it might take on the task of creating the required town. Invariably its overtures in this respect had been rejected, hence when Erskine was mooted it was seen as the Association's opportunity to show what it could do and, although never formally identified as a New Town, it entered the Association's literature under the euphemistic designation of 'Erskine New Community'.

As things happened, the scale of the town was eventually much more limited, and new building ceased with the termination of the Overspill programme in 1983. However, between 1972 and that year some 3,391 houses were built at Erskine and the detailed breakdown is given in Appendix D. Ironically the specifications provided for the town were very similar to those used by Glasgow District Council in the construction of the equally large peripheral housing estates in Drumchapel, Easterhouse and Castlemilk[200], but there all similarity ends. The Association took infinite trouble – not always successfully – to try to keep the development of community facilities and housing in step[201] and from the earliest days took pains to nurture a genuine sense of community. 'Credit must go to Mrs Jean Hollins, housing manager at Erskine from the start, for the lively, healthy and vandal-free environment.'[202] As early as 1972, when a mere 800 houses had been built, the Secretary of State, after a visit to the town, wrote to express his congratulations for what had already been acheived. He described himself as being 'most impressed'.

Looked at today, Erskine seems in some ways to have been a reversion to the Garden City concept but in a fully modern guise. It demonstrates convincingly how the no-fines technique could be used to build to extremely high standards and, although smaller in scale, it easily withstands comparison to the best of the New Towns. That it is a fine place in which to live is demonstrated by the fact that no less than 663 of the houses have presently been sold to tenants and no doubt others would also have been purchased were the more recent houses not precluded from the advantageous terms of the current legislation.

If Overspill and, even more, economic expansion were the dominant building programmes of the 1960s and 1970s, at the end of the period, they were to some extent replaced by the smaller, but important, Redevelopment Assistance Programme. However, since much of the activity in this connection occurred in the contemporary period, it will be considered in the next chapter.

The years from the mid-1960s were, of course, the period in which successive governments, in their efforts to accelerate the expansion of public services and to stimulate the levels of economic growth which were required to support such government activity, succeeded in unleashing destructive surges of inflation. Inevitably, this made life extremely difficult for those responsible for managing the affairs of the Association and it is important, therefore, to give some account of the experience.

As early as May 1966, Council met with the Minister to determine a new rent policy and it was decided to aim at an average rent of £65 per house to be achieved by progressive increases up to 1970.[203] The procedure then was for the rent increases to be effected after discussions with the local authorities. It will be recalled that at that stage the Association was committed to producing 5,000 new houses per annum by 1970, together with up to 1,000 houses constructed for other authorities.

By September of 1966 the plans were already in disarray

because of the introduction of a Prices and Incomes 'Standstill' and Council gloomily noted that while some increases – at Aberdeen and Lanark County – had become effective, rents elsewhere were now frozen at the old level.[204] In December Council again met with the Minister and it was decided that there must be no immediate attempt to catch up when the Standstill ended, but that the increase to an average rent of £65 should be brought about in two stages, in 1967-68 and 1969-70. Already, however, the need for a greater rent income was being discussed.[205]

Early in 1967, while pleased with the Association's estimated achievement of 4,480 starts for 1967-68 the Minister was urging Council 'if at all possible, to increase the figure to 5,000' and he indicated that rents might have to go up 'to a more realistic figure' in which case there would have to be 'a rent rebate scheme which would withstand all criticism'.[206]

In March and April, building operations were severely disrupted by a strike of electricians objecting to the Prices and Incomes Board's refusal to allow an increase in hourly rates. At the same time, however, the Association gave details of the proposed rent increases and issued a Guide to Tenants in Respect of the Rent Rebate Scheme.[207] By May many protests were flooding in in respect of the proposed rent levels and Council agreed to try to fix rents on an area by area basis in an effort to meet the wishes of the various local authorities.[208]

Early in 1968 Council noted that building operations had been excluded from the restrictions which had been placed on local authority capital expenditure as a result of the devaluation of the currency.[209] However in the following month a letter from the SDD informed them that henceforth all bodies borrowing from the Consolidated Fund would be obliged to repay loans in six-monthly instead of annual instalments. This move was occasioned by sharply increasing rates of inflation and was accepted with reluctance in view of the pressure which it imposed on the Association's cash flow position.[210]

By October of that year the Minister was expressing his concern at the mounting scale of the Association's deficit. He had discussed the proposed new rents with the Secretary of State 'and while they had misgivings as to the size of the increase, they realised that if the deficit was to be contained increased rents were necessary and the proposals were broadly acceptable'. The chairman gave assurances that everything was being done to control the Association's finances. But he pointed out that whereas the originally planned average annual rent at that stage was £55, already 'the Association had reached an average of £58 per annum and yet the deficit was greater than ever.' He suggested that there were three ways to contain the problem, namely, stop new building, increase rents substantially, or scrap the rehabilitation programme.[211]

None of these alternatives were accepted entirely, but the Minister later urged the Association to push its rents up to a maximum increase of 10s per week and to consider the possibility of annual rent increases in future. Meanwhile the planned level of revenue expenditure should be reduced immediately.[212]

By February 1969, Council noted that a ceiling deficit of £1,865,000 had been introduced for the year 1969-70. They protested that the figure should be increased because of (a) the rental loss as a result of the Prices and Incomes Policy, (b) increased interest charges resulting from higher borrowing rates, (c) the increasing cost of remedial works, and (d) the additional cost of rent rebates.[213]

In June of that year the SDD ordered that all 'non-essential repairs' be postponed in an attempt to contain the deficit and a few months later at a meeting with the chairman the Minister indicated that the 5,000 new houses per annum was no longer a target, but a limit and that starts to 1,227 houses should be deferred for the time being. Council did not like this at all and requested a meeting with all the Ministers concerned.[214]

Early in 1970 the Department agreed that some major improvement work could be capitalised to relieve the pressure on the revenue account, but cautioned that there should be no increase in expenditure without prior consultation.[215] In July fresh proposals for rent increases were immediately accepted by the new government and the Minister hoped that annual adjustments in rent would bring under control and, indeed, reduce the deficit. He 'congratulated the Council on the steps which had been taken to deal with the deficit problem and stated that this had been appreciated by the government.'[216]

In January 1971 Council considered a draft memorandum on the subject of the 'Reform of Housing Finance' and noted that they were to be awarded a 'Rising Costs Subsidy' of £6 per house per annum for five years, but considered that 'this was insufficient in amount and duration'.[217] The following month an average rent increase of £26 per year was agreed and it was noted that the government intended to introduce a standard rent rebate scheme.[218] Meanwhile, the building programme had also been curbed and it was realised in July of that year that by 1973 building would fall below 2,000 new starts per year.[219]

By late 1971, when the new rent increases were being implemented, the chorus of protest from local authorities and tenants rose to a crescendo.[220] Various delegations were received. For example, on 22nd September, Council met with the Steering Committee of Local Authorities to discuss the matter. Bailie Bauld of Clydebank said that

[221] The Association had not taken into consideration all the factors involved at present including unemployment, the effect on the cost of living of increased rents, revaluation and increased rates and the human factor. He continued that the Chancellor of the Exchequer had asked for prices to be kept down to increases of only four to five per cent and the Association should pay heed to this. He felt that increased rents would be imposing further hardship and suggested that if the Association could not see fit to abandon the increase in rents they should at least be postponed.

The chairman pointed out that Scottish rents compared very favourably with rents elsewhere and that it was essential to make the increases. Mrs Ewart indicated 'that there was no organisation that acted with more compassion towards tenants than the Association and emphasised that where cases of low income tenants became known to the Association ... the cases were investigated carefully to see whether more help could be obtained.'[222] Nevertheless the rent increases went forward without delay.[223]

In January 1972, Council noted that about 10,000 tenants would be affected by the miners' strike and learned of the arrangements which were in hand for dealing with any cases of particular hardship.[224]

By December of that year, the Heath Government's economic policies were also floundering and Council's attention was drawn to the terms of the 'Counter-Inflation (Rents) (Scotland) Order, 1972.' Once again government efforts at the legislative control of inflation had caught the Association in the middle of a rent increase. On this occasion it was learned that whereas the rents of approximately 26,000 houses had been raised, the new charges for the remaining 52,000 houses could not be applied for at least the five months of the Standstill and that the cost of this was bound to be of the order of £350,000.[225] The later increases in fact became effective from 28th April 1973.[226]

As the phase advanced the orders, controls and regulations became more and more reminiscent of the war years or the immediate post-war period, and they were by no means the only similarity. In June 1973, the chairman spoke of the severe scarcity of labour and materials. 'The building manager stated that in his long experience he had not encountered a situation where there was such a severe shortage of certain materials, some of which could in time not be available at all. The main effect of the materials and manpower shortage, coupled with an inflationary period, had resulted in delays in building starts and if the starts were delayed this in turn would bring increased costs as prices and wages escalated.'[227]

By the winter of 1973, the government was moving into its terminal phase with the oil crisis and an impending miners' strike. Council noted the arrangements which the senior officers had made to cope with petrol rationing and that all possible economies would be made by cutting out unnecessary travel.[228] A few weeks later Council also learned of the steps which had been taken concerning the three-day working week introduced to cope with the energy crisis.[229]

In April 1974 the SDD informed the Association that rents were to be held at present levels until the end of the year[230] and, a few weeks later, that the limit on its total expenditure would be increased from £230m to £290m.[231] In November, rents were again frozen until the following May[232] and the year ended with Council complaining to the Minister about 'the effect of inflation on house-building costs' and pleading for more flexible borrowing powers.[233]

January 1975 saw a new programme being initiated for an additional 1,000 houses per year[234] and Council were delighted to learn that much of the effort would once more be in Glasgow. The chairman's reaction was 'that the Association was suffering from inflation as were other builders, but that (its) job was to discharge its programme and not hold back.'[235] However, a month later he was sharing 'the obvious anxiety of all members of Council in regard to the escalation of the costs of building and financing housing.'[236]

By June two circulars *Housing Needs and Resources* and *New House Building – Cost Control Procedures and Indicative Costs* were under consideration and an instruction was noted that rent increases should not exceed £26 per annum.[237] Later in the year, the lack of a significant building programme after 1978 was discussed with the Minister and he explained that 'in a year or two there might require to be a change in emphasis from new house building either for national economic reasons or in the interests ...of modernisation.'[238] In January 1976, the maximum average rent increase of £26 had become the requirement for each of the next two years[239] and a few weeks later it was learned that the Association's borrowing powers were being extended to finance the Redevelopment Assistance Programme of an additional 2,700 houses.[240] However, by the end of the year the Minister was referring to 'the changing shape and pace of the Scottish housing programme and emphasised the need for all concerned to adjust to the changing circumstances and the expected drop in public sector new housing in the coming year.'[241]

In July 1977 it was noted that building department's activities were swinging sharply from new build to modernisation, but that there was 'deep concern at the lack of work'.[242] A few months later the chairman assured the Minister that 'following a comprehensive review of staffing levels a reduction of about seven per cent in the Association's establishment would be attained by the end of the present financial year.'[243] In November, Council considered the Green Paper *Scottish Housing – A Consultative Document* and noted 'the government's intention to consider granting greater discretion to housing authorities in respect of standards to be achieved in new housing. It was also reported that the concern previously expressed by Council in regard to a lowering of standards of new housing had been submitted to the Secretary of State.'[244]

Even more worrying, however, was the way in which the Association's financial position – mirroring that of the national economy – seemed to be skidding out of control. In October the chairman had drawn the Minister's attention to the fact that the Association's borrowing requirements had risen by 250 per cent in the past four years and might be expected to double again over the next two years.[245] Capital expenditure at that time was almost exclusively funded by borrowing from the National Loans Fund at fixed rates of interest and, of course, as interest rates increased in the face of inflation so the cost of new borrowing became almost insupportable and produced an irresistible pressure for higher rents. In his Draft Revenue Estimate of October 1978, the director of finance summed the position up as follows. After drawing attention to the prevailing interest rates of 13 per cent on loans payable by annual instalments over sixty years he reported that –

[246] The total loan charges which amounted to £16½m just three years ago in 1975-76 are almost double that figure now at £31.7m in 1978-79, and are forecast to double again to £65½m by 1983-84, assuming that the present high interest rates continue ... In terms of cost per house loan charges were £240 in 1976-77 and are forecast to be £620 in 1983-84. As the former chairman stated in the recently published Annual Report 'it is inevitable that the Association's call on revenue support from the Treasury, which is already at an historically high level, will continue to increase at a pace which can only give cause for alarm.' The Exchequer subsidies which amounted to £17m in 1976-77 are expected to be £26.6m this year and to be £59.9m by 1983-84 ...

The large programme of work in the next few years to be financed from borrowing at high interest rates, the volume of modernisation work to be financed from revenue, and continued inflation in repair, management and other running costs will not only lead to an increase in Exchequer subsidies but will 'decree a pattern of substantial rent increases annually for the foreseeable future'.

The winter of 1978-79 represented the nadir of the phase with industrial disputes (during the road haulage drivers' dispute the Building Department manager reported that he had no copper supplies left, but that other stocks should last for a month[247]) and severe weather (5,400 cases of burst pipes as a result of frost were reported and these cost the Association £235,000 in repairs[248]) added to the general gloom and uncertainty over the Association's financial plight and, in particular, over the planned reduction in staffing levels. It was generally a miserable period and the prevailing mood of uncertainty is ironically captured by the words of the new chairman, William L. Taylor, who, in attempting to encourage everyone in his inaugural comments to Council, stated 'that he had no intention of presiding over the dissolution of the Association.[249]

Culling selectively over the records to produce the narrative set down in the last few pages is obviously extremely unfair since it does little to illustrate the skilled and dedicated management which operated throughout many of the years in question. Moreover, one ought always to bear in mind the many significant achievements of these years. However, the fact is that the management of the national economy throughout the phase, and within which context the Association had to function, resembled nothing so much as the careering downhill momentum of a drunk man, rushing forward from time to time, but always colliding sickeningly into the next inevitable lamp post and progressively losing control over his general faculties and his sense of direction.

Perhaps no one was really to blame. Even the politicians in government over these years were simply striving to find the resources claimed by the influential pressure groups which swelled the chorus of demand for public money for this, or that interest. In so doing, were they not merely responding to the perceived requirements of the public at large? Small wonder that the printing presses were kept busy producing more currency of ever diminishing value. But it was no way to run a country!

CHAPTER SIX

The Contemporary Period

Before considering more recent events it is worth taking a brief look back at the 1970s to note some of the changes of personnel which occurred and to point out a few of the more interesting landmarks.

Following the change of government in 1970 William Gray had remained in office as chairman, but in the summer of 1972 he decided not to seek renomination and in September of that year Council wrote to congratulate him on his appointment as Lord Provost of Glasgow. He was succeeded as chairman by Gordon Muir of Cardross.[1]

Gordon Muir proved to be a hard working, knowledgeable and extremely popular chairman of modest ways, but with a great enthusiasm for the interests of the Association. One of his early actions was to sell the chairman's Daimler limousine and to replace it with a Ford and this was typical of his unpretentious outlook. It was perhaps his misfortune to be in charge at a particularly difficult period, but there is no doubting the respect and fondness with which he is still remembered. In July 1978 he was appointed chairman of the Scottish Housing Advisory Committee and the Scottish Home Ownership Forum[2] and when he attended his last meeting of Council in September of that year the deputy chairman said of him 'that the Council had been singularly fortunate to have had his wise guidance over a period of six years. They had all greatly appreciated the way in which he had presided over their meetings and they acknowledged the very great contribution he had made to the

Association.'[3] There was genuine grief throughout the SSHA when news came of Gordon Muir's untimely and tragic death in a gliding accident in September 1981.

1975 was a key year in terms of changes of senior officers, for in that year both the general manager, Mr L.W.S. Cross, and the secretary and solicitor, David Halley, retired. Mr Cross had been in office for ten years and he departed with many well-deserved tributes[4] but, inevitably, the secretary's retirement after thirty years was something of an earthquake. 'It was unanimously agreed to record the Council's appreciation of the long and distinguished service by Mr Halley over these many years and also to record the Council's sincere appreciation of the high quality of advice always available and their thanks for his devoted and loyal service.'[5] He has been described to the author as 'an old-fashioned public servant who set himself and those around him the highest possible standards of professional conduct'. Indeed, it says much for the Association that it could command such loyalty from men of his calibre.

Mr A.R. Allan was promoted to become secretary and solicitor for a short time, but when he retired in 1978, he was succeeded by Mr J.B. Fleming, another outstanding official who, from his many years at the Scottish Office, was fully familiar with the activities of the Association.[6] He too was 'of the old school' of civil servants, and it would be difficult to imagine a better example of the conscientious, competent administrator which he personified.

Mr Cross's successor as general manager was Major-General Ronald M. Somerville. Naturally, coming from a distinguished Army background, he had little experience of the type of activity in which the Association was involved: however, given the troubled waters which now had to be navigated, it may be said of him that he was the right man in the right place at the right time. His affable, friendly manner gave him the ability to establish a good rapport with tenants – with whom he was enormously popular – and with trade union representatives. It was thanks largely to the latter ability and to his sensitive handling of the matter that the staff reductions which occurred from 1978 to 1980 were effected without compulsory redundancy and with the minimum of dispute.

Nevertheless, his jovial presence and good manners fooled none of his close colleagues for, as befitted his former professional calling, he was an extremely tough and demanding master who suffered few mistakes to pass lightly. After forty years of more or less continuous growth it is not surprising that, on the one hand, the Association looked forward to the dramatic slow-down in new building with some trepidation, and on the other, was perhaps suffering from some hardening of its bureaucratic arteries. In these circumstances some discomfort was not only inevitable, in some ways, it was desirable, and with 'The General' around no one could afford to be too comfortable.

The other most notable change was the retirement in 1979 of Harold Buteux as chief technical officer. His career with the Association almost spanned the period set out in the preceding chapter and it will be understood therefore, that he was ultimately responsible for the building activities at a time when high density schemes were, in many cases, virtually an absolute requirement, and when the no-fines technique became mature, adaptable and sophisticated. That the Association emerged from the period with a reputation for high building standards in respect of every type of dwelling is very largely to the credit of Mr Buteux. His successor, Mr John Fullarton, came to the Association from the Scottish Development Department.

1977, of course, witnessed the celebration of the Association's fortieth anniversary and the occasion was marked on 8th November by a lunch attended by HRH the Duke of Gloucester.[7] Six months later the Association's one hundred thousandth house was opened at Erskine in a ceremony performed by the Earl of Dundee.[8]

Another notable landmark of these years concerns the historic border town of Jedburgh. Back in December 1971 the Town Council asked the Association to act as their agents in the redevelopment of the ancient Castlegate area[9] and once the necessary permission had been obtained the task was accepted with alacrity. Within the planned redevelopment was Prince Charlie's House,
[10] a fine 17th century crow-stepped townhouse in Jedburgh. The house was at the centre of the north-east front of Castlegate, and the SSHA's area included Cornelius, Under Nagshead, Blackhills and Veitch's Closes and Paradise Vale. The resulting restoration created an atmosphere in Jedburgh not unlike White Horse Close, Canongate, in

Contrasting scenes of old and new Jedburgh.

Edinburgh, and included nine shops, offices, workshop and 22 dwellings.

By the mid-1970s awards and commendations for Association projects had become almost a regular occurrence, but there was particular pleasure first, in 1976, when under the Royal Institute of Chartered Surveyors/Times Conservation Awards Scheme the Association was commended for the restoration of Prince Charlie's House[11]; and later, in 1979, the SSHA's redevelopment of the area attracted not only Saltire Society and Civic Trust awards[12], but international recognition in the form of the coveted Europa Nostra Medal, the only such honour accorded to a project within the UK in that year.[13] It was a vivid demonstration of the Association's ability to produce redevelopment and conservation work of the finest quality.

From the point of view of the new government elected in 1979 the main task which it had to achieve was to bring public expenditure under control in order to curb inflation. This objective could not, of course, be met overnight, particularly since wage and salary negotiators had become accustomed to allowing for high rates of inflation and it would take time to restore confidence and to break into the vicious circle of spiralling expectations. However, the new Scottish Office Minister responsible for housing, Malcolm Rifkind, lost no time in meeting with the chairman together with representatives of the Housing Corporation and explained to them that housing expenditure would have to take its full share of the cuts which would be necessary to meet the targets for reducing public expenditure. As far as the Association was concerned, it was working to a planned capital expenditure for 1979-80 of £46m and it was instructed to reduce this immediately to £40m and to assume a cash limit not greater than that level for the foreseeable future.[14]

This was, indeed, strong medicine, and proved to be almost impossible in the short term, but the government's resolve was made clear the following March when the future lines of policy on capital expenditure were set out. The Association was given a cash limit of £151m spread over the following four years as shown below.[15]

1980-81	1981-82	1982-83	1983-84
£42m	£41m	£36m	£32m

Naturally there was initial depression at this news and it was obvious that there was to be no return to the scale of new building of the past, particularly since the major modernisation programme of older houses would be bound to take an increasing share of any available resources. Moreover the policy of reducing the establishment of the Building department – begun under the previous government – was inevitably confirmed, while new legislation was in train which would compel the department to operate within a framework of competitive tenders for any substantial contract and to produce a return of at least five per cent on capital employed.[16]

In the case of the revenue account, the estimate for 1980-81 was for a total of £63.8m but the prevailing ratio of subsidy to rent in the proportion 53:47 could obviously not continue, since rent increases had not kept pace with inflation and, in real terms, had not increased at all in the previous five years.[17] From June 1980 rents rose by an average of £1.40 per week and it was certain that further increases of that magnitude would follow in future years as the proportion of revenue subsidy diminished.[18]

At first, despite all the rejigging and postponing of capital projects it was almost impossible to come within the government's targets. It was not easy. After all, the capital allocation for 1980-81 represented a 20 per cent reduction and, at face value, the limits over the next three years promised a contraction of a further 25 per cent.[19] Indeed, the truth is that the Association failed to meet its objectives, overspending by £3.3m in 1979-80[20] and, theoretically, by no less than £9.1m in 1980-81[21], but, painful though the process was, both in human terms and in terms of deferred or abandoned projects, gradually effective financial control was re-established. Gradually the doubtful habits of a generation gave way and the sense of the inevitability of inflation diminished, so that, eventually, a new and perhaps more stable equilibrium was attained. At the same time confidence, not euphoria, steadily returned as it was realised that planning could now proceed on a firmer and more certain basis. In addition, by 1982-83 it was clear that capital projects, of various kinds, still had a worthwhile place in the Association's future.

The factor which now began to relieve the pressure on the capital programme was the sale of houses to tenants. This was a contentious policy about which many of the Association's staff were less than enthusiastic, but which, as a central government organ, the Association had no option but to implement with its customary professionalism.

As we have seen, as far back as 1942, the Association had urged on the Secretary of State the necessity of taking·steps to increase the level of home ownership among ordinary Scots, but in the post-war era these intentions were forgotten as renting from the public authorities became the dominant form of house provision in Scotland.

From time to time there were some modest attempts made to stimulate home ownership by selling houses to tenants as, for example, in 1961 when Inverness Town Council invited the Association to join with it in a scheme of that kind within the town.[22] Indeed, in the following year the Association agreed to allow tenants to buy a few houses which had been built for managerial staff in various parts of the country.[23] However, these were mere gestures and generally the Association considered itself to be in the business purely of providing houses for rent.

The Conservative Government 1970-74 made the first significant moves towards a sales policy by giving authorities permission to introduce sales schemes. At first the Association was reluctant to be involved[24], but, as ever, it was bound to follow government policy and, over the next few years, and after several surveys of tenants and experiments, evolved a limited sales programme.[25] Initially, several pilot schemes were introduced and it is interesting to note that one of the first of these was at the old Sighthill experimental estate in Edinburgh where several members of Association staff applied to buy their houses. Essentially the policy at that time was to try to encourage sales within suitable selected areas, but to decline to sell houses such as multi-storey flats or maisonettes, where particular management problems might result. Elsewhere, tenants could also buy houses if they applied, but they were given no particular encouragement and had no right to buy outside the specified areas. At that time the terms of sales were either at full market value or with a 20 per cent discount if a five year pre-emption clause was involved, and at all times the agreed price had to be sufficient to offset the outstanding debt on the house. Inevitably the latter condition meant that the newer houses in particular were bound to be as expensive as an equivalent house purchased from the private sector.[26]

In fact there was a fair degree of interest from tenants[27], but with the demise of the Heath Government the momentum quickly petered out, particularly since the Association policy was not to sell houses in areas where the local authority were not in sympathy with the idea. 204 houses were sold in 1973 and 161 in the following year, but by 1975 the number of sales had dropped to a mere 6.[28]

Nevertheless, the case for a sales policy did not disappear so easily. In 1977 Professor Cullingworth and his colleagues returned to the subject in the government Green Paper *Scottish Housing*. They pointed out that the supply of houses for sale in Scotland was unequal to the potential demand and with tenure dividing 54 per cent to 33 per cent between public rented accommodation and owner occupation, the distribution in Scotland was markedly out of step not only with England and Wales, but with the rest of Western Europe[29] and failed to match the growing aspirations of a significant portion of the population. Their argument was that 'if access to home ownership is to be widened then other sources of supply are required from the existing stock of other tenures'. They emphasised that 'the public sector ... contains a large pool of second-hand houses of varying ages from inter-war to modern in a variety of types of environment. Their market values would accordingly vary widely but a good many would be valued at a price sufficiently below the price of new housing to bring home ownership within reach of many people who cannot afford it at present.' The conclusion, therefore, was that the sale of some public sector housing seemed a 'reasonable instrument of a sensitive and varied local housing strategy, directed at making better use of the existing housing stock to provide the kind of housing which people want.'[30]

Given the hostility of many local councillors towards the sale of council houses, it is not surprising that the government found it difficult to support a sales policy and the recommendations in the Green Paper were deliberately vague in this respect. However, Cullingworth himself developed the case in his *Essays on Housing Policy*, published in 1979. He again pointed out that the problem in Scotland was the inability to obtain a 'filtering' process into home ownership because of the small size of the private stock and, particularly, because of the lack of houses which could be afforded by relatively low income families. 'What is needed is an increase in the supply of cheap, satisfactory houses for owner-occupation. One way of achieving this is by the sale of older public authority houses'.[31] Discussing the Scottish position in particular he stressed that there was a chronic gap between 'nasty old housing and good (but expensive) new housing' confronting the potential buyer of modest means and that this in fact forced most to become public sector tenants.

[32] In short, housing choices are distorted by supply. If households are to be given the real opportunity to choose the tenure they prefer, then considerable adjustments are needed in the pattern of real alternatives available to them. This cannot be achieved simply by new building: this is inevitably relatively expensive and, in any case, can only make a small marginal contribution. There is thus a strong case for infusing the supply with good quality, older and cheaper housing: in short, the sale of public sector houses. There is no other way in which the 'missing rung' of the ladder can be provided.

Cullingworth clearly favoured a selective sales policy, biased according to local requirements and concentrating on older houses. The incoming government, however, had no such inhibitions and moved swiftly to implement the seminal Tenants Rights' (Scotland) Act of 1980 which gave public sector tenants an enhanced range of rights including greater security of tenure and the legal right to purchase their houses with, except in the case of houses built after 15th May 1975, substantial discounts related to the tenant's length of occupation.

In fact, with a little prodding from the SDD, the Association had not waited for the Act to become law, but had, in June 1979, introduced its own voluntary scheme, which was a little more restrictive than the government scheme in that it again attempted to exclude several types of dwellings.[33] Some local authorities made a half-hearted attempt to persuade the Association not to implement its scheme in their areas[34], but in the event there was little resistance since it rapidly became clear that many tenants were eager to buy. For example, by September 1980, a month before the Act became law, the chief housing manager reported to Council that approximately 4,500 applications to purchase had been lodged and that missives had been concluded for no less than 946 houses.[35]

At first the problem was lack of the staff resources to operate the scheme, but gradually the process steadied down and a skilled team was established to advise tenants on both the advantages and risks of house purchase. The outcome is as indicated in Table 1 on page 241.

Naturally the sales process has been subject to the most careful monitoring and some of the most recent information on the subject is included in Appendix K. However, in 1984 the ressearch and development section of the Housing Management Directorate produced an extensive summary of research findings which considered, among other things, the various reasons given by tenants for purchase and the age and employment profiles of the individuals concerned. A few of the conclusions are indicated in Tables 2, 3 and 4 on page 241.

It is not the function of the present discussion to argue the case for or against house sales and beyond remarking that the policy seems to be filling precisely the 'missing rung of the ladder' identified by Cullingworth, readers are left to form their own judgements.

However, from the point of view of the management of the Association the matter of immediate significance is that demand from tenants, while varying with the economic and political climate, has proved to be substantial and 14.2 per cent of the stock has now been sold. In the short term this has meant a substantial inflow of capital to the Association each year and this has been particularly true since the building societies and other financial institutions became alert to the potential business and took over the task of supplying almost all of the mortgages. At first it appeared that the government were unprepared for success on this scale, because, of course, the inflow of new funds more than offset the planned reduction in borrowing; and in 1984 the Department intervened to transfer some £6m into home improvement grants and, initially, imposed an absolute bar on any carry forward of unspent monies from one year to another. This latter restriction was particularly irksome, since it was naturally difficult to predict in advance the exact level of sales in any given year and this made accurate planning of spending programmes somewhat difficult. How-

Malcolm Rifkind and Association chairman, Derek Mason, discuss house sales.

ever, in 1985 some marginal relaxation in this ruling was permitted and the planning task is now, therefore, rather more straightforward. Thankfully, what the Scottish Office did not do was to impose the sort of blanket ban on the use of capital derived from sales which has been applied to English local authorities, and this has meant that the Association's capital programme has remained at a thoroughly useful level and, in the specific case of the Association (as distinct from local authorities), that the money has been fully utilised to the benefit of housing.

What then has the Association's capital programme been over these recent years? Roughly one-third of the effort has gone into new building, while the remaining two-thirds has concentrated on either the comprehensive modernisation of the older houses or on general stock improvements.

As far as new building is concerned a few of the houses have been provided in the latter stages of the Overspill and Economic Expansion programmes, but the dominant thrust from 1978 to the present has gone into Redevelopment Assistance and it is appropriate now to consider this phase with more care.

By the mid-1970s it was becoming clear that the policy of building large estates on green-field sites could not continue for long and that, in any case, much of the contemporary housing problem was connected with the dereliction which now existed within older areas of towns and cities. If life was to be breathed back into these communities then the quality of life on offer to citizens simply had to be enhanced.

At first the government was perhaps uncertain how best to proceed and, when in 1975, a programme of about 1,000 houses per year 'to replace losses by local authorities due to the demolition or conversion of sub-standard houses' was discussed, the approach had something of the flavour of the old slum clearance policies.[37] This impression was reinforced within a few months when the Association recorded a total programme of 2,600 houses 'in aid of slum clearance.'[38]

However, with the Scottish Development Agency now in existence and with the new Regional and District structure of local government in operation, at long last Tom Johnston's vision of a regional approach to the planning and management of the economic infra-structure of Scotland was becoming a reality, and in 1976 attention now turned to the identification of

Table 1 *Sales to Sitting Tenants 1979-80 to 1986-87*[36]

Year	Houses Sold	Receipts (£million cash)
1979-80	80	0.2
1980-81	1892	15.6
1981-82	1973	16.8
1982-83	1884	19.9
1983-84	3093	30.1
1984-85	3213	35.0
1985-86	2218	24.8
1986-87 (provisional)	1943	22.6

Table 2. *Reasons for House Purchase*

	Purchasers (per cent)
Discount attractive	93.5
Independence of home ownership	85.0
Increasing public sector rents	85.0
Security of home ownership	77.6
Improvements to own specification	74.8
Protection against inflation	66.4
Private housing expensive	65.4
Legacy	60.1
Future profitability	43.0
Previously improved house at own expense	42.1

Table 3. *Occupational Status of Head of Household*

	Prof/ Managerial	Inter- mediate	Skilled	Semi- Skilled	Un- Skilled	Retired	House- Wife	N/A
Purchasers	10.0	23.3	52.2	7.8	2.2	2.2	–	2.2
Non-appliers	5.4	12.0	45.5	16.5	3.3	6.6	1.7	7.9
All tenants	6.5	15.4	48.1	13.6	2.7	5.2	1.2	6.5

Table 4. *Age of Head of Household*

	Under 30	30-39	40-49	50-59	60-69	70+	N/A
Purchasers	3.3	30.0	36.7	16.7	7.8	1.1	4.4
Non-appliers	12.4	21.9	16.5	18.2	20.7	8.3	2.0
All tenants	9.4	25.1	22.3	18.4	16.1	6.0	2.7

Source: House Sales Survey 1984.

Kirkland Street.

An aerial view of Leith before
re-development.

Bowling Green Street, Leith.

what were called Housing Action Areas.[39] By February of that year the term Redevelopment Assistance was being attached to the programme, showing that the planning of housing was now being firmly linked within wider plans for the social and economic regeneration typically of some of the older, decayed urban areas.[40] These sites were to be found in various parts of the country and included, for example, the central area of a small town like Arbroath. But, of course, the main task was within the cities – at Dura Street and Peddie Street in Dundee; at Bowling Green Street, Leith; and in Glasgow.

In Glasgow a major part of the Association's effort has been to participate in the sustained assault which has, in the last few years, transformed what is known as the Maryhill Corridor, until recently an area of miserable dereliction. Schemes completed in this area include Glenfarg Street (completed 1985), Kirkland Street (1985), Seamore Street (1981), and Woodside D2/D4 (1984).

Perhaps, however, the most exciting activity has been centred in the east end of Glasgow, a large district which, as recently as eight years ago, contained some of the most wretched housing conditions in the western world. News of this venture first reached Council in June 1976. 'There was considered a previously circulated report containing details of the proposals announced by the Secretary of State for Scotland on 21st May 1976 regarding a combined project by the SDA, the Association, Strathclyde Regional Council and Glasgow District Council for the comprehensive modernisation of a major area of Glasgow comprising Bridgeton, Dalmarnock and Shettleston.'[41] Soon the Housing Corporation was also involved and thus began the so-called GEAR (Glasgow Eastern Area Renewal) project.

At the time, such was the scale of decay and despair, that there were many who doubted that the necessary effort would be forthcoming. In 1978, Ian Adams had this to say of the scheme.[42]

'Physically shocking', 'like going through a bombarded city' and 'dreadful' were some of the comments made by delegates from the European Parliament at the sight of the East End of Glasgow in 1976. ...It is a daunting challenge for the area is suffering from *planning dementia*, a species of planning blight, a condition which is the result of earlier notions of planning which themselves have created more problems than they have solved and thus demand ever greater efforts by planners to solve the problem ... Already people closely involved predict failure for the project for it resembles too closely the 'single-solution' planning philosophy of the past.

The fears of Adams and others at the time were fully justified, but in the event the outcome has been stunningly successful. In fact, the real reason for what is by any standards a major achievement of crucial significance to Glasgow and its people, is the integrated and flexible planning which permitted public and private effort to proceed side by side and in harmony. In the author's opinion it provides a classic example of how the Association should be used; pump-priming by beginning the process of development and enhancement so that conditions are created which invite private involvement.

So far just over £315m of public money has been injected into the venture, as against £184m of private sector expenditure, but the idea of £87m being spent on private house building in inner Glasgow would have been utterly unimaginable just a few years ago.[43] To date the Association itself has spent approximately £43.6m within the area and this breaks down into £24.1m on new housing and £19.5m on the modernisation and renovation of older properties. 1,077 new houses have been built, 20 are in progress and a further 112 are in programme. 1,832 houses have been modernised and 217 rehabilitated, 52 of the latter for sale on the open market.

A detailed breakdown of the Association's operations within GEAR is included in the Appendices and it should, of course, be emphasised that the SSHA is only one of the contributors to the project. However, it has been a venture with which the Association is fully in tune since it, as with the Redevelopment Assistance Programme in general, has permitted the organisation to bring together its long experience in both new building and the preservation and restoration of older environments. Perhaps the high point of GEAR for the Association occurred in 1983 when Her Majesty The Queen came to open a major eighteenth century tenement at 394 Gallowgate which had been rehabilitated and blended into the surrounding new houses.

Inevitably, the scale of new house building is now much smaller than in former years and it is, in some ways, ironic that

The East End of Glasgow showing the conditions which the GEAR project was designed to tackle.

Calton re-development in GEAR.

The re-development of inner Dunbar,
Castle Street.

this has been the period in which the Association has produced some of its finest work when assessed purely in terms of architectural quality and aesthetic appeal. Perhaps this is partly due to the particular demands of urban renewal for, of course, here attention to design detail is at a particular premium; and schemes are very rarely of a scale which would encourage the use of no-fines building, hence most of the recent construction has relied on traditional techniques. Moreover, it is now a common practice for the Association to involve tenants at an early stage in the design process and this has undoubtedly contributed to making the houses not only look attractive, but to be first and foremost eminently suited to their purpose as dwellings. Whatever the reason, developments such as at Woodside or Kirkland Street in Maryhill are quite outstanding when judged by any criteria, while the recently opened schemes in Calton and Dalmarnock Road seem to the author to provide what must surely rank among the finest modern townscapes in the country.

Nor is this excellence confined to Glasgow or to Redevelopment Assistance projects. For instance, associated with the development of the new Torness nuclear power station some building under economic expansion has enabled the Association to participate in the redevelopment of inner Dunbar and some of the recent work in that ancient burgh has been quite remarkable. For example, a scheme of 25 houses and flats at Lamer Street, completed in 1983, won a Saltire Award for good design in the following year, but two similar developments at Castle Street and at Woodbush, are in the view of the author, quite magnificent examples of the art of new building within confined sites in a run-down but historically interesting setting. The use of colour in finishings and the choice and layout of the various types of building have produced a result which, in detail and overall, seems to blend effortlessly into the surrounding old buildings. Equally noteworthy is that this activity within Dunbar seems, again, to have stimulated others to become involved in the revitalisation of the town and there is thus good reason to predict that it will become once more one of the most attractive towns in the east of Scotland. No doubt the Association would love to help the process along still further, but perhaps its job is already almost done and private investment can be relied on to carry things foward. One hopes so, for the town's potential as an interesting and beautiful place in which to live is most exciting.

There are of course other examples elsewhere – such as for instance at Arbroath or at Beith in Ayrshire – which are equally worthy of mention, but space demands an, inevitably, unfair selectivity.

Another aspect of the new building programme which should be noted concerns the provision of specialist housing for the disabled or, more particularly, the elderly. The Association began, at first, to consider this subject early in 1976 under the guidance of an SDD circular on the matter.[44] With an ageing population and with many people being increasingly isolated within the community, the potential demand for appropriate housing, and especially sheltered housing, was very great, but the first reaction was simply to modify existing designs to produce suitable dwellings for elderly tenants and to incorporate a significant proportion of these within new build projects.[45] However, this was an aspect of housing which interested Malcolm Rifkind, and in May 1980 he expressed the view that sheltered housing should form a main element in the Association's building programme.[46] In this he was warmly supported by the new chairman, Derek Mason, who had earlier urged on the Minister his desire to give a new meaning to the word 'Special' in the Association's title. As a result of their joint initiative the provision of purpose-built sheltered housing became a main preoccupation and something of the order of 500 units of this type have been created each year in various parts of the country. Often they have been incorporated within other developments while others have come to form part of what is called the 'special needs' programme. Some of these sheltered housing schemes are most attractive – for example, there is a particularly fine one at Sutherland Street in Edinburgh – and invariably they are greatly appreciated by their tenants. On this subject, it should also be noted that older properties have been modified most successfully to produce excellent sheltered accommodaton.

As was mentioned earlier, approximately two-thirds of the capital programme now goes, not into new building, but into major modernisation and to the improvement of the older houses in stock. Given the age of some of the houses, and bearing in mind the house types and circumstances which

Re-development in Arbroath completed 1985.

Sheltered houses at Sutherland Street, Edinburgh.

coloured building in the immediate post-war era, it is not surprising that, by the late 1970s, many of the houses were in dire need of substantial improvement.

At first the houses which caused most concern were the Weir Steel houses and the cost of modernisation was thought to be so prohibitive that for a time the Association favoured demolition. Indeed, as was indicated previously, most of the Weir 'Paragons' were in such poor condition that there was no alternative to knocking them down. But with the more numerous Weir 'Quality' houses the tenants were adamant in their determination to prevent their communities from being broken up and the SDD were equally certain that, with a few exceptions, money would not be found to replace these houses. Under these circumstances extensive modernisation was the only answer.[47] The Weir houses as rehabilitated became known as the Weir 'Phoenix' houses, but not only was the process expensive, it was also difficult, for once the work started some fairly serious technical problems were uncovered.[48]

But the steel houses, of course, were not the only ones in need of radical attention. Almost all the non-traditional houses of the post-war years were in a similar predicament and the older 'Commissioners' houses were also in the queue. To begin with the new government in 1979 blanched at the sheer cost which was likely to be involved in this work[49] and this is understandable since the requirement of £7.8m for this purpose in 1979-80 was expected to reach £14m by 1982-83. It was not the most encouraging background to a planned attempt to cut government spending.

However, their worst fears were not realised. Not that the need for major expenditure on modernisation disappeared, or failed to grow (indeed, in 1986-87, for example, expenditure of the order of £30m can be expected in bringing older houses up to a modern standard), but what made this programme possible was the income derived from sales. This point cannot be emphasised too strongly. It is not only the former tenants who have purchased their homes who have benefited from the sales policy. The money raised by sales has very largely been ploughed back to the advantage of tenants in the older houses and estates. Admittedly, once improved, some of the houses are then bought by tenants with an eye for a good bargain, but the great majority remain to enhance the lives of those tenants

Modernised Weir Phoenix houses at Blackburn.

who are either reluctant or, more commonly, unable to contemplate purchase. The simple fact is that the sales policy has enabled the necessary major enhancement of the older stock to go forward steadily over the last few years and this has been very much in the interests of tenants in some of the Association's oldest and most unsatisfactory estates.

For example, the experience of the modernisation and regeneration of the Laighstonehall estate on the western outskirts of Hamilton is instructive. To do justice to the rehabilitation of this community in a few lines is quite impossible and anyone who is interested in the subject would be well advised to obtain a copy of the Association's booklet, *Laighstonehall, A Special Housing Story*. However, the estate, which had been built between 1947 and 1954 and which included in its 514 dwellings Weir steel, Orlit and four other house types of the period, was undoubtedly not only one of the Association's worst housing estates, but was one of the worst in the whole of Scotland when measured in terms of social deprivation. An insight into the estate comes with the fact that it was known locally as 'Wine Valley'.

[50] A low density scheme with an average of 9.6 dwellings per acre, 86 per cent of the units were cottages and 14 per cent flats. The majority were designed for large families, – 34 per cent five-apartments and 66 per cent four-apartments. Laighstonehall had the biggest concentration of large families in the Hamilton area. A large proportion of residents were in the younger age groups, 36 per cent being under the age of 15. There was also a higher than average percentage in the 15-25 age group.

An Association report on the social problem identified the main problem in Laighstonehall as being the existence of a concentration of disadvantaged families with the associated problems of poverty, unemployment, high dependence on social work support and low levels of educational achievement. The problems were said to be more acute among the larger families concentrated in the larger houses which formed distinct geographical groupings.

By the early 1970s, Laighstonehall had gained the reputation of being one of the country's worst housing areas. Housing conditions and the general environment

were poor. Open areas had become dumping grounds for discarded goods. Vandalism was rife and crime rates high. There were problems with 'gangs' and fighting in the streets. Graffiti-daubed walls added to the general unsightliness of the area.

Not surprisingly, houses had become difficult to let. At one stage, as many as ninety houses were standing empty and boarded-up. Rent arrears were at a high level. No-one wanted to move into Laighstonehall. The area had become heavily stigmatised. The Wine Valley tag originated from the daubing of walls with this name in the Westwood Crescent/Buchanan Crescent area. It appeared in newspaper headlines and from then on the name stuck...

By contrast, the adjacent SSHA scheme of Little Earnock – built originally for Glasgow Overspill – enjoyed high standards of housing, amenity and environment. Clearly, something had to be done about Laighstonehall. Though there was a big demand for the Association's limited resources elsewhere, Laighstonehall had to be accorded a high priority.

Since the scheme had been built it had been factored by the former Hamilton Town Council which had also been responsible for the lettings policy, and the beginning of recovery for the community occurred when the then chairman, Gordon Muir, visited the estate. Horrified by what he had seen, he insisted that it be brought under direct Association management, and this was done in April 1976.

No one could wave a magic wand over the scheme. It would take years to deal with the buildings. But meanwhile the infinitely more complex task was to breathe self-confidence back into the community and to get the inhabitants to participate positively in the effort. A site-based project manager, Patrick O'Hagan, was appointed; his background was in community development rather than housing. Around him was assembled a project team including representatives from housing management, architecture, administration, and a clerk of works and supported by such other professional back-up as was required from day to day. The remit was to carry out the physical and social regeneration of Laighstonehall speedily and in consultation with tenants.

Of course many others had to be involved including the local Social Work Department, the DHSS, the Police Community Involvement Unit, the local tenants' association and other agencies working in the area. The Association made two old houses available as a community centre and this provided a focal point from which to co-ordinate the various interests and activities. Gradually, and overcoming considerable initial hostility and distrust, the tenants began to participate and a Hamilton district councillor, David Peutherer, played a particularly active role in the establishment of a Laighstonehall Steering Committee to get local officialdom and the residents working together.

So far, so good! But for all these efforts to bear fruit the essential requirement had to be the restoration of the physical fabric of the community. In the first instance 106 of the Weir houses had been condemned and demolition of these began in 1977. They were to be partially replaced by new houses built in two phases, while the remaining 408 houses were to receive major modernisation. By 1980, however, the project was in deep trouble because the capital to sustain the work was simply not available. 'About half of the modernisation work had been completed by this time. Houses awaiting modernisation included Wilsons and Orlits which were badly in need of attention. A considerable number of houses were standing empty. The Association came in for criticism locally because of

Weir houses due for demolition at Laighstonehall.

doubts about the completion of the programme. There were signs that community participation was in danger of becoming fragmented.'[51]

What saved the day for Laighstonehall – although this might not have been generally appreciated at the time – was the success of house sales. As income from sales increased so the flow of funds to modernisation expanded and, in 1984, the work was completed at a total cost of around £5m. [52]

> The building programme, in addition to the demolition of the Weir steel houses and their replacement with 2, 4 and 6 person houses, included the conversion of traditional, 8 person flats into 1 and 2 person flats... All of this work in addition to landscaping and other environmental improvements, has led to a significant change in the appearance of the area...
>
> As in any housing regeneration project it is possible to conclude, with hindsight, that action at a much earlier stage might have prevented Laighstonehall sliding into physical and social decline. The regeneration programme, however has undoubtedly improved the conditions of tenants living there. Local residents speak of Laighstonehall as now being 'a completely different place' from what it was a few years ago. The Wine Valley stigma has been successfully removed.

Mercifully, the SSHA had very few estates which had deteriorated to the depths of Laighstonehall and work which has been done to restore schemes in different localities up and down the country should ensure that nothing absolutely similar will recur. However, it should be understood that the fact that the estate was a low density site made it a comparatively manageable problem. Altogether of a different scale are the dilemmas imposed by peripheral estates built in the 1950s such as at Arden or at Faifley near Clydebank.

A glance at the nature of Faifley will illustrate the point. This estate consisted of 2,373 dwellings, three quarters of which were owned by the SSHA with the remainder belonging to Clydebank District Council. The density is about 66 dwellings to the hectare and the Association's stock was originally made up of 476 cottages and 1,310 two-, three-, and four-storey flats. This community had not 'run-down' on the scale of Laighstonehall, but it was on the brink and its decline had to be

Laighstonehall today.

250

arrested, hence, in 1981 a multi-disciplinary strategy team consisting of housing management staff, an architect, planner and landscape architect was formed and instructed 'to identify the problems and solutions and to draw up a programme of priorities and plans for implementation'.

Again, anyone interested in this type of management problem should get their hands on a copy of the booklet *A Future for Faifley: A Strategy for a Problem Estate* which illustrates the way in which the required information on the community was assembled in the early stages of the formulation of policy. Today rather more resources are available for Faifley than the team originally expected and modernisation is now under way. However, one of the interesting findings was that with many of the original tenants still in residence and now, therefore, rather elderly, there was a severe mismatch between the tenants and the dwellings – *ie* many older tenants were in the cottage houses while young families were in flats. Moreover something of the order of 70 per cent of the applicants for tenancy nominated to the Association were single parents. In these circumstances management of exceptional skill had not only to precede modernisation, but to accompany it step by step. How successful the redevelopment of Faifley will be remains to be seen; it will certainly be expensive. But since such estates in any case involve a huge drain on maintenance expenditure simply to keep them habitable, the major rehabilitation of these communities is not only essential on social grounds, it is financially prudent.

The present Scottish Office Minister with responsibility for housing, Michael Ancram, who went to Faifley 'to see for himself', has correctly identified the priority which ought to be accorded to such districts. Not surprisingly, therefore, the *Policy Review* document published in the summer of 1986 set the Association the objective of *the preparation, on an estate by estate basis, of a co-ordinated strategy for the improvement of the stock based on an assessment of foreseeable resources, needs and priorities.*[53]

There is, therefore, every reason to assume that this kind of work will go forward until it has been properly completed – probably by the early 1990s – so that every tenant will then have the right to rent or buy his home in an attractive, modern environment – at least so far as it lies within the power of the Association to achieve such an aim. But, of course, where an SSHA estate is located beside a decaying local council scheme – decaying perhaps because the resources to effect improvement have not been generated – then a limit is imposed on the scope for advance. In such instances there would seem to be a case for permitting the Association to acquire and upgrade the houses in question, but so far, this notion does not seem to have attracted Ministers. That many district councils would welcome support of this kind cannot be doubted; hence one can only hope that the wisdom will eventually prevail of using to the widest benefit of the community the management and rehabilitation skills which have been acquired. It cannot be emphasised too strongly that this is, at the moment, almost a self-financing policy, hence it is very difficult to see where the objection lies to its extended application. Within a few years, however, as the rate of sales begins inevitably to slow down, the opportunity of sustaining this activity may have passed and it is thus important that the government does not dwell on the matter too long and makes the prompt decision necessary to maintain momentum.

As will have been clear from the foregoing discussion, the modernisation of estates involves much more than technical skills. Also of crucial importance is the housing management function. As we saw earlier housing management was built up from the war years under the leadership of Miss Pollock, and this facility has been developed and extended under the hand of the present director of housing management, Len Ferguson. Today 72,755 houses, 85.6 per cent of the total, are directly factored, and the level of professionalism among the staff concerned is quite remarkable. In recent months the author has made several informal visits to various Association developments in different parts of the country and in the company of local management staff. On each occasion the running commentary on the communities concerned – almost on a house by house, family by family basis – has been quite staggering and has revealed not only a high level of training, but a most impressive degree of dedication. Of course things do not always go according to plan. Of course tenants do get upset from time to time over real or imagined grievances; and matters are not always dealt with as promptly or as satisfactorily as one would wish. (After all, it is a large human organisation with all the fallibilities implied by human endeavour, and his house is something about which a tenant is bound to have very strong feelings.) But the simple fact is that the level of genuine care and conscientious effort which goes into managing the Association's houses and estates up and down the country, and to meeting the problems experienced by tenants, is immensely impressive.

Part of this professionalism stems from the effective selection of appropriate applicants for staff positions, but good training is also an important factor. Having sat in on some of the training sessions associated with the introduction and operation of the new housing benefit system one could not fail to admire the careful, realistic and imaginative guidance which was given. What this meant was revealed at the end of one of the very rare Appeal Hearings, when the agent representing the appellant – his client's claim had just been rejected – remained behind to remark that he had been most impressed by the way in which the tenant had been treated at each stage. 'You have no idea how refreshing it is to come up against an organisation where the attitude taken is just right from day one through to appeal.'

Ann Arthur, Assistant Senior Housing Assistant, Motherwell, visiting a tenant.

The office at Erskine.

In fact, appeals are now virtually a thing of the past and this may be a measure of the confidence which everyone has in the care and fairness with which Association staff operate the system.

Another remarkable unsolicited tribute to the quality of Association housing management occurred early in 1986 with the publication of a Mori poll conducted as part of an investigation into housing in the Glasgow area. In answer to the question 'how satisfied or dissatisfied are you with this particular house/flat as a place to live?' the responses were as follows.

	Satisfied %	Dissatisfied %
All	82	15
Housing tenure		
Council tenant	77	21
Owner occupation	95	4
Private rent	75	18
SSHA	93	6

Source – Mori poll for GDC; Q8

These figures really speak for themselves.

Since the present government came to power in 1979 the ratio of subsidy to rent on the revenue account has altered dramatically. Whereas, in 1979, rent accounted for £26.5m while subsidy was £30.9m, by 1986 the respective figures had become £63.9m from rent and £23m from subsidy. However, it should be remembered that as the general subsidy has diminished both as a proportion and, dramatically, in real terms, so specific subsidy to tenants in the form of housing benefit has increased. Today almost 50 per cent of Association tenants are in receipt of relief in this form.

In the same period, on the expenditure side of the account and because of the prevailing high interest rates over these years, debt repayments or loan charges (the Association's mortgage bill) has jumped from £35.9m to £61.8m. At the same time repair and maintenance has risen only from £16.7m to £18.9m, a substantial cut in real terms. This has, of course, only been possible to sustain as a result of the major modernisation programme funded from the capital budget.

Nevertheless it is worth reflecting for a moment on the

Association's Planned Maintenance System, for this is certainly one of the success stories of recent years.

In the late 1960s, conscious of the growing problems of maintaining a rapidly expanding housing stock, the Association sought to obtain better value from its maintenance expenditure through improved management procedures. It began with the organisation of painterwork into cycles of inspection, contracting and supervision. Later, other maintenance work was added into a five year cycle taking account of the whole fabric of the house in the development of a comprehensive Planned Maintenance System. In a sense the system which evolved can best be described as good asset management.

To some extent, the credit for this development goes back to Harold Buteux, for in his paper mentioned previously, *Housing for a Hundred Years or More*, he set out the value of prolonging the useful life of the houses by good design and by rationalisation of components in such a way as to invite effective maintenance over a long period. In addition, he was devoted to fostering the flow of accurate information and did everything that he could to stimulate the use of computers, including the establishment of a joint SSHA/Edinburgh University research project on the subject.

By the early 1970s the Association was acknowledged to be a front-runner in the field and was asked to contribute to various study groups as a result of which three significant publications were produced on maintenance practice –

1 *Practice in Property Maintenance Management* – MOPBW (1970).
2 *Building Maintenance* – MOPBW (1972).
3 *Computers and Housing Maintenance* – LAMSAC (1975).

These reports set standards in maintenance practice for the next decade and many of their recommendations derived from the Association's research and methods at that time. By the late 1970s the Association had published its first handbook on Planned Maintenance, setting out the detail of the system.

In 1972 the first computerised Property Register was introduced. Based on the original DEC10 Mainframe the system has operated consistently within the limits of its original design. Since then, of course, developments in information technology have been vast and, over the past three years, a new Property Information System (PIMS) using data base principles has been developed. When it becomes fully operational the amount and detail of information available should enable the Association to direct its investment with even greater effect.

A complementary information source which has proved to be an invaluable aid to the recent stock improvement programme is the technical archive library. This is a micro-film library of original contract drawings and bills of quantities which not only provides basic information for refurbishment and maintenance contracts, but acts also as a data source for PIMS.

Given that the prime objective is to maximise the potential life of the stock it was obviously necessary to estimate the probable life span of the houses and then to arrange the timing and level of maintenance over a prolonged programme. The system devised over the past five years to accomplish this task became known as Development Profiling. It was an extension into the future of the existing five yearly cycle of PM Inspections and it was, therefore, relatively simple to introduce. Although the first applications of the system were used to assess the timing and level of total maintenance demand, when fully deployed it should also be possible to assess values of differing investments on a consistent basis. Future developments of this system will link the production of profiles with the descriptive data in the property data base. This second development of Planned Maintenance and the reasoning behind it is described in the Association's most recent handbook *Planned Maintenance – The Long Term Care of Housing Stock*.

As required under its corporate objectives, the Association expertise on this kind of subject is made freely available to other housing agencies, both in the UK and overseas. In addition to the published handbook, numerous seminars have been conducted while, in the last year or so, delegations from Sweden, India, Hong Kong and Singapore as well as from many UK housing authorities and the Audit Commission for England and Wales, have come to examine the Association's work in this field.

Writing on the subject recently in an internal paper, Frank Colston of the Association's Technical Directorate had this to say–

Traditional response maintenance, by itself, is wholly

inappropriate to the dimension and value of the housing asset in the national economy.

The sowing of that seed, will in time change what was previously termed maintenance by the industry, into a process increasingly aimed at deliberate and pre-planned whole life care. Examination of the term, whole life care, will define practice, but clearly this must provide an accurate picture of demand to identify immediate and future resource requirements, give a framework to continuously estimate potential life, and be the means to the best value for investment of whatever level of resources are available...

Unless methods of finance acknowledge not just the amount of original construction cost, but also the size and pattern of future maintenance demand, the result will be at best needlessly expensive or at worst a wasteful shortening of the life of large sections of the housing stock.

Perhaps that provides as good a statement of the philosophy as any. But, of course, to implement much of the system the Association is fortunate to have a skilled and highly efficient Building department. Today, the Building department is much smaller than in the old days when it was known as the Direct Labour Organisation, but its activities are still extremely significant and its performance in 1985-86 is illustrated below.

As was mentioned previously, the Building department is now legally obliged to work within very tight controls. For example, on all capital work in excess of £50,000 it is obliged to enter into competitive tendering with private contractors, and

Building Department Financial year 1985-86

	Valuation £	Cost £	Surplus £	% of Val
New construction	57,277	47,666	9,611	
Major modernisation	6,237,510	6,141,984	95,526	1.53
Maintenance jobbing	8,180,977	7,797,258	383,719	4.90
Maintenance painterwork	451,599	379,538	72,061	15.96
Insulation	19,155	18,963	192	1.00
Planned maintenance	4,576,145	4,329,563	246,582	5.40
	£19,522,663	£18,714,972	£807,691	4.14

the same is true of maintenance work valued above £10,000. Given the effect of inflation since the regulations were introduced in 1980, this effectively means that progressively less and less work is open to straightforward negotiation. In 1985-86, in fact, the Department tendered for 130 capital contracts, of which it won 14. Not surprisingly, therefore, the government's *Policy Review* document had this to say.

[54] Since the application to the Association of Part III of the Local Government Planning and Land Act 1980 in April 1982, its Building Department has managed to acquit itself more than adequately under the DLO Regulations. It has complied with the competition requirements and has had little difficulty in securing the necessary rate of return. Its volume of work ... has been maintained at much the same level as in 1982. (£18m-£19m). This means it has not only managed to win an increasing proportion of its work in competition with private contractors (18.5 per cent in 1982-83, 38 per cent in 1984-85), but also it implies its costs are competitive and its overheads are being tightly controlled.

One is not certain about the 'little difficulty', since the task has required painstaking and effective management by those concerned, but there can be no argument about the usefulness of having such an efficient organisation to hand. The mere likelihood of the Department tendering is enough to concentrate wonderfully the minds of private contractors up and down the country and to ensure that tenders come forward which are realistic. At the time of writing there were an average of 916 operatives employed, supervised by 89 site staff and supported by a head office complement of 53. There were 47 apprentices, together with a number of craft based trainees under the Youth Training Scheme. The present building manager is Roy Davidson.

To bring matters fully up-to-date, in 1981, William Taylor, who had had a long and distinguished career in local government, stepped down as chairman. Perhaps the government wanted a younger man, more in sympathy with their radical policies. The choice was Derek Mason, a chartered surveyor by profession and a former Glasgow Councillor. His shrewd judgement is behind much that has been achieved in recent years, and not the least of the matters for which he can take credit is the harmonious manner in which the Council functions under his leadership. The deputy chairman is Charles Sneddon, former Provost of Bo'ness, and current Convener of the Central Regional Council. The other members of the present Council of Managment are Mrs Terry Cruickshank, a former Association tenant from Rosyth, greatly respected by members and officials alike for her unfailing and conscientious interest; Brian Broomfield, an Aberdeen businessman; Tom McCalmont, a veteran trade unionist and housing expert, who was responsible for the McCalmont Report on Tenant Transfers; Norman Renfrew, a dentist and former Provost of Perth; and the author.

In 1984 the general manager, Ronnie Somerville, and the secretary, Jack Fleming, both retired, leaving with many well-merited tributes. Their replacements were Derrick Marks, the former chief executive of Motherwell District Council – a quiet man with the type of experience which enabled him to slot easily into the job – and Robin Stevenson, a lawyer, who came to the Association after a career in the management of a national newspaper and as managing director of a private company.

One of the more significant ventures of Major-General Somerville's tenure of office was a radical reconstruction of the management structure. Following a detailed study by independent management consultants and in an effort to encourage some decentralization of decision-making processes, the Association territory was divided into three geographic regions, the North region covering everything north of the River Forth, the South region, responsible for everything south of the Forth – including the southern part of Strathclyde, and the West region* which covers Glasgow and northern Strathclyde. The respective regional managers appointed were Bill Jessop, Bill Landels (succeeded by Ian Williamson) and Mary Hope. These appointments were interesting in that they revealed how the various professions could converge at the top of the Association, for the first was an architect, the second an administrator, while the third had her background in housing management.

To support the regional structure a reduced central establishment is maintained at head office and this is organised into four

*In 1977 a West Regional office had been established in Glasgow and this may have encouraged the subsequent development of a full regional form of organisation.

directorates. John Fullarton, the director of technical services, Robin Stevenson, secretary and director of administration, and Len Ferguson, the director of housing management, have all been mentioned previously. The fourth is Ian Ireland, the director of finance. Collectively these senior officers, together with the three regional managers and the building manager, meet under the general manager as the executive board and, normally with John Timms, the public relations officer also present, they all attend Council meetings to report directly and to give any required advice. Decisions on policy and, of course, the responsibility for these decisions, are entirely a matter for the members of Council.

CHAPTER SEVEN

Retrospect and Prospect

To what then does it all add up? What is the sum of the Association's achievement over the past fifty years? What difference have its activities made to the people of Scotland? And, were they alive, what would Walter Elliot, Sir David Allen Hay and the other founding fathers of the SSHA think of it all?

Obviously, and by any standard, the housing conditions of the people of the kingdom are today incomparably better than was the case in 1937. Since then, approximately 1.25 million houses have been built across Scotland and, of these, the SSHA have provided 110,838, about 9 per cent of the total (March 1986). An interesting point of comparison, which perhaps gives some notion of the scale of this effort, is that the new towns of East Kilbride, Glenrothes, Cumbernauld, Livingston and Irvine have between them built 65,600 houses, but, of course, whereas the latter are concentrated into the five localities, the Association's houses are spread throughout the length and breadth of the country – some in remote communities, in small towns or burghs, and thousands within or around the main cities. In addition, many other dwellings have been modernised at the hands of the Association and this was particularly true in the 1960s and 1970s.

Another comparison is with the private sector. Over the years of the Association's existence the combined output for the private market has been approximately 325,000: hence for every three houses built by private builders in Scotland, the Association has provided a little more than one house (in the last

Before and after views of the transformation of Spence's houses at Forth.

fifteen years, of course, the figures have moved dramatically in favour of private enterprise).

These parallels perhaps give some sense of the significance of the Association, not only as a house provider, but as an engine within the Scottish economy. In addition to employment created directly, obviously many manufacturing, legal, architectural, surveying, contracting and building companies have earned a substantial portion of their business from the Association's activities, and some understanding of what this has meant, and means, may be derived from the point that almost every penny has been and is spent within Scotland.

Looking back across the years, there is admittedly some regret that the Association was not permitted to take on in its intended form the great venture envisaged first by Elliot and subsequently by Tom Johnston. But history is much less concerned with the 'what might have beens' than with what actually happened, and from any point of view the Association's contribution to the modern fabric of Scotland is both significant and impressive. Moreover, that contribution cannot simply be measured in terms of numbers of houses built or restored.

As a glance at Appendix A will confirm, in the years from 1945 to 1976 the Scots became overwhelmingly a people housed by the local authorities. For much of that time the scale of private construction was small and, for instance, it was not until the 1960s that the total private output began consistently to exceed that of the Association. The reasons for the inadequacies of private building earlier in the century were discussed fully in the first chapter and there is no point in repeating them. However, what is clear is that without the Association house provision in Scotland would have been virtually a local authority monopoly so far as the great majority of ordinary Scots were concerned.

Even allowing for the presence of the SSHA, the fact is that in many parts of the country housing did become monopolistic and all the abuses which one would expect under these circumstances did prevail from time to time. In saying that there is no intention to denigrate the caring and honourable work of thousands of decent, well-intentioned and successful local councillors up and down the country over the years. Nor is it one's wish unfairly to abuse competent and conscientious professional housing staff in local authorities, since it is freely acknowledged that many councils do provide their tenants with an excellent service. However, the truth is that monopolies which confront consumers with little or no choice almost invariably give rise to poor standards, and this is no less true of housing than of any other commodity or service. Naturally, one can think of many council estates where standards are first class – it would indeed be a dreadful thing were that not the case – and there have, in recent years, been many major improvements. But equally, if anyone cared to compile such a list, it would be easy to point to disastrous estates. Too often standards of design, construction and management have been miserably low and tenants have had to endure conditions which owed far more to false political priorities, to misguided economic strategies or to the perceived short-term interests of employees, than to any genuine attempt to meet the desires or hopes of consumers.

As we have seen, not all Association estates were (or are) perfect. Nor has the organisation always been wisely or well used. For example, there is no doubt that had it been free to select its own preferred house types in the post-war era, far fewer prefabricated non-traditional houses would have been built, and many tenants would today be living in houses of rather better quality. Moreover, it is also true that Association operations have often been constrained by the preferences and policies of various local authorities and this has rarely been to the advantage of the citizens concerned. For example, it is the author's view that the restraints which were imposed on the Association by the City Corporation in the 1940s and 1950s, and at various periods later, were not to the benefit of Glasgow or to thousands of Glaswegians. Indeed, it could be argued that the City's recent remarkable recovery is at least in part the result of allowing the Association to operate within the City for almost the first time in a manner which more closely approaches its own instincts, and by so doing, to encourage others to follow suit.

However, when all that has been said, there are perhaps three major historic contributions which the Association has made, each of which may be regarded as of enormous importance to the people of Scotland.

First, it has been able to provide a point of comparison and contrast with local authorities. In other words, the Association has set a standard – however imperfectly at times – against which local housing committees, staff and tenants could assess the quality of service provided within their districts. Inevitably that aspect of the Association's influence did not always make it popular in local official circles, but for many of Scotland's working people over the past half century, the SSHA was not only the only alternative, but the only measure against which their housing could be judged. To the extent that it acted as a corrective or a spur to municipal housing operations, the SSHA's activities must be regarded as invaluable. Indeed, it is not too much to say that in many parts of the country, particularly in the industrial communities, the only hope of relief, variety or improvement in housing quality, tenant choice or management standards, rested on the possibility of a significant Association development. To put it another way, without the Association, very many Scots in certain parts of the country would have been entirely dependent on the housing provided by the local council, whether the latter was good, bad or indifferent. To the extent that it ameliorated that situation, introduced an element of choice of tenure, offered some variation in design and demonstrated effective management procedures, thousands of tenants who have never lived in an Association house may nevertheless have derived benefit from the SSHA's presence in their neighbourhood.

Second, as a central government organisation, the existence of the Association has enabled government, through the Scottish Office, to pursue central housing policies of various kinds with far greater efficiency than if it had always been necessary to operate by means of the filter of local authorities. For example, governments of different political hues have been able to direct resources via the Association towards very specific targets. In the late 1940s and 1950s the coal mining industry and forestry and other rural workers were helped in this way. Later the emphasis was switched to the overcrowded cities and the Glasgow Overspill programme, though not particularly success-ful, should be included as an element of this work. Later still, from the 1960s, economic and industrial growth points became at times precise targets through the 'Economic Expansion' programme, and more recently 'Redevelopment Assistance' and 'Special Needs' have also demonstrated the SSHA's capacity to meet carefully selected objectives. Moreover, it should be understood that this ability to intervene directly to meet geographic, economic, or social requirements has enabled governments to redistribute resources from the centre and according to need. Whether it was a question of assisting, say, the north east or the Grangemouth area to cope with economic growth; whether it was to help a poorer or deprived area in the manner which taxed the original founders of the Association; or whether it was to act on behalf of a specific social group, such as the elderly; the Association's existence has given governments the means to direct assistance precisely in the intended direction. Quite apart from such an option being desirable in terms of pure political management, its very precision must make it one of the more economically efficient tools available to the State.

Another interesting example of the SSHA's usefulness as a vehicle through which resources can be redistributed is illustrated by the contemporary modernisation programme. In the latter part of the 1970s the Association was permitted to obtain some 3,000 or so old houses, many of them inter-war Glasgow council houses in the GEAR area or in other parts of the City. Their comprehensive rehabilitation is now complete, but this has meant that capital derived from Association sales – perhaps in the north east of Scotland – has been put to work to the advantage of communities in a quite different locality, but in genuine need of help. It is difficult to envisage a more direct or accurate method of organising this kind of transfer of resources and, as has already been explained, it is an approach that the present government might usefully further encourage.

But housing policy, of course, has not simply consisted of building new dwellings. As was illustrated in the 1950s and more recently, the Association's existence has enabled governments to exert a direct and major influence on housing financial policies. In the late 1950s the objective was to bring rents generally up to a more realistic level and although this was not then fully achieved, there is no doubt that the Association's rent levels provided a means by which governments could influence the standard. Similarly, in recent years, not only has the Association been able to give a lead in respect of sales, it has also been able to illustrate the efficiency of shifting from general revenue subsidy to specific housing benefit geared to the needs of individual tenants.

It follows therefore, that whether or not one approves of the individual policies pursued by this or that government, the fact is that the Association has provided central government with the means of direct intervention at key points throughout the past fifty years. Prior to local government reorganisation, when housing was the responsibility of a multitude of often tiny, and always variable, local authorities, this facility was crucial. Arguably, it still is.

Third, the Association has enabled – again, however imperfectly – certain standards of both construction and management to be established. As we have seen this function has not always been achieved as efficiently as those responsible for the Association would have wished, usually because of some external constraint imposed from government or elsewhere. However, through its experimental work in the 1940s and 1950s, by its development of the no-fines technique of construction, by the careful and rigorous standards of research, design and supervision imposed particularly throughout the high rise era, by its pioneering of modernisation and rehabilitation techniques, and by keeping itself at the forefront of methods of planned maintenance, the Association has done much to demonstrate and enhance the physical quality of housing throughout Scotland. This point was not lost on the many Ministers who have, over the years, assumed responsibility for Housing within the Scottish Office. There are many instances of Ministers drawing attention to the Association's ability to set an example whether in greater energy efficiency through improved design, in devising techniques to circumvent scarce materials, in more economic or efficient use of resources, or in any one of dozens of other directions.

Nor should it be imagined that this influence has been directed solely at the public sector. Repeatedly in recent months the author has examined schemes which are close to or bordering on private developments and one could not but be aware of the pressure to which the private builders were subjected in having to try to at least match Association standards. In many cases they failed – sometimes by a substantial margin – but the upward pressure on standards is invaluable and has done much to improve the quality of Scottish housing.

The Association itself has always been conscious of its leading role and there is no doubt that this explains much of the continual striving for excellence which emerges so clearly from any inspection of its records. Council members and senior officials always considered that it was their responsibility to arrive at the best available method of doing anything, even when they were being compelled to work within unsatisfactory restrictions, or were required to operate in ways which they regarded as inadequate. What this sometimes meant was that, because they were conscious of the many eyes which were upon them, they endeavoured to find the best way to cope with situations which they regarded as being inherently unsound. Anyone who doubts that ought to take a walk round Wyndford where they will find an exceptionally high density estate not only functioning, but functioning well. Better still, look at Hutchesontown and contrast the tragedy of Area E with the Association's Area D. The suffering and distress represented by a decaying concrete wilderness is just cause for anger and outrage, but as the temper cools it is worth asking why it did not happen next door. Why is it that a strong and vibrant community still thrives in Area D? And if the Glasgow 'Smiley Man' on the tenants' mural in the foyer of 474 Old Rutherglen Road has only half a smile, why does he smile at all? Surely it is because the Association not only made the buildings work, but has gone on making them work and has thus given the tenants the chance to make decent homes for themselves. Of course, it ought not to have happened that way. Of course, such buildings ought never to have been constructed. But in the hands of the Association they have succeeded. Quite apart from the benefit of this in terms of the quality of life of the tenants directly concerned, the financial reward should not be over-looked. As the *Policy Review* noted in 1986 'Virtually all SSHA stock is in lettable condition and nearly 99 per cent is earning rental income.'[1]

Moreover, a main part of this success has to rest not so much in the different building structures, but in the exemplary standards of housing management. As we saw, starting with Miss Pollock and continuing under the guidance of Len Ferguson, an outstanding level of estate management expertise was developed and this has also provided a model for others. Indeed, if the strength of the Association is the sum of its

Sheltered tenants in their kitchen at Erskine.

various parts – administrative, technical and building – perhaps the true heart of the modern organisation resides in its accumulated housing managment skills, for certainly they combine to form a priceless asset. Communities and estates are organic, constantly changing, growing, flourishing and ageing. Like gardens, they require continuous and careful attention. The ability to provide such care is the Association's real strength and every day it demonstrates this to all who care to see throughout the length and breadth of Scotland.

Taken together these three main contributions make up a formidable sum and one can only, therefore, conclude that Elliot and the others would have every reason to be pleased with the record so far.

No institution can survive on its history or afford to dwell on past glories for too long. Today and tomorrow are the main considerations and it is, therefore, worth finally reflecting for a moment on the future.

As was mentioned in the previous chapter, in 1985-86 the Scottish Development Department carried out a major policy review of the Association and anyone who wishes to read further on the subject might care to obtain a copy of the Review document. There is no point in repeating here the various findings, but the main conclusion was that the Association continued to occupy 'a significant place in public sector housing in Scotland'[2] Accordingly the following objectives were set out.

[3]   In accordance with government housing and related objectives:

1   To continue to assist authorities to meet local housing needs, primarily by:
    a managing its own stock efficiently; and
    b contributing towards the provision of Special Needs accommodation;

2   To recognise tenants' aspirations for home ownership and where possible to give priority to transfer of its assets from the public to the private sector, in order to break up single tenure estates and enhance diversity and choice of tenure;

3   To promote and demonstrate innovative developments in the management and provision of public sector housing;

The tenants' group helping to design the houses for Dalmarnock.

Kate Thomson, Community Artist, and local children in front of the tenants' mural in the foyer of 474 Rutherglen Road.

4   To promote tenant involvement in the management of the estates in which they live;

5   To minimise the demands it makes on public housing resources both capital and revenue;

6   To offer value for money in all its operations and services.

Thereafter detailed policies were explained on New Build,

The design group at work on the plans for the award winning Kirkland Street development.

Privatisation Initiatives, Housing Management, Estate Strategies, Agency Work, Finance, Management Structure and Controls. Possible constraints and other matters worthy of investigation were also discussed.

As far as New Build is concerned, obviously the major building programmes are a thing of the past, particularly since private home ownership seems bound to continue to expand. Present and future generations will want to be home owning and it would be unrealistic to attempt to stand in the way of such aspirations. Housing for Special Needs is, of course, a different matter and it remains to be seen whether or not the government's estimate of 300 houses a year from 1990 is adequate to meet the requirements of an ageing population. In addition, it is possible that specific help may have to be given to particular areas and the sensible intention is, therefore, to retain a residual economic expansion facility in reserve.

In the case of House Sales, clearly the government wants to see 'continuation of an energetic sales policy'[4] and that is certain to be forthcoming, particularly if the Association is given the extended power to use the resources generated to upgrade old council houses in the manner advocated in previous pages. Two further points are, however, worth making in this context. As has been mentioned, a large proportion of Association tenants are in receipt of housing benefit or other forms of social assistance. An improvement in employment levels would help, but the fact is that in the foreseeable future the majority of tenants are simply not going to be in a position to contemplate purchase and a large stock of houses for rent is going to continue to have to be maintained. In these circumstances some refinement of the sales policy seems justifiable. For example, under the present legislation tenants have an absolute right to buy their houses. In certain circumstances this means that an individual flat in a block of flats can be sold, leaving in train a series of management and maintenance problems. Equally, of course, it is true that flats have been difficult to sell in this random fashion, whereas a cleared block might be much easier to market in its entirety. Against this background, in an ideal world certain tenants, while retaining the right to buy, might reasonably not have the right to buy the house in which they currently live, in order to enable a more sensibly organised policy to be followed. Presumably the government has not accepted such an argument for fear of providing loop-holes for an authority which wished to thwart or impede the general sales policy. In the case of the Association this is a groundless concern, but perhaps until the general principle of allowing people the freedom to choose for themselves their preferred form of tenure is accepted across a broader spectrum, common-sense will continue to have to be subservient to political tactics.

Otherwise the Association emerged from the detailed scrutiny of the *Policy Review* with its reputation intact and with little to excite concern or apprehension. It is still, and will remain, a valued instrument of government in Scotland, though perhaps within a different structure. The most radical suggestion came in the foreword to the Review document written by the Secretary of State himself. Mr Rifkind wrote –

One way of keeping tenants informed. A Dundee tenant with a copy of 'Tenants News'.

5 ...In considering my response to the main findings and recommendations of the *Policy Review*, I have been conscious of the need to look at the role of the SSHA in the wider context of overall housing activity in Scotland, over which government exercises control. While each of the main bodies concerned has its own distinctive approach and contribution to make to the housing needs, there is common ground and some overlap in their activities. There have also been significant changes in recent years in the pattern of housing tenure, provision and management as a direct result of the successful pursuit of this government's housing objective.

In view of this broader canvas and the changing circumstances, the government is actively considering the basis for the early promotion of a closer working relationship between the SSHA and the Housing Corporation in Scotland. If this proves fruitful, a full merger in the longer term might be a desirable option. At this stage, however the government has no committed views. I believe that it is right to take the opportunity offered by the current Review of the SSHA to indicate the issues that need to be addressed. Full and open consultation on the way forward will take place as soon as specific proposals have been developed for consideration.

How this will ultimately develop remains to be seen, but certainly some rationalisation of public sector house provision is bound to occur sooner or later. The notion of a closer relationship between the Association and the Housing Corporation in Scotland, perhaps ultimately a full merger, is interesting because clearly each has much to offer the other. The youthful vigour, freshness and independence of many of the housing associations might act as something of an infusion into the older veins of the Association and encourage still more decentralization of administration. Equally, there is an unrivalled reservoir of housing management and technical expertise within the SSHA which would enormously strengthen Housing Corporation activity, particularly once the emphasis of its operations moves – as it must – from new projects to the management of an existing stock. It is an attractive prospect. As this story has explained, the case for a particularly Scottish variation to national housing strategy has been valid throughout much of the present century and, although things are changing, it remains a significant factor. The Scottish dimension to policy will be potentially that much more potent and fruitful if indeed a closer relationship is established. Obviously, however, much will depend on the attitudes taken by individuals. Change, even the threat of change, creates uncertainty and nothing encourages the establishment of entrenched positions so swiftly as the real or imagined sense of a potential loss of personal power or influence. It would be sad if such were to happen in this case and, at the time of writing, one can only express the hope that both organisations will approach their discussions with the goodwill to succeed.

Such thoughts are for the future. The concern of this book has been with the past and to tell the story of an organisation of which many Scots are only vaguely aware. But the SSHA's significance and contribution to the development of modern Scotland is unique and of immense value. If this volume does anything to make that more widely understood it will have served a useful purpose.

Meanwhile, let the final word belong to John Ruskin, for his sentiment seems to speak as well for the individuals who have contributed to the Association from first to last as for the buildings for which they are responsible.

[6]   We require from buildings, as from men, two kinds of goodness: First, the doing their practical duty well: then that they be graceful and pleasing in doing it; which last is itself another form of duty.

References

I have relied heavily on the work of other authors for much of the material in Chapter 1. In particular Ian H. Adams *The Making of Urban Scotland*, Croom Helm (1978), Douglas Niven *The Development of Housing in Scotland*, Croom Helm (1979), and Marion Bowley, *Housing and the State*, Allen and Unwin (1945), were extremely useful and I fully acknowledge my debt to the writers concerned.

Elsewhere, the sources are mainly primary and I wish to set down my appreciation of the various Association Secretaries who, from first to last, have maintained the records in an impeccable manner. Collectively, and in terms of their organisation, the archives are something of a historian's dream. The Minutes of the Council of Management, Monthly Reports and Annual Reports are gathered into bound volumes and, in most cases, the pages are numbered. For this reason I have been able to refer to the appropriate volume and page number rather than the original reference number, since the latter would be much harder to track down. Abbreviations are recorded as follows.

Minutes of the Council of Management–	MCM (date)
Monthly Reports–	MR (date)
Annual Reports–	AR (date)
Minutes of Ordinary & Extraordinary General Meetings–	MOEG (date)

CHAPTER ONE

1   In particular the relevant sections of I.H. Adams, *The Making of Urban Scotland* (1978) and Douglas Niven, *The Development of Housing in Scotland* (1979)

2   Many examples, but see J.H. Muir, *Glasgow in 1901* (1901) or *Glasgow, 1858 – Shadow's Midnight Scenes and Social Photographs* (1976), or Andrew Gibb, *Glasgow – The Making of a City* (1983) for a modern account

3   Adams, *op cit*, p160

4   S. Chapman, (ed) *The History of Working-Class Housing* (1971), essay by John Butt *Working-class Housing in Glasgow, 1851-1914*, p57

5   *Ibid*, p63

6   J. Melling, (ed), *Housing, Social Policy and the State* (1980), essay by Melling on *Clydeside Housing and the Evolution of State Rent Control*, p143

7   Chapman, *op cit*, p82

8   Report of the Royal Commission on the Housing of the Industrial Population of Scotland, Urban and Rural; 1917, Cmnd 8731, p346

9   Marion Bowley, *Housing and the State* (1945), pp261-2

10 See R.C. Report, *op cit*, Chapter 3

11 *Ibid*, pp8-9

12 Bowley, *op cit*, p262

13 R.C. Report, *op cit*, p292

14 J. Melling, *op cit*, has an interesting discussion of the various movements in Glasgow

15 Niven, *op cit*, p27

16 Bowley, *op cit*, p16

17 *Ibid*, pp24-5

18 J. Burnett *A Social History of Housing* (1978), p227

19 *Ibid*

20 Bowley, *op cit*, pp40-43

21 Niven, *op cit*, p28

22 Annual Report of the Department of Health for Scotland, 1932

23 Bowley, *op cit*, p264

24 Annual Reports, D of H for Scotland, 1924, pp48-9; 1926, p48; 1929, p10

25 *Ibid*, 1929

26 Burnett, *op cit*, p234

27 Bowley, *op cit*, p265

28 *Ibid*

29 Scottish Housing Advisory Committee – *Planning Our New Homes* (1944)

30 Bowley, *op cit*, p267

31 Scottish Housing Advisory Committee, *op cit*, Chapter VIII

32 Henry Meikle (ed) *Scotland* (1947), p49

33 Social Trends (various eds)

34 *Ibid*

35 See, for example, the interesting essay in P. Addison, *Now the War is Over* (1985)

36 I am indebted to my father for this one, since he was the minister in question

37 Addison, *op cit*, p54

38 Mary E.H. Smith, *Guide to Housing* (1983), p13

39 Adams, *op cit*, p177

40 Addison, *op cit*, p57

41 *Ibid*

42 Smith, *op cit*, p16

43 *Ibid*, p20

44 Adams, *op cit*, p226
45 *Ibid*, p227
46 *Ibid*, p225
47 *Ibid*, p228
48 *Ibid*, p180
49 See A. Sutcliffe (ed) *Multi-Storey Living, The British Working-class Experience*(1974), essay by E.W. Cooney, pp151-81
50 Social Trends (various eds)
51 Green Paper – *Scottish Housing* (1977), p3 and Regional Trends (1985) Table 2.17, p58
52 Any number of economic text books will provide data in support of these comments. See, for example, the various editions of A.R. Prest (ed) (& D.J. Coppock) *The U.K. Economy* (from 1966). Also Burnett, *op cit*, pp273-9
53 Social Trends No 5 (1974) Table 90, p132
54 *Ibid*, Table 161, p180
55 Smith, *op cit*, p25
56 *Ibid*, p21
57 *Ibid*, p23
58 Prest, *op cit*, provides relevant economic statistics, as does Social Trends. Also J. Black – *The Economics of Modern Britain*, Fourth ed (1985) – Table 1.7, p31 (growth), Table 1.9, p47 (inflation), Table 2.2, p12 (growth), Tables 18.1, p161, and 18.2, p163 (inflation). (The official 1980 inflation figure was 18.0%, but the actual peak was above 20%)
59 Regional Trends, *op cit*, Table 3.1, p60
60 Green Paper – *Scottish Housing* (1977), pp4-5
61 Regional Trends, *op cit*, Table 3.3, p61; *Scotsman* 28 January 1987 for the latest Scottish figures
62 Niven, *op cit*, pp94-5
63 *Ibid*, p94
64 Adams, *op cit*, p276

CHAPTER TWO

1 Ebenezer Howard, *Garden Cities of Tomorrow* (reissued 1986)
2 For much of my information on Rosyth, I am indebted to the unpublished dissertation *The Changing Face of Rosyth: A Case for Conservation* written in 1984 by Doreen Smith and held at Queen Margaret College
3 Adams, *op cit*, pp205-6
4 *Ibid*, p206 – quoting from *Glasgow Herald* 19 June 1912
5 Memorandum and Articles of Association of SNHC, Scottish Record Office (DD6/243)
6 F. Sinclair – *Scotstyle – 150 Years of Scottish Architecture* (1984) p77
7 Quoted in the booklet *A Mirror of Scottish Housing*, written by Charles McKean and published in 1984 by the SSHA to mark the Festival of Architecture; p2. The note on Rosyth in this page provided some of the background information which I have used in the text
8 John S. Gibson *The Thistle and the Crown: A History of the Scottish Office* (1985), p70
9 Janet A. Smith, *John Buchan and his World* (1979), p81
10 Stephen Roskill, *Naval Policy Between the Wars*, Vol 1, (1968). Ch VIII gives a full account of the Washington Conference and its effects, and the same author's *Churchill and the Admirals* (1977) discusses Churchill's opposition to the cruiser programme
11 B.W.E. Alford, *Depression and Recovery? British Economic Growth 1918-1939* (1972), p57
12 Gibson, *op cit*, p70
13 *Glasgow Herald*, 1 October 1925
14 SRO DD6/245 (HO/56/3/2)
15 Gibson, *op cit*, p70
16 *Ibid*, p71
17 *Ibid*, p72
18 SRO DD6/246 Memo submitted to Cabinet by Secretary of State (HO/56/6/2)
19 SRO DD6/245 (HO/56/3/2)
20 SRO DD6/243 (HO/56/3/1)
21 SRO DD6/246 (HO/56/6/2)
22 SRO DD6/251 (HO/56/1/1) Minute of Agreement dated 30 June and 3 July 1926
23 *Ibid* 8, Letter to Treasury
24 SRO DD6/243 (HO/56/3/1) and DD6/248 (HO/56/10/2), the latter including specifications and tenders
25 SRO DD6/245 (HO/56/3/2)
26 SRO DD6/246 (HO/56/6/2)
27 Gibson, *op cit*, p71
28 Martin Gilbert, *Winston S. Churchill*, Vol V 1922-1939, p301; letter Churchill to Baldwin, 2 September 1928
29 A.M. Mackenzie *Scotland in Modern Times 1720-1939* (1941) p336
30 Gibson, *op cit*, pp76-9
31 *Ibid*, p78
32 Mackenzie, *op cit*, p333

33 Bowley, *op cit*, p265
34 SRO DD6/1131, Paper of 18/1/37
35 SRO DD6/251
36 AR 1937-47
37 Gibson, *op cit*, p84
38 *Ibid*, pp79-80

CHAPTER THREE

1   MCM 1937-38, p1
2   *Ibid*. (Story of Mr King measuring the distance to the various banks is contained in p6 of the SSHA's booklet *A Chronicle of Forty Years 1937-1977*, published in 1977 to mark the Association's fortieth anniversary and prepared from material researched by David H. Halley)
3   *Ibid*, p3
4   AR 1937-47, p12
5   MCM 1937-38, p2
6   *Ibid*, p3
7   *Ibid*
8   *Ibid*, pp4-5
9   *Ibid*, pp28-9
10 AR 1937-47, p10
11 MCM 1937-38, p22
12 *Ibid*, p30
13 *Ibid*, p29
14 *Ibid*, p37
15 *Ibid*, p30
16 *Ibid*, p40
17 *Glasgow Herald*, 5 May 1938
18 Dorothy Laird, *Queen Elizabeth the Queen Mother*, (1966), p185
19 *Motherwell Times*, 6 May 1938
20 Housing Special, 1971
21 Adams, *op cit*, pp234-5, and Official Report, 28 June 1938, vol 337, no 136, col 1679
22 MCM 1937-38, pp64-5 and AR 1937-47, pp11-12
23 MCM 1937-38, p22
24 *Ibid*, p25
25 *Ibid*, pp26-7 for a discussion of the original debate on 'no-fines'
26 AR 1937-47, p9
27 *Ibid*, p10
28 MCM 1937-38, p105 and MCM 1938-39, pp26-7
29 MCM 1938-39, p88

30 AR 1937-47, p15
31 *Ibid*, p12
32 *Ibid*, pp12-13 and MCM 1939, p36
33 MOEG 1937-47, p3
34 *Ibid*, p7
35 AR 1937-47, p8
36 MOEG 1937-47, p9
37 MCM 1939, p24
38 *Ibid*, p31
39 *Ibid*, p91
40 Gibson *op cit*, pp138-9
41 MCM 1939, pp89-90
42 AR 1937-47, p27
43 MCM 1939, p97, p117 and in subsequent reports
44 AR 1937-47, p23
45 *Ibid*, p24
46 *Ibid*, p41
47 *Ibid*
48 *Ibid*
49 *Ibid*, p41 and p61
50 *Ibid*, p61
51 *Ibid*, p62
52 *Ibid*, pp138-9. (The Annual Reports for each of the war years contain a mass of interesting detail on wartime working conditions as, of course, do the Monthly Reports and the Council Minutes. It has been possible in the text merely to give the flavour of the material on this subject)
53 The original number of houses identified in September 1939 for completion was 1366 – as indicated AR 1937-47, p29 – but 32 houses at Johnstone, 58 at Kilmarnock and 54 at Motherwell were withdrawn from the programme for various reasons, while 4 extra houses were included for Greenock; hence the eventual programme was 1226 which, when added to the 186 houses completed before the war, gives the 1412 houses quoted in the Report for 1944, AR 1937-47, p147
54 AR 1937-47, pp83-4 and pp 133-4
55 *Ibid*, p134 and p147
56 *Ibid*, p63 and p86
57 AR 1940-42
58 AR 1937-47, p430
59 *Ibid*, p25 and MCM 1940 various places
60 AR 1937-47, pp60-61 and MCM 1941 pp 50-55
61 I am indebted for this quote and some of the other material on the Kirkwall Post Office to the pamphlet written by Mr R.H. Macintosh, OBE (Building Mana-

ger, SSHA 1951-74) entitled *The No-Fines Story*, pp8-9. AR 1937-47, p93 and p137 carry the official comments

62 MCM 1939 p17
63 *Ibid*, p47
64 *Ibid*, pp66-7
65 *Ibid*, pp76-7
66 *Ibid*, p114
67 *Ibid*, p124
68 MCM 1940, p45
69 *Ibid*, p31
70 *Ibid*, p52
71 *Ibid*, p61
72 *Ibid*, meeting of 27 September
73 MCM 1941, p29, p38 and p46
74 MCM 1940, p99
75 MCM 1943 and 1944
76 MCM 1940, p62
77 *Ibid*, pp99-100
78 Many references, but see, for example, MCM 1940, p62 and MCM 1941, pp93-4. Most of the MCMs of the war years include the quarterly medical reports
79 MCM 1940, p84
80 *Ibid*, p93
81 *Ibid*, p84
82 *Ibid*, p92
83 *Ibid*
84 MR 1943, Report of 30 July
85 MCM 1942, p90
86 MCM 1940, pp100-01
87 MCM 1941, p30
88 MCM 1942, p52
89 *Ibid*, p57
90 *Ibid*, p74
91 MR 1943, Report of 30 July
92 *Ibid*, Reports of 1 October and 26 November
93 MCM 1945, p39
94 *Ibid*, p77 and meeting of 21 December
95 MCM 1939
96 AR 1937-47, p43
97 MCM 1941, p31
98 AR 1937-47, p76
99 *Ibid*, p65
100 *Ibid*, p87
101 *Ibid*, p65
102 MCM 1941, p69
103 *Ibid*, p87
104 *Ibid*, p95

105 AR 1937-47, pp87-8
106 *Ibid*, pp98-100
107 *Ibid*, p102
108 *Ibid*, p143 and p209
109 *Ibid*
110 *Ibid*, p143, pp209-10, and p279
111 *Ibid*, p144
112 MR 1943, p28
113 AR 1937-47, p210
114 *Ibid*, p350
115 *Ibid*, p351
116 *Ibid*, pp351-2
117 AR 1948-55, p14
118 AR 1937-47, p89
119 *Ibid*, p138
120 *Ibid*, pp89-93
121 *Ibid*, p90
122 *Ibid*
123 *Ibid*, p144
124 *Ibid*, pp135-6
125 *Ibid*, p144
126 MCM 1944, p13, MR 1944, p80
127 AR 1937-47, pp210-11
128 *Ibid*, p280
129 *Ibid*, p281
130 *Ibid*, pp353-4
131 *Ibid*, p281
132 *Ibid*, pp354-5
133 AR 1948-55, pp15-16
134 MR 1943, p112
135 MCM 1943, p24
136 AR 1937-47, pp206-7
137 MCM 1944, p35 and p64
138 AR 1937-47, pp136-7
139 MCM 1944, pp40-41
140 *Ibid*, p41 and AR 1937-47, p198
141 AR 1937-47, p348; AR 1948-55, p11; and see, for example, MCM 1945, p45 for reaction to comments in the House by the Minister for Works; p90 for dealing with tenants' complaints; p119 for reaction to Parliamentary Questions. MCM 1946, p9 on reduction of rent; p18 on letter from Greenock Town Council expressing thanks for successful remedial measures; p19 Press comment on Ministry of Works houses for miners
142 MCM 1950, p55
143 MCM 1944, p58
144 *Ibid*, pp59-60

145 Thomas Johnston, *Memories* (1953), p148
146 Gibson, *op cit*, p102
147 MCM 1942, p15
148 *Ibid*, p21
149 *Ibid*, ·pp46-50
150 *Ibid*, pp78-9
151 MR 1943, pp14-24
152 *Ibid*
153 Niven, *op cit*, p85
154 *Ibid*, p74
155 MR 1943, p6
156 MR 1944, p83
157 *Ibid*, p40
158 MR 1943, p137
159 *Ibid*, p77
160 MCM 1944, p24
161 *Ibid*, p26
162 AR 1937-47, pp187-9
163 MR 1944, pp150-8
164 *Ibid*, pp150-51
165 See for example progress lists MCM 1945, p2 and p62
166 MCM 1945, pp103-4
167 *Ibid*, pp110-11
168 *Ibid*, pp134-8

CHAPTER FOUR

1 AR 1937-47, pp187-9 (The relevant sections of the meeting with the Secretary of State on 31 July 1944 are quoted in Chapter 3, page 124)
2 Tom Johnston, *op cit*, p166
3 T.C. Smout, *A Century of the Scottish People 1830-1950* (1986), p274
4 Christopher Harvie, *No Gods and Precious Few Heroes: Scotland 1914-1980* (1981), p106
5 Douglas Niven, *op cit*, p77
6 Tom Johnston, *op cit*, p169
7 MCM 1945, pp147-8
8 MCM 1946, pp9-10
9 R.D. Crammond, *Housing Policy in Scotland* (1966), p26
10 *Ibid*, p10
11 AR 1937-47, pp272-3
12 MCM 1946, pp35-6
13 *Ibid*, p54

14 *Ibid*, p50
15 *Ibid*, p59
16 *Ibid*, p64
17 *Ibid*, p66
18 *Ibid*, p71
19 *Ibid*, p83; MR 1946, p278
20 *Ibid*, p89
21 *Ibid*, pp77-8
22 MCM 1947, p8
23 MCM 1946, p89
24 *Ibid*, p104
25 AR 1937-47, pp363-4
26 AR 1948-55, pp1-2
27 MCM 1947, p17
28 See, for example, *Ibid*, p57
29 MCM 1947, pp60-61
30 AR 1948-55, pp3-4
31 *Ibid*, p4
32 *Ibid*, pp27-8
33 Christopher Harvie, *op cit*, p107
34 MCM 1947, p62
35 See, for example, MCM 1948, p48 – minute of meeting with Mr Robertson
36 AR 1948-55, pp121-2
37 *Ibid*, p225
38 *Ibid*, pp251-3
39 MCM 1945, p32
40 MCM 1948, p13
41 MCM 1949, p29
42 *Ibid*, p43
43 *Ibid*, p49
44 MCM 1950, p1
45 *Ibid*, p13
46 *Ibid*, p22
47 *Ibid*, p18
48 MCM 1948, pp17-18
49 *Ibid*, p27
50 *Ibid*, p22
51 MCM 1949, p6
52 *Ibid*, p89
53 MR 1946, p330
54 AR 1948-55, p122
55 MCM 1949, p54
56 *Ibid*, p42
57 MCM 1950, p44 and p57
58 MCM 1951, p2
59 *Ibid*, p17
60 *Ibid*, p43

61   *Ibid*, pp22-3
62   *Ibid*, pp57-9
63   MCM 1952, p36
64   *Ibid*, p42
65   *Ibid*, p36
66   AR 1948-55, p412 and p497
67   MCM 1952, p24
68   *Ibid*, p52
69   *Ibid*, p17
70   *Ibid*, p6
71   *Ibid*, p21 and p67
72   MCM 1951, p27
73   *Ibid*, p47
74   MCM 1953. p4
75   *Ibid*, pp39-40
76   *Ibid*, pp14-15
77   *Ibid*, pp46-9
78   MCM 1954. p7
79   R.H. Macintosh, *op cit*, pp13-14
80   *Ibid*, p15
81   MCM 1954, p16
82   AR 1948-55, p28
83   MCM 1946, pp44-5
84   *Ibid*, p54
85   AR 1948-55, p13
86   MCM 1947, p68
87   AR 1948-55, p7
88   MCM 1946, p46
89   MCM 1949, p13
90   AR 1948-55, p227
91   MCM 1950, p3
92   *Ibid*, p23
93   *Ibid*, p28
94   *Ibid*, p49
95   MCM 1951, p7
96   *Ibid*, p24
97   *Ibid*, p43
98   *Scotsman*, 24 November 1954
99   MCM 1951, p34
100 *Ibid*, p43
101 MCM 1952, p4
102 *Ibid*, p5
103 MCM 1952, pp60-61, MCM 1953, p9, p13, p19 and pp25-6
104 MCM 1953, p14

CHAPTER FIVE

1   MCM 1955, p3
2   Adams, *op cit*, p228
3   MCM 1958, pp30-31
4   See Adams, *op cit*, p226-30 for a discussion of this problem.
5   MCM 1954, pp44-5
6   *Ibid*, p43
7   MCM 1952, p36
8   R.H. Macintosh, *op cit*, p16
9   MCM 1954, p34
10   *Ibid*, p48
11   *Ibid*, p50
12   MCM 1955, p22
13   *Ibid*, p25
14   Macintosh, *op cit*, p19
15   MCM 1955, p24
16   *Ibid*, p33
17   *Ibid*, p34
18   *Ibid*, p25
19   *Ibid*, p38
20   MCM 1956 p9
21   MCM 1954, p45; MCM 1955, p12
22   MCM 1955, p17
23   MCM 1957, p31 and MCM 1958, p45
24   MCM 1956, p33
25   MCM 1957, p22 and p37
26   MCM 1954, p25
27   MCM 1957, pp44-5
28   *Ibid*, p59
29   MCM 1958, p62
30   Adams, *op cit*, p229
31   MR 1963, pp6-10 (p10 for quote)
32   MCM 1958, p22
33   MCM 1957, p31; MCM 1959, p18 and p27
34   MCM 1958, p60 and MCM 1961, p4
35   MCM 1961, p25, p34 and MCM 1966, p76
36   R.D. Crammond, *op cit*, Chapter IV for a full discussion of this subject
37   DHS Circular 7/1962, dated 12 February 1962
38   Official Report, Scottish Grand Committee, 4 July 1961, columns 16 and 17
39   John S. Gibson, *op cit*, p137
40   MCM 1957, p17
41   AR 1956-61, pp69-70
42   MCM 1957, p55
43   MCM 1958, p3

44 AR 1956-61, p180
45 For example, MCM 1958, p20
46 MCM 1958, pp30-31
47 R.D. Crammond, *op cit*, p78
48 MCM 1958, p33
49 *Ibid*, p42
50 *Ibid*, p32
51 *Ibid*, p46
52 *Ibid*, p53
53 *Ibid*, p59
54 *Ibid*, pp62-3
55 *Ibid*, p59
56 *Ibid*, p64 and p71
57 *Ibid*, p71
58 MCM 1959, p21
59 MCM 1960, p27
60 *Ibid*, p63
61 *Ibid*, p12
62 *Ibid*, pp34-5
63 *Ibid*, p68
64 MCM 1962, pp44-5 and p59
65 AR 1956-61, p136
66 *Ibid*, p219
67 MCM 1959, p16
68 MCM 1957, p6
69 *Ibid*, p29
70 MCM 1955, p45
71 MCM 1958, p50
72 MCM 1959, p32
73 *Ibid*, p38
74 For example, MCM 1961, p56
75 MCM 1960, p77
76 MCM 1961, p1
77 AR 1956-61, p272
78 MCM 1962, pp58-9
79 AR 1962-67, p1, p57 and p113
80 MCM 1963, p61
81 MCM 1963, p102 and MCM 1964, p1
82 MCM 1965, p39
83 MCM 1960, p27, p33, p40 and p55
84 *Ibid*, p70
85 *Ibid*, p8
86 MCM 1958, p71
87 MCM 1959, pp20-21
88 MCM 1961, p7
89 MCM 1962, p20
90 MCM 1963, p71
91 MCM 1960, pp38-9

92 *Ibid*, pp9-10
93 MCM 1961, pp34-5 and p61
94 MCM 1963. p53
95 MCM 1962, p8
96 *Ibid*, p67
97 *Ibid*, p81
98 MCM 1963, p10
99 *Ibid*, p72
100 MCM 1962, p45 and p51
101 *Ibid*, p64
102 *Ibid*, p69
103 *Ibid*, p70
104 *Ibid*, p76
105 MCM 1963, p25 and MR 1963 pp48-9
106 *Ibid*, p46
107 *Ibid*, p52
108 Extracted from MR 1963, pp237-46
109 MCM 1963, pp82-83
110 *Ibid*, p90
111 MCM 1964, p13
112 *Ibid*, p48
113 *Ibid*, p54
114 *Ibid*, p55
115 *Ibid*, p61
116 *Ibid*, p62
117 MCM 1965, p71
118 MCM 1966, p44 and P75
119 *Ibid*, p81
120 MCM 1969, p61
121 MCM 1968, p26
122 *Ibid*, p79
123 *Ibid*, p84
124 *Ibid*, p111
125 MCM 1969, p31
126 *Ibid*, p137
127 MCM 1963, p83
128 MCM 1964, p26
129 *Ibid*, p30
130 MCM 1965, pp1-3
131 *Ibid*, pp54-5
132 *Ibid*, p99
133 MCM 1966, p13
134 *Ibid*, p22
135 *Ibid*, p44
136 *Ibid*
137 *Ibid*, p53
138 AR 1968-75, p4
139 *Ibid*, p26 (Page numbering for this volume of reports

is somewhat odd, with only textual pages being numbered)

140 *Chronicle, op cit*, p27
141 AR 1962-67, p249
142 *Ibid*, p315
143 MCM 1966, p80
144 MCM 1967, pp14-16
145 AR 1962-67, pp315-6
146 AR 1968-75, p25 (Figures for 1970 extracted from p37 since the figures shown for that year on p25 are estimates)
147 MCM 1967, p35
148 AR 1968-75, p13
149 *Ibid*, p25
150 MCM 1967, p2
151 MCM 1959, p34
152 MCM 1963, pp13-14
153 AR 1962-67, pp133-4
154 MCM 1964, p65 and Annual Reports 1964-70
155 MCM 1962, p33
156 MCM 1965, p1
157 AR 1968-75, pp4-5
158 *Ibid*, p28
159 Quoted in *Chronicle, op cit*, p29-30
160 MCM 1968, p14
161 *Ibid*, p60
162 *Chronicle, op cit*, p22
163 MCM 1968, 41
164 *Ibid*, p60
165 *Ibid*, p94
166 MCM 1958, p18
167 MCM 1967, p7
168 *Ibid*, pp78-9
169 MCM 1971, p26
170 MCM 1968, p57
171 MCM 1969, p109
172 AR 1968-75. p51
173 MCM 1971, p48
174 MCM 1969, p2
175 *Ibid*, p84
176 MCM 1971, p7
177 MCM 1972, p47
178 MCM 1965, p13
179 MCM 1968, p9
180 MM 1969, p109
181 *Ibid*, p111
182 MCM 1966, p79
183 MCM 1967, p92; MCM 1968, pp57-8 and MCM 1969, p110
184 *Chronicle, op cit*, p6
185 *Ibid*, p43
186 For example, MCM 1968, p67
187 For example, MCM 1967, p100
188 *Ibid*, p125 and various places through Minutes to 1974
189 MCM 1971, p95
190 MCM 1969, p44
191 *Ibid*, p33
192 *Chronicle, op cit*, p33
193 MCM 1971, pp122-8
194 MCM 1974, p78
195 MCM 1975, p21
196 MCM 1973, p115
197 *Ibid*, p117
198 *Mirror, op cit*, p26
199 MCM 1976, p85
200 *Mirror, op cit*, p24
201 See, for example, MCM 1972, p92; MCM 1976, p3 and MCM 1978, 45
202 *Chronicle, op cit*, p35
203 MCM 1966, pp42-3
204 *Ibid*, p63
205 *Ibid*, pp91-4
206 MCM 1967, p15
207 *Ibid*, p31, pp32-3 and p34
208 *Ibid*, p67
209 MCM 1968, p9
210 *Ibid*, p16
211 *Ibid*, pp94-5
212 MCM 1968, p107
213 MCM 1969, p20
214 *Ibid*, p99
215 MCM 1970, pp27-8
216 *Ibid*, p77 and pp113-16
217 MCM 1971, p11
218 *Ibid*, pp14-15
219 *Ibid*, p56
220 *Ibid*, pp72-9
221 *Ibid*, pp87-9
222 *Ibid*, pp89-90
223 *Ibid*, p94
224 MCM 1972, p3
225 *Ibid*, p113
226 MCM 1973, p36
227 *Ibid*, p52
228 *Ibid*, p114

229 MCM 1974, p5
230 *Ibid*, p35
231 *Ibid*, p53
232 *Ibid*, p105
233 *Ibid*, p113
234 MCM 1975, p3
235 *Ibid*, p10
236 *Ibid*, p22
237 *Ibid*, p59
238 *Ibid*, p84
239 MCM 1976, p4
240 *Ibid*, p20
241 *Ibid*, p70
242 MCM 1977, p54
243 *Ibid*, p69
244 *Ibid*, p86
245 *Ibid*, p71
246 MR 1978 Vol 2, p321 (p2)
247 MCM 1979, p2
248 *Ibid*, p18
249 MCM 1978, p79

CHAPTER SIX

1   MCM 1972, p60 and p67
2   MCM 1978, p65
3   *Ibid*, p74
4   MCM 1975, p56
5   *Ibid*, p34
6   MCM 1978, p49
7   MCM 1977, p42
8   MCM 1978, p37
9   MCM 1971, p131
10 *Mirror, op cit*, p28
11 MCM 1976, p53
12 MCM 1979, p2
13 *Ibid*, p67
14 *Ibid*, p26
15 MCM 1980, p23
16 MCM 1979, p45
17 *Ibid*, p55
18 MCM 1980, p3
19 *Ibid*, p26
20 *Ibid*, pp61-2
21 MCM 1981, p84

22 MCM 1961, p3
23 MCM 1962, p39
24 MCM 1970, p95
25 MCM 1971, p45, p114; MCM 1972, p49
26 MCM 1972, pp57-8
27 *Ibid*, p105
28 MR 1978 (Vol 2), p311
29 *Scottish Housing,*Cmd 6852, *op cit*, p13
30 *Ibid*, pp69-70
31 Cullingworth, *Essays on Housing Policy (1979)*, p41-2
32 *Ibid*, p107
33 MCM 1979, pp27-8
34 For example, MCM 1979, p58
35 MCM 1980, p75
36 Policy Review, SDD July 1986, Working Annex, 2, Table 9 (With figures for 1985-86 added)
37 MCM 1975, p2
38 *Ibid*, p47
39 MCM 1976, p4
40 *Ibid*, p9
41 *Ibid*, p30
42 Adams, *op cit*, p233
43 Figures extracted from GEAR Project Progress Statement 1986
44 MCM 1976, p3
45 *Ibid*, p10
46 MCM 1980, p38
47 MCM 1975, p87
48 For example MCM 1976, p59 and pp72-3
49 MCM 1979, p26, pp47-8, p53, p64
50 *Laighstonehall; A Special Housing Story*, (SSHA 1984), p5
51 *Ibid*, p27
52 *Ibid*, pp28-9
53 Policy Review, *op cit*, p5, Objective xiv
54 *Ibid*, p17, Para 2.6.16

CHAPTER SEVEN

1   Policy Review, *op cit*, p2
2   *Ibid*
3   *Ibid*, p3
4   *Ibid*, p4
5   *Ibid*, p1
6   John Ruskin, *Stones of Venice*, Vol 1, ch 2

Completed houses – Scotland

	Local Authority (incl Scottish Special Housing Association & Scottish National Housing Companies)	Private Sector	Totals All Agencies
1919	–	–	–
1920	817	1,140	1,957
1921	4,342	2,237	6,579
1922	9,523	2,527	12,050
1923	6,462	1,667	8,129
1924	2,993	3,274	6,267
1925	4,822	5,227	10,049
1926	9,501	5,906	15,407
1927	16,923	5,484	22,407
1928	15,071	5,172	20,243
1929	14,316	5,199	19,515
1930	7,918	4,546	12,464
1931	8,315	4,153	12,468
1932	11,631	5,913	17,544
1933	15,808	8,155	23,963
1934	15,216	9,684	24,900
1935	18,814	7,086	25,900
1936	16,044	7,757	23,801
1937	13,341	8,187	21,528
1938	19,162	7,311	26,473
1939	19,118	6,411	25,529
1940	10,474	3,732	14,206
1941	4,714	692	5,406
1942	3,072	224	3,296
1943	2,717	92	2,809
1944	2,383	170	2,553
Total	253,497	111,946	365,443

Completed houses – Scotland (contd)

	Local Authority	New Town	Scottish Special Housing Association	Other Housing Associations	Government Departments	Total Public Sector	Private Sector	Total All Agencies
1945	1,351	–	77	–	–	1,428	141	1,569
1946	3,321	–	490	–	–	3,811	499	4,310
1947	8,919	–	1,854	20	2	10,795	1,354	12,149
1948	16,615	–	2,932	14	109	19,670	1,541	21,211
1949	20,004	60	4,116	72	493	24,745	1,102	25,847
1950	20,989	158	3,167	91	624	25,029	782	25,811
1951	17,971	120	2,906	139	647	21,783	1,145	22,928
1952	22,393	485	4,745	285	797	28,705	2,242	30,947
1953	29,719	1,316	4,957	217	946	37,155	2,393	39,548
1954	29,748	1,466	4,117	115	799	36,245	2,608	38,853
1955	24,210	1,323	3,745	131	1,137	30,546	3,523	34,069
1956	22,084	1,073	3,133	148	887	27,325	4,576	31,901
1957	24,239	951	3,136	105	493	28,924	3,513	32,437
1958	22,622	1,474	3,277	93	643	28,109	4,061	32,170
1959	18,665	1,551	2,493	4	348	23,061	4,232	27,293
1960	17,913	1,519	2,071	127	433	22,063	6,529	28,592
1961	16,823	1,265	1,453	53	489	20,083	7,147	27,230
1962	16,245	1,576	967	65	124	18,977	7,784	26,761
1963	17,699	1,649	1,816	32	399	21,595	6,622	28,217
1964	24,814	2,608	1,734	12	341	29,509	7,662	37,171
1965	21,823	2,996	1,765	154	825	27,563	7,553	35,116
1966	21,343	3,870	2,302	118	526	28,159	7,870	36,029
1967	27,092	3,941	2,189	181	557	33,960	7,498	41,458
1968	26,756	3,207	2,048	288	970	33,269	8,720	41,989
1969	27,497	3,656	2,779	183	187	34,302	8,327	42,629
1970	28,045	2,790	3,525	244	302	34,906	8,220	43,126
1971	23,125	2,394	3,058	332	260	29,169	11,614	40,783
1972	16,335	1,519	1,739	413	151	20,157	11,835	31,992
1973	14,432	1,589	1,328	245	224	17,818	12,215	30,033
1974	13,016	2,099	1,067	480	435	17,097	11,239	28,336
1975	16,086	3,636	3,062	766	402	23,952	10,371	34,323
1976	14,361	3,980	2,813	1,152	517	22,823	13,704	36,527
1977	9,119	3,167	2,042	546	314	15,188	12,132	27,320
1978	6,686	1,510	1,711	1,127	282	11,316	14,443	25,759
1979	4,755	2,018	1,084	544	206	8,607	15,175	23,782
1980	5,048	1,288	1,119	881	33	8,369	12,242	20,611
1981	3,770	1,516	1,779	1,928	1	8,994	11,021	20,015
1982	2,342	729	645	1,167	17	4,900	11,530	16,430
1983	2,311	667	508	1,271	6	4,763	13,178	17,941
1984	2,120	233	280	2,076	14	4,723	14,116	18,839
1985 (P)	1,983	201	622	1,075	17	3,898	13,869	17,767

Sources SHS (annual and quarterly versions)
and Housing Returns Publication
- Figures are published annually in *Scottish Housing Statistics*

House completion under various programmes (With Yearly Adjustments)

Year	General Needs		Miners		Overspill		Redevelopment Assistance		Economic Expansion		Special Needs		Total	Built for Others	Built for Sale	Total Completions
	Built	Acq	Built	Acq	Built	Acq	Built	Acq	Built	Acq	Built	Acq				
1937-38	–												–			–
38-39	2												2			2
39-40	358												358			358
40-41	612												612	800		1412
41-42	276												276	354		630
42-43	108	1											109	18		127
43-44	56												56			56
44-45	291												291			291
45-46	66												66			66
46-47	536		24										560			560
47-48	1768		274										2042			2042
48-49	1746		1550										3296	9		3305
49-50	2485		1643										4128	92		4220
50-51	1662		1629										3291	147		3438
51-52	2001		1340										3341	347		3688
52-53	3423		1562										4985	197		5182
53-54	3707		1045										4752	390		5142
54-55	4019		574										4593	359		4952
55-56	2784		392										3176	328		3504
56-57	3168		146										3314	91		3405
57-58	2801		137										2938	129		3067
58-59	2759		222										2981	95		3076
59-60	2227		54		212								2493	311		2804
60-61	1509				215								1724	130		1854
61-62	865				420								1285	135		1420
62-63	711				534								1245	178		1423
63-64	781	4421			1060								6262	167		6429
64-65	826				966								1792	209		2001
65-66	969				670				60				1699	136		1835
66-67	1265				112				519				1896	409		2305
67-68	990				451				680				2121	636		2757
68-69	455				497				1217				2169	420		2589
69-70	618	120			317				2116				3171	568		3739
1970-71	239	10			228				3215				3692	520		4212
71-72	122	6			354				2419				2901	125		3026
72-73		36			420				1032				1488	282		1770
73-74		48			329				777				1154	149		1303
74-75					230				1030	52			1312	137		1449
75-76					701				2308	249			3258	1015		4273
76-77					646				2037	62			2745	465		3210
77-78					369		266	759	1203	144			2741	322		3063
78-79	47				429		472	26	450	169			1593	646		2239
79-80	37				472		473	1091	222				2295	182		2477
80-81	51				113		897	102	195				1358	61	71	1490
81-82					125		1410	209					1744	19	40	1803
82-83					84		356	624	14				1078	6		1084
83-84							278	100	98		86		562	–		562
84-85							195	116	99		124	3	537	55	21	613
85-86		4					328		149		92	12	585	–		
	46340	4646	10592	–	9954	–	4675	3027	19840	676	302	15	100067	10639	132	110838

	General Needs Total	Miners Total	Overspill Total	Redevelopment Assistance Total	Economic Expansion Total	Special Needs Total	Total	Built for Others	Built for Sale	Total Completions
Deduct Repurchase	50986	10592	9954	7702	20516	317	100067	10639	132	110838
	–	–	–	–	–	–	–	2	–	2
	50986	10592	9954	7702	20516	317	100067	10637	132	110836
Deduct Demolished	–300	114	–1	–2	–	–	–417	–	–	–
Deduct Sales to Others	–41	24	–	–	–156	–	–221	–	–	–
Deduct Sales to Tenants							–14399	–	–	–
Add: Repurchased from Tenants	+3	–	–	–	–	–	+3	–	–	–
Adjustment for Conversion	+42	–	–	–	–	–	+42	–	–	–

Note These figures do not exactly match those in Appendix A, since they relate to the Financial Year

APPENDIX C
Multi-storey stock – West Region

Location	Type	No of Blocks	No of Storeys/Dwellings	Programme	Completion Date
Glasgow, Anderston Cross	JHDU	1	15 Storeys/128 Dwellings	GN	13.12.69
Glasgow, Anderston Cross	Cruden	2	9 Storeys/ 96 Dwellings	GN	9.6.78
Glasgow, Broomhill	Mark 6A	5	18 Storeys/510 Dwellings	GN	29.10.67
Glasgow, Broomhill	Tracoba	3	8 Storeys/ 96 Dwellings	GN	13.12.68
Glasgow, Carron Street	Mark 3	4	15 Storeys/224 Dwellings	GN	12.10.64
Glasgow, Carron Street	Mark 10	3	8 Storeys/ 93 Dwellings	GN	31.3.66
Glasgow, Collina Street	Tracoba	1	19 Storeys/113 Dwellings	GN	3.8.70
Glasgow, Fortrose Street	JHDU	1	9 Storeys/ 53 Dwellings	GN	30.7.64
Glasgow, Gorget Avenue	Tracoba	3	8 Storeys/ 96 Dwellings	GN	30.5.69
Glasgow, Hutchesontown	Mark 6	4	24 Storeys/552 Dwellings	GN	23.4.67
Glasgow, Hutchesontown	Tracoba	3	8 Storeys/ 96 Dwellings	GN	13.2.70
Glasgow, Langlands Road	Mark 3	2	15 Storeys/112 Dwellings	GN	27.1.63
Glasgow, Toryglen	Mark 1	2	10 Storeys/ 60 Dwellings	GN	19.3.57
Glasgow, Toryglen	Mark 2	2	10 Storeys/ 60 Dwellings	GN	29.6.59
Glasgow, Toryglen	Mark 3	2	15 Storeys/112 Dwellings	GN	23.6.64
Glasgow, Wester Common	Tracoba	4	19 Storeys/452 Dwellings	GN	16.5.70
Glasgow, Wyndford	Mark 3	5	15 Storeys/280 Dwellings	GN	18.12.63
Glasgow, Wyndford	Mark 4	4	26 Storeys/600 Dwellings	GN	10.6.68
Glasgow, Wyndford	JHDU	1	9 Storeys/53 Dwellings	GN	15.6.68
Glasgow, Wyndford	Mark 10	7	8 Storeys/217 Dwellings	GN	7.8.67
Clydebank, Central Area	Mark 3	7	15 Storeys/392 Dwellings	GN	31.3.64
Paisley, Foxbar	Mark 3	2	15 Storeys/112 Dwellings	GN	18.3.62
Paisley, Linwood	Cruden	2	16 Storeys/180 Dwellings	EE	20.6.73

Summary	Total No of Blocks	Total No of Dwellings
Glasgow	59	4003
Clydebank	7	392
Paisley	4	292
West Region	70	4687

Reference GN – General Needs Programme
EE – Economic Expansion Programme

Erskine – Housing stock

Development	Total No of Houses (Built)	House Types	Programme	Completion Date
Bargarran, Phase 1	271	BD No-fines cottages & flats (193 cottages) (78 flats)	OS	8.4.72
Bargarran, Phase 2	216	BD No-fines cottages & flats (188 cottages) (28 flats)	OS	2.12.72
Bargarran, Phase 3	308	BD No-fines cottages & flats (269 cottages) (39 flats)	OS	20.10.73
North Barr, Phase 1	300	BD No-fines cottages & flats & traditional paraplegic houses (4 paraplegic houses) (272 cottages) (24 flats)	OS	5.6.75
North Barr, Phase 2	312	BD No-fines cottages & flats (174 cottages) (138 flats)	OS	5.11.76
North Barr, Phase 3	120	BD No-fines cottages (105 cottages) (11 split level cottages) (4 pend cottages)	OS	2.4.76
North Barr, Phase 4	242	Wimpey No-fines cottages & flats (178 cottages) (22 pend cottages) (36 flats) (6 paraplegic)	OS	28.2.77
Park Mains, Area B Phase 1	174	BD No-fines and brick cottages and houses (145 no-fines cottages) (7 no-fines pend cottages) (2 brick cottages) (17 3 storey brick houses) (Shop – 1 brick cottage) (Doctors Surgery – 1 brick cottage) (Community House – 1x3 sty brick house)	OS	9.12.77
Park Mains, Area B Phase 2A	16	BD Brick cottages & houses (11 cottages) (5 x 3 sty houses)	OS	1.9.78
Park Mains, Area B Phase 2B	25	BD Brick cottages & flats (9 3 storey flats) (16 cottages)	OS	30.1.81
Park Mains, Area C	239	Cruden cottages & flats & maisonettes (Brick) (209 cottages) (24 flats) (6 maisonettes)	OS	15.12.80
Park Mains, Area D	183	Weir brick cottages & 3 storey houses (131 cottages) (32 3 storey houses) (20 3 storey houses with integral garages)	OS	17.4.79
Park Mains, Area G	272	No-fines and brick cottages & flats, (103 n/f cottages) (116 brick cottages) (26 3 storey brick houses) (27 3 storey brick flats)	OS	31.3.80
Park Mains, Area H	209	Brick Cottages (all brick cottages)	OS	24.1.83
Park Mains, Area J	121	Weir trad. cottages, flats and 3 storey houses (83 trad cottages) (15 3 storey houses) (23 3 storey flats)	OS	22.4.80

Development	Total No of Houses (Built)	House Types	Programme	Completion Date
Park Mains, Area K	261	BD No-fines cottages and houses, brick cottages and timber frame pend houses (211 B.D. n/f cottages) (20 n/f pend cottages) (28 brick cottages) (2 timber frame pend houses)	OS	8.1.79
Park Mains, Area L	122	Weir trad cottages, pend cottages and 2 storey houses (110 cottages) (8 pend cottages) (4 3 storey houses)	OS	20.12.77

Total No of Houses Built 3,391

Ref: OS – Overspill

APPENDIX E

SSHA in GEAR

Capital Funded Works

1 Completed Projects

Category	Location	No of Houses/Housing Mix	Cost (£000's)	Programme
New Build	Fairbairn Street	110 general needs houses and flats	1,872	Aug 77 – Nov 79
(R A Programme)	Acorn Street	50 general needs houses and flats including 10 properties designed to ambulant disabled standard	1,164	Jan 80 – Jul 81
(R A Programme)	Dechmont Street	54 general needs houses and flats including 8 properties designed to ambulant disabled standard	1,213	Dec 79 – Oct 81
(R A Programme)	Crail Street	88 cottages and flats including 30 sheltered flats and 2 wheelchair houses	2,003	Jul 80 – Dec 81
(R A Programme)	Maukinfauld Road	142 houses and flats of which 30 flats provided sheltered accommodation and 2 houses are designed for wheelchair users.	2,772	May 80 – Dec 81
(R A Programme)	Mackeith Street	42 dwellings including 27 sheltered flats.	957	Aug 80 – Jan 82
(R A Programme)	Calton 1/1A	135 dwellings of which 12 are to sheltered standard.	2,828	Jan 80 – Jan 82
(R A Programme)	Calton 1/1B	38 dwellings including 18 sheltered flats and 1 wheelchair house.	750	Jun 80 – Jan 82
(R A Programme)	Bridgeton, Main Street	123 dwellings of which 30 flats provide sheltered accommodation with 11 of these and a further 2 houses being designed for wheelchair users.	2,919	Jun 80 – Feb 82

Category	Location	No of Houses/Housing Mix	Cost (£000's)	Programme
New Build (R A Programme) continued	Lily Street	25 units comprising 18 flats, 12 of which are sheltered, and 7 mainstream houses.	497	Dec 81 – Nov 82
(R A Programme)	Calton 1/2A	119 dwellings, 30 of which provide sheltered accommodation.	2,923	Nov 81 – Jul 83
(R A Programme)	Calton 1/2B	5 general needs houses including 1 designed to wheelchair standard.	186	Feb 82 – Jul 83
(R A Programme)	Calton 2/1A	75 general needs houses and flats including 5 wheelchair properties.	2,159	Jun 84 – Mar 86
(R A Programme)	Dalmarnock Road A	71 units comprising 47 houses, 2 of which provide accommodation for wheelchair users, and 24 flats. Certain houses and flats are designed to amenity and ambulant disabled standards.	1,891	Aug 84 – Jun 86
			24,134	
Modernisation	Bridgeton Phase1	102 GDC Inter-war flats	697	Mar 78 – Sep 79
(R A Programme)	Bridgeton Phase 2	100 GDC Inter-war flats	782	Aug 79 – Oct 80
(R A Programme)	Bridgeton Phase 3/4	157 Inter-war flats of the 153 flats acquired from GDC, 12, 4 Apt flats were converted during modernisation into 12, 2 apt and 4 3 apt flats.	1,286	Nov 79 – Sep 81
(R A Programme)	Bridgeton Phase 5	78 GDC Inter-war flats.	660	Mar 80 – May 81
(R A Programme)	Calton A	60 GDC Inter-war flats.	400	Aug 78 – Nov 79
(R A Programme)	Calton B	72 GDC Inter-war flats.	592	Jul 79 – Sep 80
(R A Programme)	Calton C/D	144 GDC Inter-war flats.	1,105	May 80 – Apr 81
(R A Programme)	Calton E	48 GDC Inter-war flats.	414	Jul 81 – Jun 82
Modernisation (R A Programme) continued	Beattock St/Powfoot St	90 Inter-war flats. The 86 flats acquired from GDC were converted during modernisation to form 90 units.	876	May 79 – Nov 80
(SNHC Modernisation)	Shettleston Phase 1	57 SNHC houses	456	Aug 78 – Feb 80
(SNHC Modernisation)	Shettleston Phase 2	136 SNHC dwellings comprising 44 flats and 92 cottages.	1,279	Oct 79 – May 81
(SNHC Modernisation)	Shettleston Phase 3	131 SNHC cottages and flats.	1,189	Dec 81 – Oct 83
(SNHC Modernisation)	Shettleston Phase 4	145 SNHC cottages and flats.	1,320	Oct 83 – Nov 85
(R A Programme)	Lily Street Phase 1	30 GDC Inter-war flats of which 20 are designed to provide sheltered accommodation.	230	Jun 80 – Apr 81
(R.A. Programme)	Lily Street Phase 2	162 GDC Inter-war flats. Modernisation included the provision of 1 disabled person's flat and 10 amenity flats.	1,627	Feb 83 – Oct 84

Category	Location	No of Houses/Housing Mix	Cost (£000's)	Programme
(R A Programme)	Westmuir Street	36 GDC Inter-war flats.	300	Jun 80 – Nov 81
(R A Programme)	Old Shettleston Road	168 GDC Inter-war flats	1,672	Jan 83 – Oct 84
(R A Programme)	Troon Street	116 GDC Inter-war cottage flats, 54 of which were upgraded to amenity standard during modernisation.	1,224	Jan 85 – Mar 86
			16,109	
Rehabilitation (R A Programme)	Finnart Street	26 flats converted from 48 flats acquired from GDC	274	Jul 77 – Nov 78
(R A Programme)	Tullis Street	24 flats acquired from GDC	335	Jan 79 – Apr 80
(R A Programme)	Abercromby Street	18 units converted from 27 tenement flats.	262	Aug 81 – Jun 82
(R A Programme)	Winning Row	24 tenement flats.	621	Jun 80 – Nov 81
(R A Programme)	394 Gallowgate	4 flatted units	80	Feb 82 – Jul 83
(R A Programme)	Bain Street Phase 1	45 storey tenement flats	629	Nov 81 – Jun 83
(R A Programme)	Bain Street Phase 2	24 4 storey tenement flats	485	Jan 83 – Oct 83
			2,686	
Rehabilitation for Sale	Bridgeton, Main Street	31 tenement flats	489	Mar 79 – Aug 81
(R A Programme)	Tollcross Rd/Crail Street	21 tenement flats	306	Nov 83 – Dec 84
			795	

2 Projects in Programme

Category	Location	Description of Work	(£000's)	Programme
New Build (S N Programme)	Finnart Street	46 dwellings of which 20 are designed to amenity standard and 2 for wheelchair users	1,360	Oct 86 – Jan 88
(S N Programme)	Muslin Street	27 dwellings comprising amenity wheelchair and general needs houses and flats	546	Jun 87 – Jul 88
(S N Programme)	Dalmarnock Road B	39 units comprising 16 amenity, flats and 23 houses, 4 of which are designed for wheelchair users	1,070	Mar 87 – Jun 88
			2,976	
Stock Improvements	Abercromby Street	Window Renewal	59	1986/87
	Lily Street Phase 1A	Dampness Remedial Works	310	1986/87
			369	
Environmental Improvements	Lily Street Phase 2	Landscaping	75	1986/87
	Bridgeton, Main Street	Landscaping	85	1986/87
			160	

Summary

SSHA in Gear

Capital Works

New Build

1,077 houses completed at an approximate cost £24m
20 houses in progress costing approximately £0.5m
112 houses programmed at an estimated cost of £3m

Modernisation

1,832 houses modernised at an estimated cost of £16m

Rehabilitation

165 houses rehabilitated at a cost of £2.7m

Rehab for Sale

52 houses rehabilitated for sale costing £0.8m

Stock Improvements

Approximately £0.9m spent on completed projects
Projects in progress amount to £1.2m
£0.4m allocated in the current programme

Environmental Improvements

£0.5m (approximately) on completed projects
£0.2m (approximately) on works in progress
£0.2m (approximately) allocated to programme

Revenue Works

£31,000 has been invested in GEAR to date and works to the value of £191,700 are currently in progress. It is estimated that a further £99,720 will be spent on works to be carried out during this Financial Year.

	Capital	Revenue
Total Expenditure on Completed Schemes	£45,034,00	£ 31,000
Total Expenditure on Works in Progress	£ 1,882,000	£191,700
Total Expenditure on Works Identified	£ 3,505,00	£ 99,720

APPENDIX F

SSHA Fixed Assets 1969/70 – 1985/86

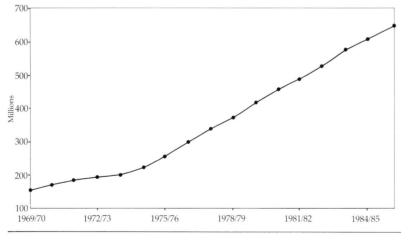

APPENDIX G
SSHA Interest Rates on Borrowings 1969 – 1985

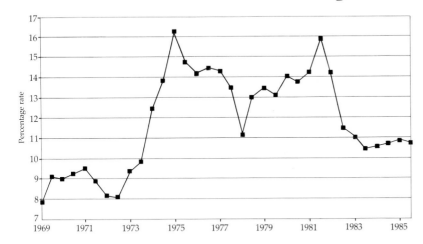

APPENDIX H
SSHA Capital Expenditure/Capital Receipts

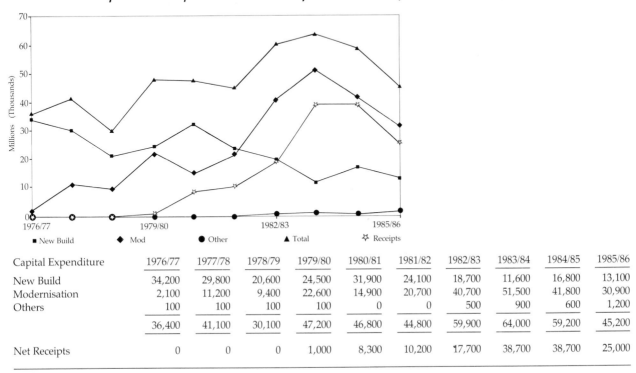

■ New Build   ◆ Mod   ● Other   ▲ Total   ☆ Receipts

Capital Expenditure	1976/77	1977/78	1978/79	1979/80	1980/81	1981/82	1982/83	1983/84	1984/85	1985/86
New Build	34,200	29,800	20,600	24,500	31,900	24,100	18,700	11,600	16,800	13,100
Modernisation	2,100	11,200	9,400	22,600	14,900	20,700	40,700	51,500	41,800	30,900
Others	100	100	100	100	0	0	500	900	600	1,200
	36,400	41,100	30,100	47,200	46,800	44,800	59,900	64,000	59,200	45,200
Net Receipts	0	0	0	1,000	8,300	10,200	17,700	38,700	38,700	25,000

Housing Revenue Account – the last 10 years

		1976/77	1977/78	1978/79	1979/80	1980/81
Income:	Rent	16,635	19,152	23,306	26,564	33,459
	Subsidy	16,959	23,635	29,345	30,891	30,323
	Other	153	186	516	479	1,254
	TOTAL	33,747	42,973	53,167	57,934	65,036
Expenditure:	Loan Charges	20,506	27,246	33,651	35,951	40,718
	Repairs & Maint	10,703	12,415	15,543	16,783	14,736
	Other	2,538	3,312	3,973	5,200	9,582
	TOTAL	33,747	42,973	53,167	57,934	65,036
FIXED ASSETS		301,125	342,014	371,919	418,530	453,550

		1981/82	1982/83	1983/84	1984/85	1985/86
Income:	Rent	42,223	51,819	56,936	59,987	63,950
	Subsidy	26,579	25,247	23,000	23,000	23,000
	Other	2,676	3,790	3,273	2,119	2,758
	TOTAL	71,478	80,856	83,209	85,106	89,708
Expenditure:	Loan Charges	47,120	50,790	54,770	57,979	61,811
	Repairs & Maint	18,457	21,537	18,837	18,722	18,929
	Other	5,901	8,529	9,602	8,405	8,968
	TOTAL	71,478	80,856	83,209	85,106	89,708
FIXED ASSETS		486,743	534,903	581,251	617,981	651,009

Characteristics of houses sold

1 *Analysis by Age*

	SALES				STOCK			
	Total Nr Sold		Total Nr sold as % of Total Sales		Total Nr of Assoc Houses		Total Nr as % of Total Stock	
Year of Construction	at Mar 85	at Mar 86	at Mar 85	at Mar 86	at Mar 85	at Mar 86	at Mar 85	at Mar 86
Up to 1950	1,176	1,487	9.9	10.6	18,737	16,812	19.0	17.0
1951-1960	2,716	3,389	22.9	24.1	35,555	35,548	35.9	35.8
1961-1970	1,994	2,294	16.8	16.3	18,719	18,758	18.9	18.9
1971-1985	5,990	6,877	50.4	49.0	25,910	28,142	26.2	28.3
	11,876	14,047	100.0	100.0	98,921	99,260*	100.0	100.0

2 *Analysis by Size*

	SALES				STOCK			
	Total Nr Sold		Total Nr sold as % of Total Sales		Total Nr of Assoc Houses		Total Nr as % of Total Stock	
Apt Size	at Mar 85	at Mar 86	at Mar 85	at Mar 86	at Mar 85	at Mar 86	at Mar 85	at Mar 86
1 + 2 Apts	73	91	0.6	0.6	6,749	6,898	6.8	6.9
3 Apts	3,059	3,656	25.8	26.0	39,786	39,989	40.2	40.3
4 Apts	6,738	7,961	56.7	56.7	44,109	44,127	44.6	44.5
5 Apts	1,742	2,026	14.7	14.4	7,214	7,178	7.3	7.2
6 Apts	241	288	2.0	2.0	980	985	1.0	1.0
7+ Apts	23	25	0.2	0.3	83	83	0.1	0.1
	11,876	14,047	100.0	100.0	98,921	99,260*	100.0	100.0

3 *Analysis by House Type*

Type	SALES				STOCK			
	Total Nr Sold		Total Nr sold as % of Total Sales		Total Nr of Assoc Houses		Total Nr as % of Total Stock	
	at Mar 85	at Mar 86	at Mar 85	at Mar 86	at Mar 85	at Mar 86	at Mar 85	at Mar 86
Cottage Detached	248	268	2.1	1.9	645	621	0.7	0.7
Cottage, Semi-detached	3,044	3,697	25.6	26.3	20,076	20,072	20.3	20.2
Cottage, Terrace Mid	4,980	5,768	41.9	41.1	26,873	26,918	27.1	27.1
Cottage, Terraced End	3,160	3,756	26.6	26.7	17,361	17,294	17.6	17.4
Flats/ Maisonettes	444	558	3.8	4.0	29,165	29,554	29.5	29.8
Multi storey	–	–	–	–	4,801	4,801	4.8	4.8
	11,876	14,047	100.0	100.0	98,921	99,260*	100.0	100.0

* Total stock includes all SSHA property, both built and acquired, ignoring house sales.

4 *Analysis of Construction Method*

Construction Type	Total No Sold	
	at March 85	at March 86
Brick/Traditional	3,897	4,725
Concrete Block	1,483	1,597
No Fines	5,472	6,408
Steel	535	705
Timber	313	412
Miscellaneous	176	200
	11,876	14,047

5 *Analysis by Area*

Sales among the Local Authority Regions vary from 10.0% to 25.7% of total stock, compared with the Association's average of 14.2%. The detailed figures are:–

	%	
Grampian	25.7	% of total stock sold in Region
Fife	24.6	% of total stock sold in Region
Highland	21.2	% of total stock sold in Region
Lothian	19.3	% of total stock sold in Region
Borders	16.4	% of total stock sold in Region
Central	13.6	% of total stock sold in Region
Shetland	13.6	% of total stock sold in Region
Dumfries and Galloway	13.0	% of total stock sold in Region
Tayside	12.4	% of total stock sold in Region
Strathclyde	10.0	% of total stock sold in Region

APPENDIX L
Awards for Design

Year	Body	Award
1964	Saltire Society	Commendation for 9-storey block at Fortrose Street, Glasgow.
1965	Saltire Society	Commendation for local traditional development at Writers Court, Dunbar.
1965	Civic Trust	Commendation for 'village green' development at Kingoodie.
1966	Civic Trust	Commendation for central re-development at Port Glasgow.
1966	Saltire Society	Commendation for use of industrial methods at Anderston Cross, Glasgow.
1967	Civic Trust	Commendation for Writers Court, Dunbar.
1968	Saltire Society	Award for central redevelopment at Wyndford, Glasgow.
1968	Saltire Society	Commendation for development in Scottish vernacular theme at Cove and Kilcreggan.
1970	Saltire Society	Award for Gap Site in historic surroundings at Culross.
1971	Concrete Society	Outstanding merit in use of concrete at Kinneil Park, Bo'ness.
1972	Saltire Society	Award for Ladyburn, Kinghorn.
1972	Saltire Society	Commendation for Aberdour Road Site, Dunfermline.
1972	Civic Trust	Commendation for Aberdour Road Site, Dunfermline.
1973	Saltire Society	Mention for Bargarran 11 development at Erskine.

1975	Saltire Society	Mention for environmental improvement at Mains of Fintry, Dundee.
1976	Royal Institute of Chartered Surveyors/ Times Conservation Awards Scheme	Commendation for reconstruction of Prince Charlie's House at Jedburgh.
1976	Saltire Society	Award for Phase 1A, Tweedbank.
1976	Saltire Society	Award for North Barr (Phase 11) Erskine.
1978	Civic Trust	Award for Castlegate, Jedburgh.
1978	Saltire Society	Award for Castlegate, Jedburgh.
1980	Europa Nostra Medal	For Jedburgh.
1980	West Lothian District	Special Design Award for Weir Phoenix modernisation at Riddochhill, Blackburn.
1980	Civic Trust	Commendation for Riddochhill, Blackburn.
1981	Saltire Society	Award for Park Mains Area G, Erskine.
1982	Saltire Society	Commendation for North Street, Peterhead.
1983	Saltire Society	Award for Lamer Street, Dunbar.
1983	Saltire Society	Commendation for entry plates at Bowling Green Street, Edinburgh.
1984	Saltire Society	Commendation for restoration of 394 Gallowgate, Glasgow.
1985	Saltire Society	Commendation for Bowling Green Street, Edinburgh.
1985	Saltire Society/RTPI	Patrick Geddes Planning Award for Glasgow, Eastern Area Renewal.
1986	Civic Trust	Commendation for Castle Street, Dunbar.
1986	Saltire Society	Premier New Housing Award for Kirkland Street, Glasgow.
1986	Saltire Society	Award, Excellence in Building, Kirkland Street, Glasgow.

INDEX

Abercrombie, Sir Patrick, 129
Aberdeen, 125, 133, 136, 144, 187, 224, 259
Aberfoyle *see* Dounans Camp
Acts *see* Parliament
Adams, Ian, 242-3
Addison Act *see* Parliament
Airdrie, 74, 81, 160
Aldington, Mrs J, 219
Algiers, 202
Allan, A.R., 232
Allan, Mr, 171
Alness, Lord, 111
American Embassy, 96
American seamen, 93-7
Ancram, Michael, MP, 252
Appleton, Sir Edward, 178
Arbroath, 125, 177, 210, 242, 245
Armadale, 74
Arnott, McLoed and Company, Messrs William, 73
Atholl Steel Houses Ltd, 54, 134-5, 142
Attlee, Clement, 151
Attwell, J., 83
Australia, 51, 172
Ayr, 125, 133, 136, 144, 186
Ayr County Council, 160, 185

Baker, Noel, MP, 94
Baldwin, Stanley, 52-3, 56
Balfour, Lord (Viscount Traprain) 75, 78, 106
Balfron, 87
Balloch, Lomond Road Hostel, 92-3, 98-9
Barlow Commission, *see* Reports
Bathgate, 64, 74, 125, 177
Bauld, Baillie, 226
Beardmore, Wm & Co Ltd, 54
Belmont Camp, 85-7
Beith, 245
Bennett, Mr, 64

Bent, J. Austen, 139, 147, 148, 149, 152, 169, 188
Bevan, Aneurin, 23
'Bevin Boys', 98
Bilsland, Sir Steven and Lady, 88
Birmingham, 183
Blackburn Aircraft Factory, 98
Bo'ness, 160, 259
Bonhill, 74
Bonnyrigg, 177
Borders Region, 1, 220
Bowley, Marion, 7
Brady, A.W., 62
Brebner, Sir Alexander, 188-9
Brechin, 125
Bridge of Weir, Lintwhite Hostel, 100-104
British Columbian Timber Commissioner, 64
British Council, 195
Broomfield, Brian, 259
Broomlee Camp, 85-91
Brown, Ernest, 111
Brown, Councillor J.C., 163-4
Brown's John, 51
Broxburn, 161
Bruce, Robert, 27, 147
Buchanan, George, MP, 126-7, 131-4, 136-8, 143, 159
Buckhaven & Methil, 125
Building Department (Direct Labour), 73, 135, 136, 143-4, 151, 153, 158, 173-4, 189, 196, 197-200, 204-5, 212-13, 228-9, 235, 257-8
Building Research Station, 65, 171
Burt, Sir George, 119
Burt Committee, *see* also Reports, 119, 121
Buteux, Harold, 188, 191-7, 200, 202, 205, 211, 215, 233, 255
Butt, Prof J., 4

Cairns, Peter, 78
Calder, Lord Ritchie, 214
Campbell, Norman J., 78, 96
Camus system, 193-4
Canada, 89
Carfin, 67-70

Carlisle, 183
Carluke, 63-4, 73-4
Chamberlain, Sir Neville, 11, 50-52, 60
Christie, Miss, 78
Churchill, Sir Winston, 51, 56, 111
Civic Trust, 234
Civil Defence, 98
Clean Air Act, 214
Clydebank, 18, 91, 106, 125, 144, 160, 173, 250-52
Clydebank, Whitecrook Hostel, 91-2, 99
Clydesdale Bank, 62, 215
Clyde Valley Regional Planning Advisory Committee, 26, 168, 173
Clyde Valley Regional Plan, 26, 129, 168
Clydesiders *see* Independent Labour Party
Coalburn, 64, 74
Coatbridge, 74, 125, 144, 160, 163
Collins, Sir Godfrey, 57
Colston, Frank, 256
Colville, Sir John (Lord Clydesmuir), 72, 76, 111
Commissioner for the Special Areas, 57, 59, 61-3, 67-70, 76
Concrete (Scotland) Ltd, 157, 195-6, 200
Corbusier, Le, 29, 30
Council for Art and Industry, 67
'Council of State', 111, 131
Coutts Morrison, J., 78, 127
Cove and Kilcreggan, 216
Coventry, 120, 183
Cowdenbeath, 203
Cowieson, Messrs, 54
Craigton, Lord, 186, 199
Crofthead, 74
Cross, L.W.S., 191, 232
Crow, Gilbert, 190
Cruden, Messrs, 208
Cruikshank, Mrs A.T., 259
Cullingworth, Prof J.B., 237-9
Culross, 178
Cumbernauld, 26-7, 30, 168, 173,

200, 261
Cumnock, 187, 203

Dalry, 74
Dalziel, James 133, 136-7
Davidson, Roy, 258
Davidson, William C., 62, 112, 123, 127, 132-3, 137, 139
Deininger, Prof, 171, 173
Direct Labour Organisation *see* Building Department
dockers, 92, 98
Dollan, Sir Patrick, 130
Douglas, 64, 74
Douglas, Alex, 70
Douglas, Sir William, 60
Douglas-Hamilton, Lord Nigel, 61, 68
Dounans Camp, 85-90
Dumbarton, 125, 187, 214
Dumfries, 134
Dunbar, 177-80, 244-5
Dunbar, Sir John Greig, 195, 212
Dunbartonshire, 161, 187, 203, 212
Dundee, 2, 4, 29, 30, 32, 55, 83, 89, 123-5, 152, 157, 168, 173, 192, 196, 242
Dunfermline, 46-7, 53
Dunkeld, 166, 178
Dysart, 149

East Kilbride, 26, 30, 219, 261
Easter Ross, 220
Easton Gibb & Sons, 44
'Economic Expansion', 176, 204, 208-9, 219-21, 240, 264
Edinburgh, 2, 83, 89, 95, 168, 195, 211, 234
    Corporation, 4, 146, 163-4, 173
    Learmonth Gardens, 81
    Lochend, 55
    St John's Road, 81
    Sighthill Experimental Site, 115, 119-22, 134, 146, 152-4, 236
    Sutherland Street, 245
    Wester Hailes, 32
Edinburgh University, 178, 255
Edinburgh, Head Office, 62, 123,

138, 187, 217-8, 259
Elliot, Sir Walter, MP, 50-53, 56-61, 67, 76, 111, 261-2, 268
Emmerson, Sir Harold, 195
Empire Exhibition (1938), 67
Erskine, 221-3, 233
Esplin, Nurse, 95
European Common Market, 37
Europa Nostra Medal, 234
Evacuation Camps *see also* camp names 75, 78, 83-91, 127
Ewart, Mrs M.S., 188-9, 214, 218

Faifley, 250-52
Fairfields, 51
Falkirk, 30, 215
Families' Hostels *see also* individual names, 100-105
Faslane, 203, 209
Ferguson, Leonard, 219, 253, 260, 267
Fife, 134, 161
Findlay, S.A., 139, 169, 191
Fintry, 87
Fleming, J.B., 232, 259
Foote, Alex, 83
Forest Products Research Laboratory, 64
Forestry Commission, 89, 144, 158
Forfar, 210
Forman, John, MP, 123, 126-7
Fort William, 177, 209
Forth, 64, 74
Forward, 77
Fraser, J.W., 96
Fraser, Tom, MP, 152, 163, 165
Fullarton, John, 200, 233, 260

Galashiels, 220
Galbraith, Commander (Lord Strathclyde), 152-5, 168, 172
gale (1968), 212-13
Gamley, Mr E.E., 215
George V, 46
George VI, 67-70
Germany, 56, 169-71
Gibraltarians, 102
Gibson, John S., 77, 182

Gilbert Ash Ltd, 197, 200
Gilmour, Sir John, 52
Glasgow, 2, 4, 5, 9, 11, 18, 26-30, 40, 52, 67, 77, 81, 83, 85, 124-6, 128-31, 157, 168-9, 186-7, 191, 195, 199, 201, 203-4, 212-13, 227, 242, 254, 259, 263, 265
    Anderson Cross, 193, 200-201
    Arden, 32, 157, 250
    Balornock, 145 Cadder Road, 145
    Carntyne, 14 Castlemilk, 222
    City Improvement Trust, 4
    Corporation, 4, 14, 26, 89, 92, 94, 130, 133, 147-8, 159, 168-9, 171-4, 182-4, 190-91, 195, 201, 213, 231, 242, 263
    Cowcaddens, 52
    Craigton, 11 Drumchapel, 32, 222
    Easterhouse, 32, 222 Fortrose Street, 193, 200 Gorbals, 52, 126
    Hillington, 81, 98
    Hutchesontown, 32, 191, 194, 197, 267 Knightswood, 14
    Maryhill, 191, 242, 244 Moss Park, 11 Riddrie, 11
    Robroyston, 55 Rosshall, 145
    Shettleston, 55, 242
    Springboig, 55 Toryglen 145-8, 152, 156, 168-9, 171-4, 192
    Wyndford, 191-2, 196-200, 216, 267
Glasgow Eastern Area Renewal (GEAR) Project, 40, 242-3, 265
Glasgow Herald, 52, 68
Glengonnar Camp, 85-91
Glenrothes, 26, 29, 200, 261
Grangemouth, 171, 265
Gray, Sir William, 217, 231
Greenock, 4, 18, 55, 74, 81, 92, 125, 129, 144
Greenock, Highlanders Academy Hostel, 92
Greig & Fairbairn, 47
Gropius, Walter, 30
Gwynne, Mr & Mrs, 70

Haddington, 176
Hall, Messrs, 205, 208

Halley, David H., 138, 188, 212, 218, 232

Hamilton, 100, 125, 136, 177, 188, 247-50

Hamilton, Fairhill Hostel, 92-100

Harvie, Prof Christopher, 130

Hawick, 125

Hay, Sir David Allan, 61, 67, 70, 74, 261

Head Office, *see* Edinburgh

Henderson, Sir George, 123, 152

Holland, *see* Netherlands

Holland, Hannan & Cubitts, 193

Hollins, Mrs Jean, 222

Holytown, 63-4, 74

Hope, Mary, 259

Horsburgh, Florence, MP, 77, 85

House Sales, 235-9, 241, 268-71

Houses for Industry Committee, 209, 219

Housing Associations, 1, 36, 272

Housing Corporation, 1, 36, 234, 271-2

Housing Special, 217

Howard, Ebenezer, 43

Hughes, Lord, 206, 213

Hull, 64

Hurlford, 74

Independent Labour Party (ILP), 52, 67, 70-72, 77, 130

'Industrialised' Building, 193-203

Inflation, 37, 151, 223-30, 234

Inglis, John A., 61

International Federation of Housing and Planning, 194

Inverness, 125, 185, 236

Ipswich, 64

Ireland, Ian, 260

Irish labour, 98, 108

Irvine, 26, 177, 216, 261

Jameson, Councillor A.D., 163-4

Jedburgh, 233-4

Jessop, William, 259

Johnston, Tom, MP, 91, 102, 111-15, 122-4, 126-7, 131-2, 134, 262

Johnstone, 64, 74, 81, 125, 176-7

Johnstone, Deafhillock Hostel, 92-9

Joint Council of the Building Industry, 66

Joint Development Group (for multi-storey building) 192-3, 200-201

Keddie, Dr J.R. Grant, 90

Keys, Dr, 95

Killearn, 87

Kilmarnock, 74, 78, 81, 125, 136, 144, 216

King of Norway, H M The, 104

King, Charles, 62

Kinsmen's Club of Canada, 89

Kirkcaldy, 144, 187

Kirkintillock, 56, 176-7

Kirkintilloch, Hillhead Hostel, 92-4, 97-8, 100

Kirknewton, 74

Kirkwall, 82

Kirkwood, David, MP, 122

Kresse, Herr Ludwig, 170

Labour Party, 126, 130-31, 162-4, 186

labour, shortages, 79-80, 117, 133-4, 140, 143, 227

Laighstonehall, 247-50

Laing, J.W., 119

Lanark County, 63, 67, 80, 106, 124-5, 134, 185, 224

Landels, William, 259

Lawrence, John, 139

Leith, 4, 242

Library of Standard Details, 205-6

Letchworth Garden City, 43

Linwood, 29, 177, 209

Livingston, 26, 218, 261

London, 19, 64, 98, 202

Mabon, Dr J. Dickson, MP, 203, 210

McAlpine and Sons, Messrs Sir Robert, 212

McBain, A.G., 137-9, 159, 162, 164-5

McBoyle, James, 137, 184, 188

McCalmont, Tom, 259

MacDonald, Mrs E., 219

Macdonald, J. Ramsay, 12

MacDougall, Mr, 70

McGovern, Mr J., MP, 77

McGregor, Mr & Mrs, 96

McIntosh, G.R., 133, 166

Macintosh, R.H., 156-8, 169-71, 215

McKinna, A., 62, 64, 78, 124, 127, 132

McLaughlin, Miss M.W., 137

Maclay, John S. (Viscount Muirshiel), 178, 190

McLuckie, Cmdr., 94

Macmillan, Harold, 24, 35

Macmillan, W. Grierson, 137, 190, 217

Marks, F.C., 259

Marseilles, 29

Marshall, William, 130

Mason, Derek, 245, 258-9

materials, shortages, 19, 23-4, 79-80, 93, 121, 133-4, 140-42, 143, 227, 229

Matthew, Prof Sir Robert, 129, 178

Maxton, James, MP, 70, 72, 77

'Maycrete' houses, 108-10

Medical Research Council, 64

Melrose, 220

menus, 97

Middleton Camp, 85-91

Midlothian, 106, 125, 134, 161, 174, 184-5

Miller, Col. Sir James, 189, 190, 216-7

Miller, James and Partners, 150

Milngavie, Clober Hostel, 100-102, 105-6

miners' houses, 5, 106-7, 134, 142, 144, 149, 158

Minto, Bob, 83

Ministries,
Air Ministry, 81-2
Ministry of Food, 95
Ministry of Fuel and Power, 106
Ministry of Health, 23-4, 60
Ministry of Labour, 57, 80
Ministry of National Insurance, 91
Ministry of Supply, 144, 158

Ministry of War Transport, 92, 94, 96
Ministry of Works, 82, 99, 108, 135, 158, 204
Mitchell, Craig, 188-9
Mitchell, Shirley, 215
modernisation, 209-12, 235, 245-52, 254
Monteath, R.C., 214
Monteith, Mrs M., 127
Motherwell, 70, 74, 81, 125, 160-62, 187
Motherwell Times, 68-70
Mottram, A.H., 47, 62, 64
Muir, Colin, 171
Muir, W.A. Gordon, 231-2, 248
multi-storey flats – Association's attitude – 116, 146-8
Musselburgh, 178
Myton-Clyde houses, 149

National Trust for Scotland, 166
Neilston, Kingston Hostel, 100-102, 104-5
Netherlands, 72, 90-91, 169-71
New Dailly, 144
Newtongrange, 150
Niven, Douglas, 14, 130
Nixon Browne, Mr J., MP, 175, 185
non-traditional houses – Association's attitude – 149-55
Northern Lighthouse Board, 144, 158
Norwegians, 104

O'Hagan, Patrick, 249
Orkney, 82
Orlit Company, 136
Orlit houses, 134-6, 142, 149, 247
overcrowding, Chapter 1, *esp* 7, 17, 57
Overspill, 26-9, 172-3, 176-8, 203, 209, 221-3, 240, 248, 264

Paisley, 192, 210, 222
Palmerston Place – Edinburgh, Head Office
Parliament – Acts of

Increase of Rent & Mortgage Interest Act, 1915, 9
Housing (Rosyth Dockyard) Act, 1915, 47
House & Town Planning (Scotland) Act, 1919 (Addison Act), 9-11, 49-50
Housing Act, 1923 (Chamberlain Act), 11-12, 50
Housing Act, 1924 (Wheatley Act), 12-15, 50, 53, 130
Housing Act, 1925, 15
Housing Act, 1930 (Greenwood Act), 16
Housing Act, 1935, 57
Special Areas (Development & Improvement) Act, 1934, 57
Housing (Financial Provisions) (Scotland) Act, 1938, 60
Town & Country Planning (Interim Development) (Scotland) Act, 1943, 22
Housing (Scotland) Act, 1944, 124, 134
Housing (Financial Provisions) (Scotland) Act, 1946, 134
New Towns Act, 1946, 26
Housing (Repairs & Rents) (Scotland) Act, 1954, 180
Valuation & Rating (Scotland) Act, 1956, 180
Housing & Town Development (Scotland) Act, 1957, 27
Rent Act, 1965, 36
Housing (Scotland) Act, 1966, 206
Local Government Planning & Land Act, 1980, 258
Tenants' Rights etc (Scotland) Act, 1980, 238
Parker, Barry, 43
Paterson, Thomas, 123, 127, 133, 163, 165-6, 172, 186, 189-90, 193
Peebles, 177
Perth, 165, 173, 259
Peutherer, David, 249
Pfefferkorn, Herr, 196

planned maintenance, 255-7
Polbeth, 74
Policy Review – *see* Reports
Pollock, Miss J.B., 106-8, 161, 187-8, 218-9, 253, 267
Pond, Leonard, 72-3, 82
Port Glasgow, 210
Post Office – *see* Kirkwall
Post-war Planning, 21-3, 110-32
Prefabs, 20-21
Prestonpans, 153
Prices and Incomes Policies, 37, 223-7
Public Works Loans Board, 53
Pumpherston, 157

Queen Elizabeth, 67-70
Queen Elizabeth II, 166, 243
Queensferry, 214

Rankinston, 144
Red Cedar Supply Company, 68
Redevelopment Assistance Programme, 223, 240-45, 264
Reith, Lord J., 26
Renfrew, Norman, 259
Renfrewshire, 64, 80, 105, 177
Rent Policy, 158-62, 180-87, 223-30, 254
Rent Restriction Act – *see* Parliament
Repatriates, 102-4
Reports,
    Barlow Report, 22, 26
    Burt Reports, 23, 119
    Distressed Areas, 57
    Dudley Report, 23
    Emmerson Report, 195
    Planning Our New Homes, 17, 23
    Policy Review (SSHA) (1986), 258, 267-71
    Programme for Development and Growth in Central Scotland (1965), 203
    Scott Report, 22
    Scottish Economy 1965-70, 204
    Scottish Housing Programme 1965-70, 204

Scottish Housing (1977), 38, 228, 237

Tudor Walter's Report, 10-11, 13, 47

Urban Deprivation Working Note 6, GB, 40

Uthwatt Report, 22

West Central Scotland Planning Committee (1975), 40

Rifkind, Malcolm, MP, 234, 245, 271

Robertson, J.J., MP, 123, 126-7, 132, 143, 146-7, 151

Ronald, D., 62, 132

Ronan Point, 202

Rose, P.J.G., 127, 132-3, 166

Ross, George, 62, 78, 138, 188

Ross, William (Lord Ross), 216

Rosyth, 11, 43-50, 81, 209-10, 259

Royal Air Force, 81-2

Royal Commission

On Housing, Ch 1, *esp* 5-9, 17-18

On Local Government, 214

Royal Navy, 44, 51, 82, 203, 209

Royal Naval Torpedo Works, 98

Royal Naval Victualing Depot, 98

Rutherglen, 210

Sales – *see* House Sales

Saltire Society, 178-80, 200, 216, 221, 234, 244

Scott Report – *see* Reports

Scottish Development Agency, 219, 242

Scottish Development Department – *see* Scottish Office

Scottish Housing Advisory Committee, 17, 23, 112, 114, 116, 119, 123, 133, 146, 151, 161, 165, 218, 231

Scottish National Housing Company (First), 46-50, 53, 58-9, 209

Scottish National Housing Company (Second), 53-5, 58-9, 64, 66, 209

Scottish Office, 22-3, 50-51, 111, 126,

190, 264-6

Department of Health, 15, 53, 62, 67, 76, 81, 85, 89-90, 104, 106, 108-9, 129, 134, 137, 149, 159-60, 171, 180, 182, 184, 186, 188, 192-3

Scottish Development Department, 29, 42, 55, 177-8, 195, 202-5, 209-10, 220, 224-5, 227, 233, 238-9, 245-6

Local Government Board, 46-7, 50

Scottish Trade Union Congress, 162

Scrymgeour Wedderburn, (Earl of Dundee), 77, 112, 233

Selective Employment Tax, 205, 208

Shaw, C.J.D. (Lord Kilbrandon), 184

Shaw-Stewart, Col B.H., 62, 74

sheltered housing, 116, 245

Shetland Isles, 1

Shiach, Bob, 156

Shipbuilding Industry, 4, 51, 54

Sighthill – *see* Edinburgh

Sinclair, Sir Archibald, 111

Skene, 220

Slamannan, 64

SLASH, 199

Smith, Rev W.C.V., 137, 162, 166, 188

Smout, Prof T.C., 130

Sneddon, Charles, 259

Somerville, Maj-Gen R.J., 232-3, 259

Special Areas – *see also* Commissioner for – 66, 72, 75-6, 79

Spence, Sir Basil, 65

Squatters' Movement, 20, 99, 104-5

Steel, Janet, 62

Stephen, Rev Campbell, MP,

77

Stevenson, Robin, 259-60

Stevenston, 74, 177

Stewarton, 177

Stirling, 78, 125, 134, 212-13

Stirling, John, 123, 127, 133

Stonehouse, 26, 219

Strathclyde Regional Council, 242

strikes, 38, 93, 224, 226-7, 229

Tain, 19-20

Tannochside, 63-74

Tarran Clyde houses, 142

Tarran, Messrs, 64

Taylor, Mr & Mrs George, 68-70

Taylor, John, MP, 185

Taylor, William L., 230, 258

Thomson, Mr, 96

Thomson, Sir Ronald J., 165, 182, 186, 190-91, 216

timber houses, 58, 64-5, 67-72, 74, 113-14, 121, 135, 142, 151, 153

timber shortages, 79, 140

Timms, John, 260

Torrance, J.F., 62

Tracoba System, 200-202

Transitional housing, 109-10

Tullibody, 145

Tweedbank, 220-21

United States, 30, 56

Unwin, Raymond, 11, 43, 46-7, 50

USSR (delegation), 172

Uthwatt Report – *see* Reports

Walter, Sir John Tudor, 10-11

War-time building conditions, 79-81

Washington Conference (1922), 51

Weir, G & J, 54

Weir steel houses, 54, 120, 133-5, 142, 149, 154-5, 246-7, 250

Welsh, J.C., MP, 61,70

Welwyn Garden City, 47
West Lothian, 64, 106, 125,
    134, 160-61
Western Isles, 3
Westwood, Joseph, MP, 23,
    88-9, 127, 132, 143
Whatlings, Messrs, 64
Wheatley, John, MP, 12-13,
    130
Wheatley Act – *see* Parliament
Whitburn, 177
Whitson Fairhurst houses,
    136, 142
Williamson, Ian, 259
Wilson, Sir Garnet, 123, 132
Wimpey, Messrs George, 204-
    5, 208
Wimpey houses, 136
Women's Voluntary Services,
    92, 94, 103
Woodburn, Arthur, MP, 130
Working Men's Hostels – *see
    also* individual names – 91-
    100

Younger, Rt Hon George,
    MP,
219-20

Zinn, W.B., 193, 202